DATE DUE

JUN 1 8 2007	

DEMCO, INC. 38-2931

Bloom's Modern Critical Interpretations

Bloom's Modern Critical Interpretations

Bloom's Modern Critical Interpretations

Robert Musil's
THE MAN WITHOUT QUALITIES

Edited and with an introduction by
Harold Bloom
Sterling Professor of the Humanities
Yale University

CHELSEA HOUSE
PUBLISHERS
A Haights Cross Communications Company

Philadelphia

©2005 by Chelsea House Publishers, a subsidiary of
Haights Cross Communications.

A Haights Cross Communications ◄— Company

http://www.chelseahouse.com

Introduction © 2005 by Harold Bloom.

Printed and bound in the United States of America.
10 9 8 7 6 5 4 3 2 1

Library of Congress Cataloging-in-Publication Data applied for.

ISBN 0-7910-8122-2

Contributing Editor: Pamela Loos

Cover designed by Keith Trego

Cover photo: Courtesy Library of Congress

Layout by EJB Publishing Services

Contents

Editor's Note

My Introduction centers upon the unfinished (and unfinishable) nature of Robert Musil's great book, and attempts to surmise why Musil cultivated so elliptical and experimental a mode.

Lowell A. Bangerter locates the novel's originality in its strange fusion of a particular cultural era with a transcendent order beyond time and place.

For Thomas Harrison, Musil's vast novel is a metaphysical experiment, a Utopian going-beyond of Marxist aesthetics, while "chance" is the over-determining element for Eric White, who interestingly contrasts Musil's art with the visual narratives of Luis Buñuel.

Burton Pike, an immensely informed scholar of Musil, meditates upon the new ways in which this novelist sought to represent the flow of experience, after which Robert Zaller explores the incestuous relationship between Ulrich and his younger sister Agathe which is the vital center of *The Man without Qualities*.

Musil's re-invention of the historical Austria-Hungary is charted by Alexander Honold, while Michael Bernstein analyzes the extraordinary book as a thought-experiment, a work-always-in-progress.

Stefan Jonsson finds ways of revealing that Ulrich transcends any possible social context, after which Austin Harrington describes the almost Platonic sense of community, a soul-sharing beyond alienation that becomes the impossible project of Ulrich and Agathe, and thus of Musil himself.

HAROLD BLOOM

Introduction

Robert Musil's literary eminence is beyond doubt. Because of the unfinished (and unfinishable) nature of his masterwork, *The Man without Qualities*, he cannot quite be placed in the company of Joyce and Proust and Kafka, or even of Thomas Mann and William Faulkner, among the High Modernists. His aesthetic splendor rivals that of Broch and Hofmannsthal, hardly a second order except in comparison to Joyce and Proust, Kafka and Beckett.

Proust and Kafka each loses by translation, rather more than Mann and Broch do, but Musil loses most, despite the distinguished and devoted efforts of Sophie Wilkins and Burton Pike. Musil's language is as unique as Paul Celan's, and Musil's styles (there are several, beautifully modulated) never stay fixed. Burton Pike contributes an eloquent "Translator's Afterword" (pp. 1771–1774) to the 1995 American edition, in which he aptly remarks that there is no author in English who could provide a model for Musil's fusion of sound and sense. It is unnerving that Musil is both essayistic and a curious blend of Taoist-Sufi in his procedures. He also combines an inward voicing with an outward panoply that verges upon prose-poetry.

Musil's actual precursor was the Shakespeare of *Hamlet*, where the representation of thinking-in-language touches a limit in the Prince of Denmark's seven soliloquies that even Musil cannot attain. Ulrich is a descendant of Hamlet, who haunts German literature as pervasively as he does the Anglo-American tradition. Incest, termed by Shelley the most

1

poetical of circumstances, is deferred throughout Part III of the novel, and evidently continues to be deferred in the six hundred and fifty pages from the Posthumous Papers that Pike translates. The consummation of Ulrich's and Agathe's mutual passion would have been a kind of suicide, probably followed by a literal double-suicide, the only way in which this unfinishable novel could have been finished. Musil's own death became the circumstance that concluded what could not reach conclusion, the full union of Agathe and Ulrich, a cosmological metaphor for the end of Musil's cultural world.

And yet the word "incest" is grossly imprecise for the love between these extraordinary siblings. What after all *is* incest in a fictive work? In Musil, the long-impending but unrealizable total relationship between Agathe and Ulrich is the ultimate trope for the new kind of secular transcendence that is the endless quest of *The Man without Qualities*. Perhaps it might have been an atonement or sacrifice to avert the death of European culture, had the actual intercourse between brother and sister taken place. Throughout Part III of the novel, and in the Posthumous Papers, Musil manifests an uncanny precision in the dangerous conversations between brother and sister:

> "And it's not at all against nature for a child to be the object of such feelings?" Agathe asked.
>
> "What would be against nature would be a straight-out lustful desire," Ulrich replied. "But a person like that also drags the innocent or, in any event, unready and helpless creature into actions for which it is not destined. He must ignore the immaturity of the developing mind and body, and play the game of his passion with a mute and veiled opponent; no, he not only ignores whatever would get in his way, but brutally sweeps it aside! That's something quite different, with different consequences!"
>
> "But perhaps a touch of the perniciousness of this 'sweeping aside' is already contained in the 'ignoring'?" Agathe objected. She might have been jealous of her brother's tissue of thoughts; at any rate, she resisted. "I don't see any great distinction in whether one pays no attention to what might restrain one, or doesn't feel it!"
>
> Ulrich countered: "You're right and you're not right. I really just told the story because it's a preliminary state of the love between brother and sister."
>
> "Love between brother and sister?" Agathe asked, and pretended to be astonished, as if she were hearing the term for

the first time; but she was digging her nails into Ulrich's arm again, and perhaps she did so too strongly, and her fingers trembled. Ulrich, feeling as if five small warm wounds had opened side by side in his arm, suddenly said: "The person whose strongest stimulation is associated with experiences each of which is, in some way or other, impossible, isn't interested in possible experiences. It may be that imagination is a way of fleeing from life, a refuge and a den of iniquity, as many maintain; I think that the story of the little girl, as well as all the other examples we've talked about, point not to an abnormality or a weakness but to a revulsion against the world and a strong recalcitrance, an excessive and overpassionate desire for love!" He forgot that Agathe could know nothing of the other examples and equivocal comparisons with which his thoughts had previously associated this kind of love; for he now felt himself in the clear again and had overcome, for the time being, the anesthetizing taste, the transformation into the will-less and lifeless, that was part of his experience, so that the automatic reference slipped inadvertently through a gap in his thoughts.

—From the *Posthumous Papers*, pp. 1399–1400,
translated by Burton Pike

As an instance of what is most original in Musil, this is both altogether typical yet also totally unique, the paradox that makes for what is greatest but sometimes maddening about *The Man without Qualities*. Some of the details in this passage I myself find unforgettable: Ulrich's brilliant evasion of "against nature," Agathe's "digging her nails into Ulrich's arm" so as to intimate "five small warm wounds," and Ulrich's subtle equation of revulsion against "the world" and a totalizing "desires for love." Is that world nature, history, society or immemorial morality? Musil insists that his reader decide that for herself.

LOWELL A. BANGERTER

Experimental Utopias:
The Man without Qualities

All of Musil's other works, including *Young Törless*, the novellas, the plays, and the essays, can be interpreted as preliminary studies to his monumental unfinished novel *The Man without Qualities*. In each creation, the author tested variations of ideas about man's relationship to the world, his self-concept, and the possibilities for realizing greater fulfillment and more perfect humanity within the context of life's experience. The analysis of the human condition, with special reference to the role of the thinking individual in modern technological society, is the common denominator of his literary art and his theoretical writings. *The Man without Qualities* is the grand culminating experiment in his creative-analytic process of exploring the unfixed domain of mortal potentiality.

Musil's masterpiece is not a traditional novel with a clearly defined plot and carefully orchestrated resolution of one or more central problems. It has been variously described as a "compendium of contemporary uncertainty,"[1] "a grand satire of the dying Austria,"[2] and "the supreme example in Western literature of the novel of ideas."[3] The author himself characterized it as a novel "of a spiritual adventure," and as a "combat document." More than anything else, however, it is his strongest illustration of the creative power of his own sense of possibility.

The uniqueness of *The Man without Qualities* lies in the fact that on one

From *Robert Musil*. © 1988 by Lowell A. Bangerter.

level it is an analysis of historical reality, while on another it is an extremely complex metaphor for something that transcends the limits of specifically defined time and locale.

With reference to the real world, Musil was concerned about the human developments in Austrian society that inevitably led in the direction of World War I. In his notes about the novel's orientation and his approach to the material, he defines its artistic focus by saying that direct portrayal of the period leading up to the war must be the real substance of the narration, the context to which the plot can be tied, and the thought that provides the orientation for everything else.

It is important to understand that what mattered most for Musil were questions of human response to a spiritual atmosphere, and not the details of events. In his interview with Oskar Maurus Fontana in 1926, he disclaimed engagement in the writing of a historical novel, insisting that the actual explanation of concrete events did not interest him. One reason for this posture was that he considered facts to be totally interchangeable. Accordingly, he declared his fascination with what is spiritually typical, "the phantom aspect of the happening."[4] For Musil, that "phantom aspect" is a timeless dimension of human experience. In the impact of events upon the individual, it is the factor that stimulates experimentation with new ideas.

Within the framework of *The Man without Qualities*, Musil treats what he sees as major problems of the immediate prewar years—the search for order and conviction, the role of the "Other Condition" in the life of the individual, the situation of the scientific person—as substance for experiments with ideas about achieving utopian forms of existence. His notes to the novel identify the most important of the projected patterns as three separate utopias. The first of these is the utopia of the given social condition, the second, the utopia of the "Other Condition" as found in love, and the third, a purely refined form of the "Other Condition" with mystical implications. In discussing these possibilities, he suggests that they differ in importance and that they can be reduced to two major utopias, that of real life and that of the "Millennial Kingdom," where the latter is a combination of the respective forms of the "Other Condition" experienced through love and mysticism.

The experiments pertaining to the first alternative receive their greatest emphasis in the early portions of the book. Exploration of the potentialities of the "Other Condition" then follows as the development of ideas for their own sake reaches its strongest intensity. Because Musil believed that attainment of the "Other Condition" could never be permanent in rational mortality, he projected an ending for the novel that would lead the central characters back into reality.

Musil's experiments with the search for utopia take the form of exposing his "guinea pig" to various stimuli and observing the results. The "guinea pig" is Ulrich, a representative specimen of technological man who is characterized by himself and others as a "man without qualities." The stimuli to which he responds include people who stand for different aspects of modern society, social, political, cultural, and intellectual situations that are typical of the times, and ideas that represent possibilities for alternate approaches to life and its questions. In each instance, the object of the experiment is to obtain a solution to a single puzzle. As the novel's male protagonist sums it up for his sister, the problem that troubles him most is concentrated in the question: "How am I to live?"

The outcome of each investigation is at once a function of and a contribution to the view of typical modern scientific man as a "man without qualities." On one level at least, the entire novel revolves around what it means to be such an individual. For Musil, a "man without qualities" is today's manifestation of the man of possibility, unfixed man in all his, ambivalence and ambiguity. In defining the title figure as a typical representative of the times, one of his friends describes him as a man who always knows what to do, a man who can look into a woman's eyes, a man who is intelligent and able to use his mental capacities well under all conditions. More striking are the polarities that exist within him. In addition to talents of strength, objectivity, courage, and endurance, he can be either impetuous or cool and cautious. He can laugh when he is angry, reject things that stir his soul, and find good in things that are bad. His relationship to the world is completely unstable, because his surroundings represent infinite changing possibilities.

It is precisely this fluidity of his nature and his lack of a strong sense of reality, however, that make the "man without qualities" the ideal vehicle for Musil's experiments. His sense of possibility is manifested in a conscious utopianism that is a direct product of his intellectual mobility. It permits him to treat life as a laboratory and to contemplate the uniting of opposites to achieve a more fulfilling existence.

Ulrich's attempts to redefine his life are projected against a rich and complex fabric of interpersonal, social, political, and psychological relationships. At the age of thirty-two, he has behind him three unsuccessful endeavors—to become a "man of importance," first as an officer, then as an engineer, and finally as a mathematician. These efforts have been in vain because he is more at home in the realm of possibility than in the mundane real world. Accordingly, in response to what he perceives as a lack of order and meaning in his existence as a whole, he decides to take a year's vacation from his normal life. During that period, he hopes to discover the causes of his surrounding reality's progressive collapse and a more suitable direction for his own future. The body of the novel is formed by the composite presentation of what he learns about himself and his environment in the course of this experiment.

To the extent that one can trace even a general story line for the completed portion of the fragment, its substance can be divided into two major sections with numerous subgroupings of connected situations, ideas, events, observations, and characters. The first main portion examines approximately half of the "vacation" year. It is primarily a description of Ulrich's efforts and ultimate failure to find an appropriate niche for himself within the context of Austrian prewar reality.

Diverse aspects of the decaying society are illuminated in a panorama of character types and behavioral patterns, as Musil depicts Ulrich's involvement in an empty political project called "the Collateral Campaign." Ulrich's participation consists primarily of passive observation of and reflection about events and situations. This fact determines the form of the narration. Essayistic integration of ideas, rather than elaboration of action and plot, receives the key emphasis.

In the second half of the narrative, the Collateral Campaign moves into the background as Ulrich abandons his attempt to find the right life for himself within the domain of material reality. His search enters a new phase in the intense exploration of the possibilities for fulfillment offered by the "Other Condition." The problem of finding the proper form of existence becomes that of self-definition as he grapples with the question of his relationship to his sister Agathe.

With this narrowing of focus comes a subtle change in the format of artistic presentation. Ulrich's examinations of a broad spectrum of ideas about love and mysticism are elaborated in long conversations between brother and sister. In the process of these discussions the siblings begin to function as complementary halves of a single spiritual unit.

How the author intended to end the novel is the subject of continuing controversy among Musil scholars. It is clear from unfinished fragments of chapters, notes from different periods of work on the novel, statements in interviews, and comments in letters that he considered many variations and possibilities for concluding his masterpiece. Nevertheless, only two things can be determined with relative certainty: First, Ulrich's experiments with both mysticism and love would fail to yield a final satisfying answer, just as the attempts to adapt to practical reality had done. Second, his "vacation" year would end with the protagonists and their world being swallowed up by the war. In the notes to the novel; where he projects the ultimate collapse of the Agathe–Ulrich relationship, Musil characterizes the combination of

Ulrich's decision to participate in the war and the miscarriage of their excursion into the "Other Condition" as the "end of the utopias."

One of the most significant features of *The Man without Qualities* is Musil's general portrayal of prewar Austria as the setting for his "adventure of the spirit." Kakania, as he calls the dying Austro-Hungarian monarchy, is a land for which spiritual inertia is characteristic. In retrospect, he describes the vanished Austria of former years as an unacknowledged model for many things, a place where speed existed, but not very much of it. Despite the genius that it has produced in the past, it has lost its cultural energy: "It was the State that was by now only just, as it were, acquiescing in its own existence." For that reason, it is ripe for some historical event that will bring about radical changes and move things in a new direction.

A major part of Musil's purpose in writing his critical analysis of the times was to demonstrate how such conditions must inevitably lead to the explosive consequences of war. In that respect, the invented characters and situations of the narrative become symbols and metaphors for broad social and political phenomena.

Despite its de-emphasis in the later portions of the novel, the Collateral Campaign provides what Werner Welzig has labeled "the thread of action that holds the work together."[5] On the surface, the project is simply an endeavor to give Austria new visibility in the world, through the creation in 1918 of a yearlong seventieth anniversary celebration of the reign of Emperor Franz Josef. It is conceived as a direct response to the planned Prussian commemoration of Wilhelm II's thirty years on the throne, an event scheduled for the same year. Within the narrative framework, committee meetings and planning sessions, individual responses to the envisioned festivities, and discussions of the action's implications are employed as vehicles for the presentation of a wide variety of representative Austrian social types. The Collateral Campaign thus becomes on a deeper level Musil's focal metaphor for the spirit of the era. That point is hammered home in the author's notes to the final portion of the work, where he says that the Collateral Campaign will lead to the war.

Musil's ironic treatment of the prevailing social, cultural, and political attitudes in prewar Vienna is extremely successful from an artistic point of view. In the diverse reactions to the Collateral Campaign he offers a stark picture of the pathological condition of an Austrian society made up of people great and small, all of whom are concerned only with their own trivial or glorious schemes while the empire staggers on the edge of collapse.

The portrayed perceptions of the grand patriotic endeavor are as disparate as the characters and the parts of the national community that they represent. Count Leinsdorf, for example, views the coming celebration as an opportunity for Austria to reclaim its true essence. Ulrich's friend Clarisse becomes obsessed with the idea of promoting an Austrian Nietzsche Year. Associated with that, she wants to do something for the homicidal maniac Moosbrugger. For still another figure, the appropriate action is the establishment of an Emperor Franz Josef Anniversary Soup Kitchen.

At the same time, broad factions within the society greet the whole idea with skepticism and suspicion. Already-existing tensions are intensified when ethnic minorities come to regard the project as a Pan-Germanic plot, while extremists in the other direction view it as threatening to destroy the German nation both spiritually and intellectually.

Marie-Louise Roth has summarized effectively the function of the proposed patriotic demonstration in exposing the society's mortal weaknesses. She says:

> The Collateral Campaign that was invented by Musil illustrates in its main representatives the false values of an era, the abstract idealism, the confusion of the spirit, the bureaucratism, the phraseology, the impersonalism, the nonsense and the sterility of all endeavors.... The leading persons of the Collateral Campaign live and act according to fossilized principles, the unsuitability and falseness of which they feel themselves.[6]

Ulrich's response to the Collateral Campaign is especially important because it illuminates the project as a parody of his own individual quest for life's meaning. As the figures who promote the cause of celebrating the prolonged reign of their "Emperor of Peace" continue to search for a powerful focus for the undertaking, Ulrich makes his own suggestion as to what the movement should accomplish. Speaking to Count Leinsdorf, he proposes that the Collateral Campaign initiate a general spiritual inventory, as though Judgment Day were coming in 1918, signaling the end of the old spiritual era and the dawning of a higher one. He concludes his presentation by stating that until an official institution is created that is responsible for precision and the spirit, other goals remain either unattainable or illusory.

It is significant that nobody takes Ulrich's recommendation seriously, not even Ulrich himself. Just as the very nature of the spirit of the times will not permit a true synthesis of reality and the soul on a national scale, so Ulrich's own goal for himself cannot be realized because his attitude of "active passivism" (Musil's term for passivity masked by meaningless action) prevents a similar synthesis on an individual plane.

There is stark irony in the parallel between the results of Ulrich's "active passivism" approach to his search for the right life and the accomplishments of the Collateral Campaign in its attempt to renew Austria's sense of identity. At one point the protagonist clarifies his stance with respect to external events by comparing it to that of a prisoner who is waiting for the opportunity to escape. While emphasizing the anticipation of action, the image conveys the tension that exists in a situation of static longing for something that never materializes. Pursued to one possible conclusion, it suggests that escape from confinement may occur only as the prisoner experiences his own execution. Similarly, the progress of the Collateral Campaign is limited to the maintaining of expectation concerning potential future activity. The pattern of "active passivism" is underscored most strongly in what one character calls "the slogan of action." When it becomes apparent that the semiofficial planning committee is accomplishing nothing, Count Leinsdorf utters a hollow watchcry for its continued wheel spinning. He says that something has to be done. Because the Collateral Campaign, like its secretary Ulrich, is representative of the zeitgeist, its response to Leinsdorf's challenge is the same as his. Nothing happens beyond the contemplation of possibilities.

To the extent that the movement's failure to act symbolizes Austria's passivity toward the conditions leading to the war, the outcome is the same as for Ulrich's prisoner. Release from the waiting comes about only through the empire's destruction. As Wilfried Berghahn has pointed out, that fact becomes apparent at the moment when Ulrich first learns of the Collateral Campaign's existence through his father's letter: "For the father's letter, of course, acquires the satirical function that is decisive for the novel only through the dating of the Austrian apotheosis in the death year of the monarchy. With that, the Collateral Campaign is characterized from the first moment on as a burial undertaking. Its protagonists become the masters of ceremonies for a modern *danse macabre*. They just do not know it yet."[7]

The project's function as a metaphor for the disintegration of a stagnant order is further emphasized in the lifelessness of the interpersonal relationships experienced by its actual and would be participants. As Ulrich makes his way back and forth among the "death-dancers," observing and experimenting with them, his encounters reveal both the tenuousness and fragility of existing connections and an increasing inability to establish new, meaningful bonds based on traditional concepts of love and affinity. This accentuation of isolation and alienation is visible not only in the way in which other figures respond to Ulrich, but also in the manner of their interaction among themselves.

A vivid illustration of the Collateral Campaign's lack of power to bring about unifying change is given in the figure of Ulrich's cousin Diotima Tuzzi, whose drawing room is the planning committee's headquarters. In the picture of Viennese society that Musil creates, Diotima is the bourgeois defender of a romantic vision of Austrian culture. She views the Collateral Campaign as a unique opportunity to realize on a practical level the things that are of greatest importance. For her, the paramount goal is the rediscovery of "that 'human unity' in man's life which has been lost because of the advent of modern materialism and scientific reasoning."[8] Yet her inability to achieve anything more than superficial oneness with others is demonstrated clearly in her respective relationships with her husband, Ulrich, and the Prussian Arnheim.

The impractical, idealistic notions that Diotima cultivates in her salon only estrange her from her bureaucrat spouse. Tuzzi, whom Ulrich sees as the embodiment of pure, practical manliness, is totally absorbed in his profession. He feels no kinship at all with those involved in extracurricular intellectual pursuits. Accordingly, in the scenes where he appears, he is an outsider looking in at the peculiar world of Diotima's involvement in the Collateral Campaign.

Diotima is unable to realize any sort of deep personal union with Ulrich for at least two reasons. On a purely matter-of-fact level, the two cousins possess sharply different attitudes and personalities. That is, Ulrich is the embodiment of Musil's idea of healthy, scientific man, while Diotima represents what is unrealistic and decadent in the contemporary world. More important is the fact that for Ulrich, Diotima is simply another subject for detached experimental observation. Ulrich is prepared to enter only an intellectual relationship governed by carefully controlled conditions. He suggests that they try to love each other like fictional characters who meet in a work of literature, leaving out the superficial padding that gives reality a phony appearance of fatness. Because Diotima's spiritual focus is at best counterfeit intellectual, she is incapable of playing the role that Ulrich envisions for her, and the experiment fails before it begins.

In its meaning for the novel as a whole, the most important of Diotima's vain attempts to unite with another individual is her abortive liaison with Arnheim. A Prussian industrialist and writer whom Musil modeled after Walther Rathenau, Arnheim plays the role of Ulrich's spiritual antagonist. His hollow affair with Diotima thus becomes a shadowy parody of the intense Ulrich-Agathe involvement that dominates the second half of *The Man without Qualities*.

During the course of her participation in the Collateral Campaign, Arnheim becomes a peculiar symbol for the irrationality of Diotima's perception of the project. Under the spell of his external facade, she comes to view him as a kindred spirit with whom she can bring to pass the cultural rejuvenation that she sees as the campaign's goal. Her quixotic approach to her self-made task is given its most grotesque manifestation in her grand idea that her Prussian friend must become the spiritual leader of the Collateral Campaign, despite the fact that it competes jealously with a concurrent celebration in Prussia-Germany.

On the surface, Arnheim appears to share Diotima's vision of their common cause, and he does little to discourage her growing attachment to him. As their spiritual relationship grows stronger, the Collateral Campaign becomes for the two of them an island of refuge. It takes on the dimensions of a special destiny that shapes their lives at a critical moment. As they participate in the project, they grow to share the perception that it represents an enormous intellectual opportunity and responsibility. For that reason, Diotima eventually reaches the point where she considers leaving her husband and marrying Arnheim in order to make their apparent spiritual union permanent. That plan collapses under the strain of reality's intrusion into her romantic illusion. The process of events uncovers the fact that Arnheim's real interest in her salon has little or nothing to do with the Collateral Campaign. He has simply exploited the situation to make business contacts. The envisioned union of souls founders on his pragmatism.

In its artistic function as a recurring symbol for Musil's main ideas, the Collateral Campaign spins within the novel a structural thread that binds together key character groups and situations. Parallel to it, although receiving less emphasis, is a second strand of thought that fulfills a similar purpose, reinforcing the author's statements about the prewar Austrian world by illuminating it from an entirely different direction. The resulting contribution to the narrative fabric is one of harsh, chaotic color in sharp contrast to the more subdued, passive hues of the Collateral Campaign's characteristic inaction.

At the center of this more threatening representation of the spirit of the times is a symbol for what one critic has called "the insanity of a world out of control."[9] It takes the form of the homicidal maniac Christian Moosbrugger.

Like the Collateral Campaign, Moosbrugger provides stimuli to which the various figures respond, revealing things about themselves and the society of which they are a part. Through the brutal slaying and mutilation of his prostitute victims, he arouses peculiar feelings within others, feelings that throw into question traditional concepts of social normality. The judicial system's visible inability to ascertain his mental competence and his accountability for his actions becomes a grotesque caricature of what is happening on the other levels of the novel. His apparent rationality in the courtroom parallels the facade of reason that conceals the tragic internal decay of the social order. According to Musil, Moosbrugger reflects the pertinent conditions within the surrounding environment, as if they were seen in a broken mirror.

Ulrich's views concerning him are especially important for the elucidation of Moosbrugger's meaning for the work. For Ulrich, Moosbrugger is the inevitable product of the world's collective irrationality. In one instance, the thought occurs to him that if it were possible for mankind to dream in unison, the resulting vision would be Moosbrugger.

Because the murderer's behavior is not bound by the restrictions of reason, he is able to participate in the life of a realm beyond material reality, where the "goodness" of an action is determined entirely by individual perception. In that respect, he becomes a perverse manifestation of transcendence into the "Other Condition," where the sense of possibility is unfettered by a traditional morality based upon external social standards. As Johannes Loebenstein has observed: "In this murderer ... Ulrich sees all of humanity's possibilities combined together in a radically paradoxical unity."[10]

Just as Arnheim functions as Ulrich's antagonist in the practical, material world, so Moosbrugger plays the role of his opposite in the domain of the spirit. A significant aspect of Ulrich's search for fulfillment is his attempt to establish his complete identity by finding and uniting with the missing feminine component of his soul. His experiments with a number of different women bring him no closer to that ideal until he finally rediscovers his spiritual "Siamese twin," in his sister Agathe. In the figure of Moosbrugger, on the other hand, the image of a society that rejects and destroys spiritual completeness is given its strongest elaboration. What the murderer achieves in killing his victims is the excision of the unwanted feminine dimension from his own being. That fact is made abundantly clear in the narrator's description of one of the murders.

In the scene in question, Moosbrugger is presented lying rolled up in a ticket booth, with his head in the corner, pretending to be asleep. Next to him lies a prostitute who has attached herself to him during the night. The narrator labels her Moosbrugger's "accursed second self." When the psychopath tries to slip away from her in the dark, she holds him back, wrapping her arms around his neck. His response is to pull out his knife and stab her with it. When she falls with her head inside the booth, he drags her out, stabbing her repeatedly until he is satisfied that he has "cut her completely away from himself."

The behavior of Moosbrugger's victim is especially meaningful for the scene that is presented here. It signals that within the destructively insane world symbolized by the murderer the feminine element seeks undeterably for the union that he rejects. That idea is given even greater emphasis in the descriptions of Ulrich's interactions with Clarisse, Moosbrugger's strongest female spiritual counterpart.

During the course of the novel, Clarisse becomes progressively more obsessed with the idea of a personal mission to transform European society. Within the context of that fixation, she comes to view herself as a "double being." Intrigued by her husband Walter's fear that she is going insane, she associates the awareness of man's inherent doubleness with that insanity, and she concludes that modern "normal" society has lost its knowledge of humanity's true nature. Pointing to what she sees as a precedent in classical antiquity, she talks about representations of Apollo as both man and woman, insisting that human beings, like the Greek gods, are dual in nature. When Walter presses her to define her own duality more specifically, she responds that she is both man and woman. From this time on, she identifies more and more strongly with the concept of the hermaphrodite.

Clarisse's conscious association of insanity with the redemptive power of the dual individual draws her to Moosbrugger. She begins a crusade to set him free. Within her thoughts he becomes a particularly potent example of the double man. Specifically, she views him as the embodiment of her own mission to unite within herself the opposing extremes of the male element, identified in her mind with the figures of Christ and Nietzsche respectively. For that reason, she tries to persuade Ulrich to help her break Moosbrugger out of prison. She believes that if he can be freed, the redemption of the society will be the result.

To a large extent, Clarisse and Moosbrugger are symbols for what Musil saw as the ultimate focal idea of the novel, carried to its pathological extreme. The starkness of their portrayal sets off through contrast a more contemplative, philosophical development of the author's concept of human duality. The latter is presented during the progress of what the narrator describes as "a journey to the furthest limits of the possible, skirting the dangers of the impossible and unnatural, even of the repulsive, and perhaps not always quite avoiding them." This "journey" is Ulrich's final attempt to find the missing portion of his own identity. It takes place as he seeks to enter the "Other Condition" through the increasingly intense relationship with his sister.

In an important passage from his notebook, Musil suggests that the nucleus for *The Man without Qualities* is contained in an early poem that he wrote, entitled "Isis and Osiris" (Isis and Osiris). Both for its relevance to the discussion of the Ulrich–Agathe portion of the novel, and as one of few surviving examples of Musil's early awkward experimentation with lyric forms, the poem is presented here in its entirety:

Isis and Osiris

On the leaves of the stars the moon-boy lay
Sleeping silvery dim,
And the sun-wheel on its way
Turned around and gazed at him.
    From the desert came the red wind's wail,
    And along the coast there is no sail.

And his sister softly from the sleeper
Cut his manhood free, did it consume.
And she gave her soft red heart then for it,
Placed it on him in his organ's room.
    And in dream the wound again grew whole.
    And she ate the lovely sex she stole.

Lo, then roared aloud the sunlight,
As the sleeper started from his sleep,
Stars were tossing, just as rowboats
Moored on chains will surge and dart
When the mighty tempests start.

Lo, his brothers, rage asmoulder,
Chased the robber winsome, fair,
And he then his bow did shoulder,
And the blue space broke in there,
Woods collapsed beneath their tread,
And the stars ran with them filled with dread.
    Yet none caught the slim, bird-shouldered maiden,
    Not a one, despite how far he ran.

He alone, the young boy whom she called at night,
Finds her when the moon and sun are changing,
Of all hundred brothers none but this,
And he eats her heart, and she eats his.

There is a direct textual link between *The Man without Qualities* and the myth presented in the poem. In a conversation with his newly rediscovered sister, Ulrich attempts to describe the startlingly intense attraction that exists between them. In doing so, he refers to a variety of myths, including that of the human being divided into two, Pygmalion, Hermaphroditus, and the legend of Isis and Osiris. He points to these models as examples of a historic human craving for a double of the opposite sex.

The basis for the connection between the poem and the second half of the novel lies in Musil's interest in the Egyptian sun god Osiris and his sister-wife, the moon goddess Isis, as archetypal symbols for the love between brother and sister. The author was fascinated by these particular figures because Isis represents the irrational, metaphysical dimension, while her brother is identified with the opposing material and rational elements. Unification of these separate halves, graphically signified in the poem by the exchange of hearts and in the novel by Agathe's longing to trade bodies with Ulrich, connotes the merging of fundamental antithetical tendencies of mortality through the power of love.

As ultimately developed within the novel, the longing for completion of the self, which is the focus of "Isis and Osiris," is Musil's most extreme projection of the sense of possibility. It is the motivation for Ulrich's attempt to join Agathe in the Utopia of the "Other Condition" through actualization of what Marie-Louise Roth has called "the felt inkling of unity between spirit and nature, subject and object, the dream of termination of the duality between 'I' and 'you.'"[11]

Ulrich's first meeting with his sister after their father's death sets the tone for the intimate union that develops between them. The two siblings encounter each other similarly clothed, so that Agathe immediately characterizes them as "twins." As Ulrich forms his initial impression of her, an idea surfaces that is explored in ever-intensifying variation through the remainder of the novel. While considering her attributes, he notes that she is neither patently emancipated nor bohemian, in spite of the peculiar clothing in which she has received him. The more he attempts to penetrate to the essence of her nature, the more he is struck with the idea that there is something hermaphrodite about her.

In the descriptions of subsequent encounters, ever-more emphasis is placed upon the notion that Agathe is Ulrich's female alter ego. One scene presents him as seeing himself approaching in the figure of Agathe as she enters a room. To be sure, this other person is more beautiful than he is, and she has an aura about her that he does not see in himself, but he cannot help but think that she is really himself, repeated and somehow changed. It is this feeling that she embodies the longed for missing aspect of his identity that moves Ulrich to suggest to her the experiment of living together in a new kind of union beyond the restraints of conventional social reality. His vision of their spiritual merging in the ideal realm that he calls "the Millenium, the Kingdom of a Thousand Years" suggests the attainment of fulfillment in absolute interdependence, not only with each other, but also with the world as a whole.

The process of unification is one of withdrawal from the concerns of material reality into a condition of shared contemplation. Together, Ulrich and Agathe explore many ideas about man's physical and spiritual nature, his actual and possible situation in the world, and the means by which the individual may transcend the traditional limits of mortal existence. Dense conversations about love, mysticism, and morality are part of the "search for a state in which the individual is enhanced, in which his ego rises and does not fall."[12]

In the Agathe–Ulrich dialogues Musil presents the elements of his theory of a psychology of feeling, the bases of which are his interpretations of Nietzsche's ideas concerning private and general morality, the era of comparison, the logic of dreams, suffering and compassion, love and justice. In many instances, complete chapters are devoted to essayistic elaboration of theoretical points and abstractions, interrupting the flow of the narrative with material that Musil eventually recognized as being out of place in the novel. Even for the careful reader, these passages form an unnecessary barrier to the clear understanding of the author's artistic objectives.

Through the exchange of ideas, Ulrich and Agathe draw nearer to each other, until they begin to think in concert. As their relationship approaches the peak of its intensity, the narrator describes them as feeling as if they were a single entity, working together in a harmony similar to that of people who play the piano four-handed, or people who read the same material together aloud. On a mystical, dreamlike level, they seem to melt together and become one being, sharing a common personality.

The peculiar ambiguity of their situation at this point is underscored in the designation that they give to themselves: "the unseparated and not united ones." It suggests that their union, despite its spiritual depth, is fragile and unstable. Recognition that the bond between them may collapse causes them first to contemplate suicide, then to continue the experiment to its final extreme. Agathe gives the signal for the beginning of its last stage when she says that they will not kill themselves until they have exhausted every other possibility for resolving their situation. The climactic event of the novel is a combination of physical and spiritual union, in which incest serves as a catalyst for the final shattering of all boundaries between brother and sister. In one of the novel fragments, Musil describes them as coming together physically like animals seeking warmth. In the process of sexual union, a spiritual merging occurs on another level, and each of them has the feeling of having assimilated the other. Time and space lose their meaning as the lovers transcend all previous experience and enter the absolute realm of the "Other Condition."

Although the protagonists of *The Man without Qualities* do achieve self-completion temporarily, it is clear that Musil did not envision them finding a permanent escape from conventional reality in their mystical utopia. As he expressed it to Oskar Maurus Fontana during their celebrated interview, the attempt to prolong the experience fails because the absolute state cannot be maintained.[13] In that assessment, as in the novel itself, he gave a lasting indictment of a world progressing toward war, in which only a "man without qualities" could survive.

NOTES

1. Werner Welzig, *Der deutsche Roman im 20: Jahrhundert* (Stuttgart: Kröner, 1970), p. 9.

2. Wolfdietrich Rasch, "Robert Musil und sein Roman *Der Mann ohne Eigensehaften*," *Universitas* 9 (1954), p. 147.

3. Peters, *Robert Musil, Master of the Hovering Life*, p. 190.

4. Fontana, "Erinnerungen an Robert Musil," in *Robert Musil: Leben, Werk, Wirkung*, p. 338.

5. Welzig, *Der deutsche Roman im 20: Jahrhundert*, p. 192.

6. Marie-Louise Roth, "Robert Musil im Spiegel seines Werkes," in *Robert Musil: Leben, Werk, Wirkung*, p. 33.

7. Berghahn, *Robert Musil*, p. 95.

8. Peters, *Robert Musil, Master of the Hovering Life*, p. 205.

9. Gumtau, *Robert Musil*, p. 65.

10. Loebenstein, "Das Problem der Erkenntnis in Musils künstlerischem Werk," in *Robert Musil: Leben, Werk, Wirkung*, p. 94.

11. Roth, "Robert Musil im Spiegel seines Werkes," p. 21.

12. Wilhelm Braun, "Robert Musil," in *Encyclopedia of World Literature in the Twentieth Century* (New York: Ungar, 1983), vol 3, p. 337.

13. Fontana, "Erinnerungen an Robert Musil," p. 339.

THOMAS HARRISON

Robert Musil: The Suspension of the World

In history we no longer follow the course of a spirit immanent in the events of the world, but the curves of statistical diagrams.
— Italo Calvino, "Cybernetics and Ghosts"

If one takes seriously arguments such as those of Ernst Mach, Nietzsche, and other philosophers around the turn of the century concerning the epistemological illegitimacy of all interpretations, then reality in the broadest, metaphysical sense comes to lose its definition. In place of the recognized artificiality of ideological constructs there arises a "new infinity of the natural," confronting a person, in Musil's words, with "the burden of gazing into the midst of the as yet undetermined relationships of things."[1] This burden is the very starting point of Musil's fiction, vividly dramatized in his first novel, of 1906, *The Perplexities of the Pupil Törless*. The perplexed gaze of *Törless* is the dramatic correlative of a loss of theoretical method, experienced by philosophers of the time as the most pressing task of the intellect.[2]

At bottom, the confusions experienced by this pupil in the course of his adventures at boarding school stem from a critical sounding, or philosophical essayal, of those symbolic languages that the "normal" social world, through its plenipotentiary, the academic institution, is trying to teach him. On one

From *Essayism: Conrad, Musil, & Pirandello.* ©1992 by The Johns Hopkins University Press.

level his questions concern the actual content conveyed by the intellectual disciplines. History, logic, mathematics, and physics—even the moral codes and adult common sense Törless resolves to accept at the end of the novel— do not draw a convincing picture of what "is the case" in the world. Neither, by consequence, do they furnish directives for action. On this level Törless reflects Musil's reaction to the various positivisms, phenomenologies, and transcendentalisms he was studying in the course of obtaining his doctorate in philosophy, as if he had already decided that the only question worthy of an intellectual was the simple question of "right living" (*GW* 1:255, *MWO* 1:303 [62]). And yet this final and only real issue depends upon all the others.[3] Neither Törless nor the man without qualities of the later novel will be able to respond to this issue without first determining the status of knowledge. Törless demands that values be based on facts, or on precisely what the traditional sciences are unable to grasp.

On another and deeper level, however, the pupil's confusions arise from a suspicion concerning the very form of the symbolic disciplines, as if that were the ultimate cause of the inadequacy of their contents. Törless's real confusions do not concern the applications or rules of the academic sciences so much as the legitimacy of their interpretive claims. Do these disciplines explain experience, or do they merely schematize its causes and effects, in laws and forces, in measurable quantities and mechanical operations? And how do these disciplines legitimize their methods? "When someone is trying to teach us mathematics," Wittgenstein remarks, as if voicing the frustrations of the pupil, that person never begins "by assuring us that he knows that a + b = b + a."[4] It is thus the failure of language in all its forms which disturbs Törless—not the fact that what a certain language says may be "false" but that saying itself has not assumed a proper voice (*GW* 6:65; *YT* 86). Within the various symbolic languages he seeks the referent: the objective world about which they speak.

If Törless concerns himself with symbolism at all, it is only because he wants to decipher the world invariably invoked but never encapsulated by the explanations one is offered. There is nothing "mystical" in his or his author's concern; it is a desire for the same objective knowledge at which science itself aims. "If mathematics torments me," Törless explains to Beineberg, his mystical friend, "it's because I'm looking for something quite different behind it from you—what I'm after isn't anything supernatural at all, it's precisely the natural that I'm looking for" (*GW* 6:83; *YT* 112). But "the natural"—its subtle infinity—is precisely what has gotten lost, inextricably buried in the accounts of philosophy, science, mathematics, and logic. Part of the problem lies in the fact that the theoretical disciplines have not adequately theorized their own methods, furnishing no convincing criterion for what counts as valid data of study. For, if one agrees with Mach that experience is a sum total of sensations (as Törless's author generally does), then dreams, feelings, and the motions of "innerness" are equally, if not more, objective elements of this experience than the abstract processes and laws into which the academic disciplines have translated it. In his attempt to find a way within this forest of voiceless and symbolically transmuted sensations,

> Törless was assailed by a sort of madness that made him experience things, processes, people, all as something equivocal. As something that by some ingenious operation had been fettered to a harmless explanatory word, and as something entirely strange, which might break loose from its fetters at any moment now.
> True: there is a simple, natural explanation for everything, and Törless knew it too; but to his dismayed astonishment it seemed only to tear off an outer husk, without getting anywhere near laying bare what was within. (*GW* 6:64; *YT* 85)

Törless's ultimate confusion stems from a suspicion that the intellectual mediation of the real only envelops the real in silence, no interpretation ever penetrating beyond the surface of experience and no inscription proffering its potential meaning.

His suspicion is therefore double, and carries over to Musil's later novel, *The Man without Qualities*: that the processes of the world are irreducibly ambiguous, while the codes that transcribe them are not. What begins to take shape in these reflections is a meditation on the cognitive validity of ontology, a sense that both the subject and the object of all cognitive acts may actually be functions of a third and more primary process. Unlike his author, Törless could not have known anything about this primary process and only alludes to it as a still inarticulate problem. In the speculations of Mach, the philosopher on whom Musil wrote his dissertation, however, this primary process assumes the dignity of the "third and most important problem of science": the mobile relation of "psychophysics," or "the law of the connexion of sensations and presentations."[5] Like other thinkers at the beginning of the century, Törless is bewildered by the discovery of the inherent "perspectivism" of the understanding, by a budding intuition that things themselves are inextricable from the codes in which they are articulated. For "the real thing, the problem itself," still firmly lodged in Törless at the end of the novel, is this shifting mental [*seelische*] perspective upon distance and closeness.... This incomprehensible relationship [*Zusammenhang*] that according to our shifts of standpoint gives happenings and objects sudden values that are quite incommensurable with each other, strange to each other. (*GW* 6:139; *YT* 188)

By the second page of the novel Musil alerts us to the potentially paralyzing consequences of this hermeneutical confusion. The young Törless gazes at life "only as through a veil." He experiences the outer world as "only a shadowy, unmeaning string of events, indifferent stations on his way, like the markings of the hours on a clock-face." This bewilderment, or *Verwirrung*, extends even to the adolescent's own relation to himself, to that subjective core he is so intent on grasping throughout his experimental experience:

> Between events and himself, indeed between his own feelings and some inmost self that craved understanding of them there always remained a dividing-line [*eine Sheidelinie*], which receded before his desire, like a horizon, the closer he tried to come to it. Indeed, the more accurately he circumscribed his feelings with thoughts, and the more familiar they became to him, the stranger and more incomprehensible did they seem to become, in equal measure.

Throughout his experience Törless searched for a "bridge, some connexion, some means of comparison, between himself and the wordless thing confronting his spirit" (*GW* 6:8, 25, 65; *YT* 12, 34–35, 87).

Musil does not succeed in resolving this bewildering problem in the years following *Törless*; he accepts it as given. What does change, however, in the twenty-four years separating *The Man without Qualities* from *Törless* is an attitude, from visible and earnest distress to ironic pleasure in intellectual entanglement. It is this shift that allows for the generic conception of *The Man without Qualities*, a tale no longer of a naked psyche struggling with a voiceless world but of a sophisticated society's self-discussions; not of an individual "trying to lip-read words from the twisted mouth of someone who's paralyzed and simply not being able to do it" but of the unending conversations of a vociferous and articulate community (*GW* 6:89; *YT* 119). Representation is still in crisis; however, the entire culture has now recognized it as "a mysterious disease of the times." That phrase is the title of a chapter in the later novel which refers to the epoch of Törless, from 1895 to 1906, as one still imbued with hope and glimmers of genius, and suggests the difference between *Törless* and *The Man without Qualities*. By August 1913, when the action of *The Man without Qualities* unfolds, what had gotten lost is a "prognostic," an "illusion":

> Like what happens when a magnet lets the iron filings go and they tumble together again.... Ideas that had once been of lean account grew fat. Persons who had previously not been taken altogether seriously now acquired fame. What had been harsh mellowed down, what had been separated reunited.... Sharp borderlines everywhere became blurred ... the good was adulterated with a little too much of the bad, the truth with .error, and the meaning with a little too much of the spirit of accommodation (*GW* 1:57–58; *MWQ* 1:62 [16]).

Törless's personal bewilderment has assumed cultural proportions and institutional form. To discover a method for right living, the mature Törless of the later novel must begin by sorting through some of these differences and adulterations, this "good" and "bad." And to do this means first to dismantle the ideological apparatus in which the two conditions have become confused.

The first two parts of the colossal and unfinished *The Man without Qualities* are framed as a dramatic, allegorical encounter between a highly trained intellectual, Ulrich, the man without qualities, and the prewar culture, represented by the flaccid, idealistic ruling class of an empire in extremis. The reason these sophisticated liberals of the Austro-Hungarian Empire have decided to pool their mental resources is in order to plan a jubilee for the seventieth anniversary of their emperor's reign. And yet, without anyone conceiving of it in quite these terms, the reign of Emperor Franz Joseph has come accompanied by a virtually insuperable burden, the burden of an archaic and disorganized bureaucratic tradition, superimposed on mutually incompatible subcultures soon to declare their animosity in the outbreak of World War I. The centralized government of this "Emperor of Peace," as the jubilee has decided to call him, represents "merely a world that had not been cleared away," a fossilization of custom, perspective, and law. And yet, by adopting the progressive thinking of the bourgeoisie, this ruling stratum fully intends to persist in its domination of the political and intellectual world. The crowning task of the committee charged with staging the celebration is to discover a "new idea" to guide the age, one that will also show Austria "the way back to its own true nature" (*GW* 1:86–88; *MWQ* 1:97–100 [20, 21]). The ironic relation between conservatism and revolution goes even deeper than this, however, for the revolution has a reactionary origin. The Austrians have decided to celebrate 1918 only after having received wind that the German Reich is preparing to celebrate its own merely thirty-year reign in the very same year. Like its own bureaucracy, then, the Austrian campaign is "collateral" to an original fact; it is the "Collateral Campaign" (*Parallelaktion*), the "inexistent center of the novel."[6]

The Collateral Campaign, a net ensnaring the minds of the various characters of this novel, epitomizes the confusion of Vienna and all of Europe at the beginning of the century concerning its own political, moral, and metaphysical foundations. Only the man without qualities and the novel's narrator are concerned with epistemology, the science underlying all others. As a result, both those directly enlisted in the campaign ("the spirit's stewards on earth") and the sundry characters along its fringes (Clarisse, Walter, Meingast, Hans Sepp) end up seeking, each in inadequate ways, a new interpretation by which to sum up the world, a universal morality to replace or update the programs of the past. The imminent need is for a revaluation of values. An even more pressing need, but recognized as such only by Ulrich and the narrator, is a revaluation of the very means of evaluation. "At that time," writes the narrator, glancing askance at the impending war, "there were hundreds of ... unanswered questions, all of the greatest importance. They were in the air; they were burning underfoot. The time was on the move.... But one simply didn't know what it was moving towards. Nor could anyone quite distinguish between what was above and what below, between what was moving forwards and what backwards" (*GW* 1:100, 13; *MWO* 1:114, 8 [24, 2]). The echo of Nietzsche's famous description of the disorientation of the world upon the death of God ("Whither are we moving? ... Backward, sideward, forward, in all directions? Is there still any up or down?") is not incidental, for, like Nietzsche, Musil attempts to chart the vagrancy of this world unhinged from its "sun"—a sun, one begins to suspect, it never really had.[7]

One of Musil's most striking metaphors for the campaign's efforts to fetter the world to a harmless explanatory word is that of a "dot" with which people equip themselves to stare at in secret. All who submit a proposal to Ulrich, the honorary secretary of the Collateral Campaign, are unequivocally committed to a precise interpretation of the world. They have kept their eyes glued their whole lives long on

> a secret dot [*Punkt*] that everyone else refuses to see, although it
> is so obviously the very dot from which originate all the
> calamities of a world that will not recognize its saviour. Such fixed

points, where the person's center of gravity coincides with the world's center of gravity [providing, in mystical terms, a union of *Seelesgrund* and *Gottesgrund*], may be for instance a spittoon that can be shut with a simple catch ... or the introduction of Öhl's shorthand system ... or conversion to a natural mode of living, which would call a halt to the way the world is running to waste, as well as offer a metapsychical theory of the movements of celestial bodies, a plan for simplifying public administration, and a reform of sexual life. (*GW* 1:140; *MWQ* 1:162–63 [ch. 37])

The dots are metaphors for ideological reduction. As one moves up the scale from these anonymous quacks to the illustrious executive members of the campaign, the points of view become larger, more encompassing, and more spongy. Less preposterous perhaps than those outlined above, the proposals entertained by the intellectual elite of Vienna are no less facile. Count Leinsdorf envisions world harmony in the union of capital and culture (*Besitz und Bildung*); General Stumm thinks what is needed is to put some military order back into the civilian mind; Arnheim has a personal stake in the *Interresenfusion Seele-Geschäft* (the fusion of interests of soul and business); Meingast proposes a return to the creative power of will; Clarisse seeks reason in madness; Diotima, the hostess of the group's soirees, follows a more practical route, perusing the card catalog of the library before resolving on the idea of developing more workable relations of Eros than she has thus far enjoyed. Some of these are moral programs, others philosophical ones; all of them aim at formulaic control.

Chapter 108 of *The Man without Qualities* reveals the weak point of not only these formulas for world harmony but all systematizations of existence. They include some "irrational, incalculable remainder" (*irrationalen unberechenbaren Rest*) as an ultimate factor in their explanations. Religions conceive of this *Rest* as the inscrutability of God; Meingast calls it will, General Stumm understands it as honor, discipline, and "Service Regulations Part III." In the intuitive system of Bonadea's nymphomania it is called "the heart," which tempts her to commit sexual indiscretions. Although even the ingenuous Bonadea had a system, however, Austro-Hungarian politics possessed none (*GW* 2:522; *MWQ* 2:270 [109]). The terminal disease of "Kakania" (Musil's dysphemism for the *kaiserlich-königlich* empire), of which the above-mentioned thinkers are symptoms rather than cures, is its lack of an encompassing system.

The ability to invoke a system to justify one's behavior is called possessing a worldview, a *Weltanschauung*. And this ability, Musil adds, is something that modern citizens have lost (*GW* 2:520; *MWQ* 2:268 [108]).

No doubt the loss is partly due to the fact that positivists, physicists, psychologists, and philosophers had already exposed the hidden omissions, or *Reste*, of inclusive explanations of the world.[8] Nor can there be any doubt that Musil contributes a greater share to the theoretical critiques of systems than any other novelist of the century. And no less important than his perception of ideological failure are his analyses of its consequences.

A world that no longer submits to a Weltanschauung comes finally to be experienced as a series of "remainders." The collapsing structures reveal themselves to be reliant on a plethora of first principles upon which nothing can be rationally built. If to General Stumm the intellectuals of his age seemed never to be content, it is on account of this very realization: because "their thoughts never came to rest, and beheld that eternally wandering remainder in all things, which never comes into order" (*GW* 2:519; *MWQ* 2:267 [108]). Two of these intellectuals, the protagonist and the narrator of *The Man without Qualities*, hold out indefinitely, contesting the speculations of their contemporaries precisely in the measure to which they offer facile formulations of this wandering residue, compressing the world into a dot or propounding Weltanschauungen in an age that no longer allows for them.

At this point in his investigation of systematic understanding Musil moves from a metaphor of a remainder, or residue, to a metaphor of clothing. In the same way that the systematic articulation of the residue in all things seems to impart shape to the nature of reality, so the choice of one's clothes lends personality to one's character. Admittedly, in the harmonious aesthetic experience of a well-clad body, one tends to overlook the difference between the domains so coupled. On the other hand, clothes, "if lifted out of the fluidity of the present and regarded, in their monstrous existence on a human figure, as forms *per se*, are strange tubes and excrescences, worthy of the company of a shaft through the nose or a ring extended through the lip." The remainder of this enchanting communion of signifier and signified—the final and unacknowledged factor in every explanation, is the arbitrariness of the linkage itself. It occurs no differently, Musil remarks, when a tangle of lines on a piece of paper emits some sublime meaning. The disclosive power of these figures is no less uncanny than if a halo were suddenly to pop up behind a man's head as he was putting a sandwich on his plate at a tea party. And yet "such a power of making the invisible, and even, indeed, the nonexistent, visible is what a well-made dress or coat demonstrates every day!" (*GW* 2:526; *MWQ* 2:274–75 [109]).[9]

This metaphorical exchange between form and content transcribes a strange hermeneutical circle. Based though it be on an arbitrary leap of the imagination, or on an enabling tertium quid, the disclosive effect of clothing is anything but imaginary. Clothes reveal something about us after all, for the simple reason that we chose them to begin with, preinvesting them with special significance. Clothes are "debtor-objects" (*Schuldnerdinge*): By extending them credit, we get reimbursed at an exorbitant rate of interest. "In fact," and here Musil draws a deduction on the basis of his metaphor, "there *are* only debtor-objects. This quality that clothes have is also possessed by convictions, prejudices, theories, hopes, belief in anything, thoughts, indeed, even thoughtlessness possesses it, insofar as it is only by virtue of itself that it is penetrated with a sense of its own rightness" (*GW* 2:526; *MWQ* 2:275 [109]). Judgments have as convoluted a relation to the issue they address as clothes to the person who wears them. Garments of mind, as of body, are not significant in themselves but only as the consequence of some prior belief.[10]

This circular system of faith and preinvestment pervades "belief in anything." "*Credo ut intelligam*," Musil writes a few pages after his passage on debtor-objects, is the condition for the very possibility of knowledge. Before I am able to understand, I must believe. Only through a prior decision to believe do I begin to benefit from the signifying power of the symbolic language. Conviction does not result from reflection; it enables that reflection to take direction. The belief "that in some point of knowledge one possesses absolute truth," as Nietzsche noted, is the conviction that originates the very notion of truth. "Such a belief presumes, then, that absolute truths exist; likewise, that the perfect methods for arriving at them have been found; finally, that every man who has convictions makes use of these perfect methods." Or to paraphrase the determination of the best logicians: the "first stage of logic is judgment, whose essence consists ... in belief."[11] Every origin prefigures its end, and each investment establishes a line of credit.

As in many other passages of *The Man without Qualities*, here Musil gives figurative expression to arguments discursively unfolded by the philosophers of his time. But, as usual, his metaphorical flashes illuminate more than immediately appears. The larger ramification of consciousness is functional practice. Like Heidegger, Musil understands "preunderstanding" as a requirement of action at large. "In love as in commerce, in science as in the long jump, one has to have faith before one can win and reach one's aim." A person does not usually recognize, for example,

> that he must believe he is something more in order to be capable
> of being what he is; he must somehow have the sense of that
> something more above him and around him, and yet at times [as
> with a Weltanschauung] he may be suddenly deprived of it. Then

he lacks something imaginary. (*GW* 2:528–29; *MWQ* 2:277–78 [109])

This extension of an epistemological suspicion to the domains of practical action underscores the dependence of even the most spontaneous ethics on quasireligious, quasi-aesthetic operations. To give this principle a more modern formulation is to say, with Althusser, that "there is no practice except by and in an ideology."[12] Not only to understand, but even to act, one must jump from an *Abgrund* to unfounded principles.

An example of the anxiety this situation can provoke in a person who demands coherence between life and thought can be found on Thörless's obsession with the unreal reality of mathematical operations. The fact that rational calculations can be successfully made on the basis of imaginary numbers (such as i, the square root of -1) exposes the uncanny function of those remainders accompanying cognitive endeavors and the data they yield. Törless carries his perplexity straight to his math teacher, who tries to dispel the student's questions by invoking Kant's *Critique of Pure Reason*, a work, he says, that "treats of the grounds determining our actions" (*die Bestimmungsstücke unseres Handelns*) and furnishes "those mental necessities [*Denknotwendigkeiten*] ... which ... determine everything although they themselves cannot be understood immediately." But, after reading Kant, Törless is all the more sure: "There's nobody who knows where the first mesh is that keeps all the rest in place" (*GW* 6:77, 82; *YT* 103, 110).

Thus it would seem that a hermeneutical analysis of belief leads in one of two directions, either to a circle of broken connections or to an originary and primordial silence. For life to be possible this silence must be filled at all costs, even the cost of error. And this is precisely what happens. The filling is accomplished by a primal delusion (*Verblendung*) called understanding. Only by means of this *Verblendung*, writes Musil, do we manage "to live alongside the most uncanny things and remain perfectly calm about it because we recognize those frozen grimaces of the universe as a table or chair, a shout or an outstretched arm, a speed or a roast chicken." This reduction of the universe into the solid and pragmatic constituents of a stable worldview amounts to a "vivisection" that Musil retraces in thought.[13] If we ordinarily succeed in living between one open abyss of sky (*Himmelsabgrund*) above our heads and one slightly camouflaged abyss of sky beneath our feet, it is only thanks to the fact "that in between them we treat a stratum of forms [*Schichte von Gebilden*] as the things of the world." When one takes stock of this conscious stratification of the surroundings, one concludes that it is an extremely artificial state of mind that enables man to walk upright between the circling constellations and permits him, in the midst of the almost infinite unknownness of the world around him, to place his hand with dignity between the second and third buttons of his coat.

And, in order to achieve this state of mind,

> not only does every person need his own artifices [*Kunstgriffe*] ... but these personal systems of artifice are ... artfully built into the institutions for the maintenance of society's and the community's moral and intellectual equilibrium [*Gleichgewichisvorkehrungen der Gesellschaft und Gesamtheit*]. (*GW* 2:526–27; *MWQ* 2:275–76 [109])

Metaphysically speaking, the "infinity of the natural" has always been the horizon for life; but through a series of perceptual reductions it has been compressed into a Weltanschauung, or relegated to the status of the worldview's unknowable remainder. Whatever the system devised, it offers a fictitious economy, built of the hypothetical "entities" imagined by the codification.

There is undoubtedly something arbitrary about this stratum of forms constitutive of an interpreted world. Whether they be an oven, a smile, a political choice (or Heidegger's *Vor-* and *Zuhandene*), they segment the real into partial unities. Psychologically, they are the qualities (the *Eigenschaften*) defining a person's character; philosophically, they are the synthetic results of inductive and deductive reasoning; morally, they are the concepts of "duty," "responsibility," and "freedom." One wonders whether such concepts take shape purely by chance or on the basis of some historical apriority? In Musil's time the issue at stake was called the phenomenological constitution of the world: the appearance of experience as always already shaped for human purposes. The question of the actual logistics of this constituted appearance is then open to discussion. Two voices in this debate bear particular relevance for Musil: Ernst Mach and Edmund Husserl.[14]

Experience in itself, writes Mach in the *Analysis of Sensations* (1886), is an indeterminate fluctuation of sensations without any laws of its own, without substances, identities, causes, or repetitions. "Nature exists only once, it knows no repetition of the same cases." Logical order and scientific patterns are merely read into this nature as the mind translates it into concept, that is, through a simplification, schematization, and idealization of facts. Physical necessity does not exist, Mach affirms; "there exists only logical necessity," which is in turn a psychological necessity, or requirement of thought.[15] The result is that the random flux of experience is structured as a stratum of forms, causes, effects, and regularities which goes by the name of reality (or actuality, *Wirklichkeit*), which, needless to say, is structured differently in different communities of mind. What goes by the name of reality is "in great measure *conventional* and *accidental*," and in no way an accurate reflection of the way things are.[16]

Husserl, a staunch critic of Mach on a number of scores, shares Mach's belief that the world is symbolically shaped by consciousness. Before the world can be experienced at all it must have already submitted to a "transformation." The ordinary or traditional course of human experience "compels our reason to pass beyond intuitively given things ... and place at their basis a 'physical truth.'" And yet this course of experiences and the "physical truth" that it comes to posit "might also have been differently ordered." If, for instance, an experimental formation or scientific principle had never been articulated, "the physical world might have been other than it is with systems of law other than those actually prevailing." In general one can conclude that "the whole *spatio-temporal world* ... is ... *mere intentional Being*," or "reality" as the mind happens to intend it. History and nature do not consist in a hard order of fact, as the "natural attitude" has it; their appearance is constituted by consciousness. Objective reality, or the "being which for us is first," is therefore "in itself second." With regard to its own essence, reality "lacks independence." It "is not in itself something absolute ... it has no 'absolute essence' whatsoever." Once one grants the mental constitution of experience, then "'*the real world*,' as it is called, the correlate of our factual experience ... presents itself as *a special case of various possible worlds and non-worlds*."[17]

Even so, the phenomenal world is not merely a fabrication of consciousness, as though one pole of the psychophysical relation were doing all the work. There is "another" Mach in addition to the first one (and in addition to this Husserl), who recognizes that sensations are not always indeterminate and fluctuant but sometimes perceived from the start in clusters. As in the experience of a melody, these relationships, organizations, and connections are given in the perceptions of sensations themselves, not added to the sensations by thought. Immediate experience can occur in a phenomenology of patterns, partial unities, or *Gestalten*.[18]

At the end of his dissertation Musil notes that there is "a conflict in Mach's own views" according to which experience is defined as pure indeterminacy, on the one hand, and, on the other, as intrinsically patterned. Musil remarks that, while the logical ordering of reality by means of science is undoubtedly fictional in procedure, the procedure is not entirely arbitrary or independent of "objective facts." It is experience itself that offers blatant regularities; science merely attempts to furnish theoretical correlates of such perceptions. "This regularity which first induces us to deduce a necessity is thus found in facts," writes Musil. "And naturally it cannot be eliminated from facts by means of idealization; on the contrary ... it is at the basis of every step accomplished by such idealization; idealization is motivated in facts." The necessity Mach calls purely logical is therefore "not necessity proper; on the contrary, it is necessity only if to begin with there exists that other necessity which resides in facts, even if we never completely grasp its real structure with the means at our disposal" (*B* 124, 122–23; *MT* 80, 79, 80).

There is thus another, not merely mental, necessity also at work in the formation of reality in patterns, regularities, and repetitions. It is a necessity which might best be understood in the context of a metaphysics characteristic of this entire European epoch: vitalism, or *Lebensphilosophie*.

According to the general lines of this philosophy of life which bridges the period between Nietzsche and Henri Bergson, the idealization of facts is a symptom of life itself as a self-formative process. Experience is self-production and "will to form," a thrust toward expansion and growth which actualizes itself in appearances and values. This self-formation is also a type of self-representation, an activity of "fictionalization." As life becomes and articulates itself, perspectives, positions, and productions overcome their predecessors, literally making the real unreal and the unreal real. In this framework consciousness is only *one* of the operators of fictionalization, partaking of a process already inherent to experience. It simply happens to be the easiest place to see this perspectival production of the world occurring.

It is this self-productive process of life which causes the institution of functional, pragmatic relationships between a plurality of possibilities, actions, elements, and structures mutually determining each other. Practice gives birth to its own regulations. "It is not thought," remarks Musil in one of his essays, "but merely the need for practical orientation which compels the formation of stereotypes [*Formelhaftigkeit*], in fact, the stereotypes of concepts no more than those of gestures and sensory impressions, which after a couple of repetitions become as numb as the representational processes tied to words.[19] In the same reading character is at once a fictitious and historical unity: "a tendency to repetition one has acquired involuntarily" (*GW* 1:252; *MWQ* 1:299 [62]). History has its own necessity independent of mind; it simply happens to be an "unlawful necessity" (*ungesetzliche Notwendigkeit*), or a contingent mechanicity endowed with merely practical motivation.[20]

The Man without Qualities invokes this metaphysics of patterns, structures, and unities as often as it does a metaphysics of fluctuation, indeterminacy, and irrationality. What seems always to happen in experience, for instance, is that "every play of forces tends ... towards an average value and an average condition, a compromise and a state of inertia." It is as if, alongside its thrust toward self-transformation, experience has an equal tendency to perdure in whatever state it happens to have achieved. The forms and values in which life has been actualized thus frustrate its own will to form. What then grows susceptible to one's mistrust, thinks the man without qualities, "is the cut-and-dried way that life is divided up and the ready-made forms it assumes, the ever-recurring sameness of it [*das Seinesgleichen*], the preformations passed down by generation after generation, the ready-made language not only of the tongue but also of the sensations and feelings" (*GW* 1:251, 129; *MWQ* 1:298, 149–50 [62, 34]). As form gets the better of content, the condition of becoming fossilizes into that of being. The creative mobility of experience congeals into an image of itself, a self-representation or approximation. And this petrification of a state of affairs composes the reality on which a community bases its reality principles. Indeed, "its likeness occurs" or "the like of it happens" is the title of Part 2 of *The Man without Qualities* (*Seinesgleichen geschieht*), the five hundred pages housing the bulk of the novel's narrative events, those fictional but all too actual "occurrences" of human experience.[21] History evolves as a manifestation of its own self-appearance, as random congealments of the real into mere self-likenesses.

The implications of this practically motivated necessity are many. Regardless of one's creative efforts and original leaps, in the course of time "one's ordinary and non-personal ideas intensify quite of their own accord and the extraordinary ones fade ... with all the certainty of a mechanical process." Whether what attempts to take shape is a thing, a lifestyle, or even an intuition, its self-codification belies its more extensive potential. Sometimes, for example, one may seem to have an entirely personal mental experience. The minute one articulates it, however, it "no longer has the form of the thought [*des Gedankens*] in which it was experienced, but already that of the thing thought [*des Gedachten*]," and, unfortunately, this form is "a non-personal one, for the thought is then extroverted and adjusted for communication to the world." When we pride ourselves on having discovered the solution to a problem through a flash of inspiration, we claim responsibility for an act that occurs no less mechanically than that of a dog trying to get through a narrow door with a stick in its mouth: "it goes on turning its head left and right until the stick slips through."[22] Likewise, the clue to every human personality resides in an "impersonal element," in "certain simple and fundamental patterns of behaviour, an ego-building instinct, like the nest-building instinct of birds, by which the ego is constructed of many materials according to a few methods." Indeed, for all the apparent differences among a thousand human beings, once you analyze them "all you're left with is two dozen qualities, forms of development, constructive principles [*Ablaufarten, Aufbauformen*], and so on, which is all they consist of" (*GW* 1:112, 252, 66; *MWQ* 1:129, 299, 72 [28, 62, 17]).

This selfsame pattern of forms and likenesses penetrates even the recesses of one's subjectivity. The most unique and personal experiences become data fed "on to the stage, into books, into the reports of scientific institutions and expeditions, into communities based on religious or other convictions." That is, they return to the subject in a theorized, stereotyped, and "formulized" form that is no longer the original one. It is no surprise that such formulations as narcissism, paranoia, and the Oedipus complex then structure the experiences of others. Even one's innermost passions are modeled on preexistent models. "One loves because there is love, and in the way that love has always been; one is proud as an Indian, a Spaniard, a virgin, or a lion; indeed, in ninety out of a hundred cases even murder is committed only because it is considered tragic and magnificent" (*GW* 1:150, 2:365; *MWQ* 1:174, 2:73 [39, 84]).

Whatever the cause of this stereotypical and lawless necessity that goes by the name of history—whether logical, practical, or a paradoxical law of vitalistic becoming—the question inevitably arises, for Ulrich, as it did earlier for Törless, whether what one is experiencing in those preformations is really "*my* truth": "The goals, the voices, the reality, the seduction of it all, luring and leading one on," thinks Ulrich, "all that one follows and plunges into—is it the real reality or does one still get no more than a breath of the real, a breath hovering intangibly on the surface of the reality one is offered?" (*GW* 1:129; *MWQ* 1:149 [34]). As one's "own" truth begins to appear derivative, subjectivity loses its authenticity.

If a young man is intellectually alive, reflects Ulrich, he is continually sending out ideas in all directions. "But only what produces resonance in his environment will radiate back to him and condense, whereas all the other messages are scattered in space and lost." One cannot help experiencing, he continues, a "disquieting feeling of 'everything I think I am reaching is reaching me,' a gnawing surmise that in this world the untrue, careless, and personally most unimportant utterances will echo more strongly than one's own inmost, most real ones" (*GW* 1:116, 129; *MWQ* 1:134, 149 [29, 34]). Two questions immediately arise: Does this functional process of impersonal structures afford any opportunity at all for individual expression? Or is the personal, subjective domain structured just as mechanically as the setting in which it operates? Perhaps, that is, the two are imprisoned in what the biologist Johannes von Uexküll called a functional circle (*Funktionskreis*) of receptor and effector systems (*Merknetz* and *Wirknetz*), the former prestructuring an organism's receptivity to outward stimuli and the latter its possible reactions.[23] Musil tends to lean in the second direction, conceiving of modern history as an arena of "qualities without a man, of experiences without anyone to experience them," a situation that effects a "dissolution of the anthropocentric attitude" (*GW* 1:150; *MWQ* 1:174–75 [39]).[24]

This structuralization of vital flux might be bearable if it did not enforce a normalization of the elements composing it. Necessary as history may be, all too often it manifests an unnecessary absence of originality, a conventionalism repressing its own potential. The regularities are excessive, the conformity unimaginative. Instead of realizing the "fullness of life's possibilities," culture propagates models that have long since lost their motivation. One might conceive of the organized articulation of life in two separate moments. In its productive moment this articulation is actual spiritual formation, or culture in the sense of *Bildung*, by which symbols and relationships are actively produced and function as instructive, formative principles. In a subsequent and negative moment these principles degenerate into formulas, outliving themselves in a backward glance, reducing themselves to rules of thumb, tokens of what may once have been meaningfully "the case." Culture (*Kultur*) degenerates into civilization (*Zivilization*).[25] The historical epoch depicted in *The Man without Qualities* is a world of the latter, a world already formulized, in which once vital forms now reproduce themselves in their own self-likenesses, copies of copies, duplicated and transmitted as equivalent to what they represent. At this moment of sterility history is derived from its own derivations, leaving Diotima disturbed by the fact that the cultural continuity of "problems affecting one's own humanity so closely as ... the noble simplicity of Greece, or the meaning of the prophets, resolved themselves ... into an immense variety of doubts and possibilities," or into that "affliction from which modern man is well known to suffer and which is called civilisation. It is a frustrating state of affairs, full of soap, wireless waves, the arrogant symbolic language of mathematical and chemical formulae, economics, experimental research and mankind's inability to live in simple but sublime community" (*GW* 1:102–3; *MWQ* 1:117 [24]). In the era of civilization what was once understood as the unitary unfolding of "History" has lost its cogency.[26] It has dissolved into a pluralistic inconsistency of localized practices and discourses, codes and structures, mutually incommensurable principles of development.

Through this formulization of the world, things, feelings, and people lose their "essences" and ontological status. Reality turns into a context of assignments and references, a system of relations volatilizing and simulating the being of the world.[27] Entities become variables in encompassing formulas, signifiers in normative linguistic systems. The real world of the twentieth century is not composed of Wilhelm Dilthey's "lived experience" but merely its derived and reflected forms. The probability of learning something unusual from a newspaper, as Ulrich reflects, "is far greater than that of experiencing it; in other words, it is in the realm of the abstract that the more important things happen in these times, and it is the unimportant that happens in real life." Thus what may have once been viewed as a solid and authentic basis for the production of meaning—whether a value, a personality, an intention, a body of knowledge, a faith, a desire, a feeling, or a decisive historical event—has turned into an element in a self-referential system. Even something as material and tangible as water begins to lose its historical self-evidence. Long ago it was believed to be "akin to air." Then "water-sprites, elves, mermaids and nymphs were invented. Temples and oracles were founded on its banks and shores":

> And there now was water, a colourless liquid, blue only in dense layers, odourless and tasteless .... although physiologically it also included bacteria, vegetable matter, air, iron, calcium sulphate and calcium bicarbonate, and this archetype of all liquids was, physically speaking, fundamentally not a liquid at all but, according to circumstances, a solid body, a liquid or gas. Ultimately the whole thing dissolved into systems of formulae that were all somehow connected with each other, and in the whole wide world there were only a few dozen people who thought alike about even as simple a thing as water.

Of those who bothered to think about water only a few dozen agreed; the rest proceeded to talk about it "in languages that were at home somewhere between today and several thousands of years ago" (*GW* 1:69, 112–13; *MWQ* 1:76, 129:30 [18, 28]).

The formulization of the world produces both an automatism of perception and a proliferation of forms devoid of their once self-evident function.[28] Realities give way to Husserl's "unities of meaning," virtual significances, secondary elements of an uncertain primary process. The formulas encapsulating such unities are no longer sustained by "spiritual motivation"; they originate that motivation by chance and suggestion. In fact, the very notions of motivation—of governing intention, personal experience, and even a "subject"—now appear as naivetés, fictions that were credible only when thought was oblivious of its own mechanics.

To put it in the terms Musil wields so ironically (namely, those appropriate to the "skim-romanticism and yearning for God that the machine-age had for a time squirted out"), by the second decade of the century it had come to seem that spirit (*Geist*) lacked spirit. For, in post-Kantian usage, spirit means both the motivation of historical becoming and also its "phenomenology," its formal result. However ironic the context in which he places the project, Musil, like many of his contemporaries, was concerned with recuperating spirit at the "first" and deeper level—not as the arbitrary sum of its formal expressions but as the formative process itself, the self-configuring whole. At this deeper level *Geist* is a word for that all-pervading *pneuma*, or breath, diffused throughout the universe and holding all contraries together in tension, the "sympathy of the Whole" of the ancient Stoics. *Geist*, writes Musil, "mixes things up, unravels them, and forms new combinations." It was in deference to this *Geist* that the man without qualities lived so undecidedly. "Undoubtedly—he said to himself—what banished him to an aloof and anonymous form of existence was nothing but the compulsion to that loosing and binding of the world that is known by a word one does not like to encounter alone: spirit," Arnheim, his arch-antagonist, is willing to admit this much about his young colleague: "the man had reserves of as yet unexhausted soul." For in the course of time, Arnheim goes on to explain, "every human being ... dissolves his soul in intelligence, morality, and lofty ideas ... and in this his best-beloved enemy the process had not been completed" (*GW* 1:103, 153, 2:548; *MWQ* 1:118, 178–79, 2:112 [25, 40, 112]).

How can one define this soul, or spirit, that eludes its own forms of expression? Certainly not positively, as Ulrich's contemporaries attempt to do. Rather, it is the illusion of some thing still missing from the lawless relations. Negatively put, the soul "is simply what curls up and hides when there is any mention of algebraic series" (*GW* 1:103; *MWQ* 1:118 [25]). It is related to what Törless senses as the ambiguity underlying and belying all clear and distinct ideas. Why, after all, do things appear odd to him which seem perfectly ordinary to others? What is it about them that makes them seem strange? "Something about them that I don't know about," Törless concludes. "But that's just it! Where on earth do I get this 'something' [*Etwas*] from? I feel its existence; it affects me; just as if it were trying to speak" (*GW* 6:89; *YT* 119). In his intuition that everything "is fluctuating, a part of a whole, of innumerable wholes that presumably belong to a super-whole [*Überganze*], which, however, he doesn't know the slightest thing about," Ulrich senses the same thing as Törless, though less as an inlying essence than as an encompassing relation. While his contemporaries are content to abbreviate the universe into partial schemas, formulas, and systems cum remainder, Ulrich seeks that order of the whole which transcends every secondary distinction. "He wants as it were the wood and the others the trees" (*GW* 1:65, 17; *MWQ* 1:71, 13 [17, 4]).

The *Etwas* that Ulrich seeks is the entirety of *Geist*, which is missing in each of its manifestations. In Husserl's terms, Ulrich is intent on "making the world absolute in a philosophical sense" (which "is wholly foreign to the way in which we naturally look out upon the world").[29] He is searching for a "magic formula, a lever that one might be able to get a hold of, the real spirit of the spirit [*den eigentlichen Geist des Geistes*], the missing, perhaps very small, bit that would close the broken circle." But the circle cannot be closed. Nor can the essence of things, which they never had, be discovered. All that can be done is to recuperate the possibility of forming new empirical combinations: the constructive first moment of *Geist*. With his reserves of as yet unexhausted soul, Ulrich "was the expression of nothing but this dissolved condition [*dieses aufgeldste Wesen*] that all phenomena are in nowadays," an expression, that is, of the fallen moment of this *Geist* (*GW* 1:155, 65; *MWQ* 1:181, 72 [40, 17]). His task will be that of bringing about the other.

If spirit, or soul, is dissolved in intelligence and ideas, Arnheim's remark makes it clear that the soul is equally lost in moral conventions. In the last completed chapter of *The Man without Qualities* which Musil himself saw to press, Ulrich draws a firm distinction between the ordinary conception of morality—the catalog of mores that regulate human behavior—and the source of these regulations, or morality proper. Morality was for Ulrich "neither conformism [*Botmässigkeit*] nor the sum of acquired knowledge, but living out the infinite fullness of life's possibilities" (*GW* 3:1028; *MWQ* 3:431 [38]).[30] In these figures of spirit, soul, morality, and sometimes will in *The Man without Qualities*, we observe the slow emergence of tentative gestalt for the real. But it is a reality that can be manifested only in a tentative and self-constructive fashion. The *Etwas* Törless senses at the bottom of things is akin to a "moral energy" (*moralische Kraft*), a "spiritual force" (*seelische Kraft*) (*GW* 6:25; *YT* 34). "Morality is imagination," the narrator declares in the later work, and this is something that history has not come close to deploying. While the methodologies of reason, science, and technological organization have progressed at a staggering pace, the imagination that applies such methods has remained "fixed and closed." Alongside the selective systematization of selfsame forms and qualities there stands "a mound of broken shards, which are feelings, ideas, and life's potentialities, heaped up in strata just as they came into existence—always no more than side-issues—and subsequently were discarded" (*GW* 3:1028; *MWQ* 3:431 [38]).

We can now understand why Törless views the outer world only as through a veil, as an indifferent, shadowy, unmeaning string of events. Three steps have been involved: the world has been dissociated from consciousness; it has dissolved into formulas beyond which nothing substantial is visible; and this realization has instilled a moral confusion. Recognizing what Husserl calls "the detachability in principle of the whole natural world from the domain of consciousness,"[31] Törless has witnessed the "failure of that power of association which generally causes our life to be faultlessly reflected in our understanding, as though life and understanding ran parallel to each other and at equal speed" (GW 6:64; YT 85). What exists "already *realiter*" for Törless is only one among many possible determinations within "the undetermined ... marginal field of [his] factual experience at the time being." Confronting the purely "hypothetical construction of practical life," Törless considers this construction infinitely relativized by its spectrum of potential significances, by "this shifting but ever-present horizon through which the world-thesis receives its essential meaning."[32] Things have become indistinguishable from the codes in which they are articulated, without the help of an interpretive key. The question "What for?" arises and goes unanswered.

The fragmented and unpersuasive world thesis has a comparable effect on the man without qualities. The book, we remember, opens with Ulrich's plan to take a year's leave from life. Feeling like "a traveller sitting down on a bench for eternity," he decides there is no reason to do anything until he has discovered an appropriate way of using his abilities. The first picture of the man without qualities shows him attempting to apply some objective measure to this unreal actuality. Standing at the window trying to calculate the energy consumed by people "doing nothing at all," Ulrich shrugs his shoulders and thinks, "it doesn't matter what one does.... In a tangle of forces like this it doesn't make a scrap of difference." He turns from the window "like a man who has learned renunciation, almost indeed like a sick man who shrinks from any intensity of contact." His epistemological research has produced its moral effects. And yet the burden of gazing into the still undetermined relations of things marks only the beginning of Ulrich's ethical project. Striding past the punching ball that hung in his dressing room, the man without qualities "gave it a blow far swifter and harder than is usual in moods of resignation or states of weakness" (GW 1:19, 47, 13; MWQ 1:16, 49, 8 [5, 13, 2]).

We supply Ulrich's thoughts and feelings as they develop throughout the book. His life has "run out of the sense of necessity as a lamp runs out of oil," leaving him with nothing to fall back on but the "resistance of a primal instinct against this world petrified into millions of tons of stone, against this rigid lunar landscape of feeling into which one had been set down with no will of one's own." This "unlawful necessity" bears witness to a world from which "God withdrew his credit." Nowhere can one discover "any sufficient reason for everything's having come about as it has. It might just as well have turned out differently" (*GW* 2:593, 1:130, 2:259, 1:131; *MWQ* 2:361, 1:150, 2:278, 1:151 [116, 34, 109, 34]). Historical actuality was ruled by the "Principle of insufficient Reason," like the haphazard organization of a "a bad play." The same roles, complications, and plots always kept arising. The motivating concepts of actions were only "metaphors that [had] been left to congeal." Ulrich can therefore see no motive "to attach more importance to what is than to what is not" (*GW* 2:364, 574, 1:16; *MWQ* 2:73, 337, 1:12 [84, 114, 4]). The only thing to do, he decides, is to abolish reality entirely.

God, Ulrich thinks, "is far from meaning the world literally; it is an image, an analogy, a turn of phrase [*ein Bild, eine Analogie, eine Redewendung*], which he must make use of for some reason or other, and it is of course always inadequate; we must not take him at his word, we ourselves must work out the sum that he sets us."[33] In fact, only when taken literally does the figurative process of life degenerate into a petrified mass of formulas, correlates of an inflexible reality principle. And that is precisely when one should think of abolishing it. One must abolish the real and "regain possession of unreality [*sich wieder der Unwirklichkeit bemächtigen*]." To regain possession of unreality would mean to erase all the congealed metaphors and "upholstery of fatty tissue that ... makes reality look round and plump" (*GW* 2:357, 575, 573; *MWQ* 2:65, 338, 336 [83, 114]). It would mean recalculating the sum of unreal and unspirited reality principles in accordance with the selective principle of artist and reader, who leave out of the story everything they have no use for. The task, however approached (and mysticism is admittedly one, though not the most disciplined, solution), becomes that of "transforming the world's haphazard state of consciousness into a single will." At that point one would act as though in a dream or fantasy, not letting one's emotions succumb to the "medial condition" of reality but developing them instead "to their full passionate intensity." Rather than the history of the world, one would live the history of ideas, "in the manner of art," like a character in a book (*GW* 1:251, 2:573, 367, 573; *MWQ* 1:298, 2:336, 77, 336 [62, 114, 84, 114]).

All these are metaphors for metaphor itself, for experience as a figurative process, in which repossessing oneself of unreality means nothing less than restoring the "primal condition of life" (*GW* 2:574; *MWQ* 2:337 [114]). It is easy to see that this restoration envisions art as the real task of life, art "as life's *metaphysical* activity."[34] One should stress, however, that this vision implies neither an aestheticist negation of nor a subjective flight from the objective order of things.[35] For it is the objective order itself that contains this "nonsensical yearning for unreality [*Unwirklichkeit*]" as the motivating principle of its constitution (in which, one might add, the subject is never anything more than a single formation). It is this yearning for unreality which "actualizes" the real in an exclusionary forest of symbolic forms, as though showing that incorrigible tendency toward abstraction that Musil's contemporary Wilhelm Worringer derives from humanity's "spiritual space-phobia [*geistige Raumscheu*]."[36] Even the person most compulsively committed to reality has an entirely figurative relationship to concrete experience. In truth, "reality is something that the worthy practical realist [*Wirklichkeitmensch*] does not ever wholly love and take seriously":

> As a child he crawls under the table, when his parents are not at home, by this brilliantly simple trick making their living-room into a place of adventure; as a growing boy he hankers after a watch of his own; as the young man with the gold watch he longs for the woman to go with it; as a mature man with watch and wife he hankers after a prominent position; and when he has successfully attained the fulfillment of this little circle of wishes and is calmly swinging to and fro in it like a pendulum, it nevertheless seems that his store of unsatisfied dreams has not diminished by one jot, for when he wants to rise above the rut of every day he will resort to a simile [*Gleichnis*]. Obviously because snow is at times disagreeable to him, he compares it to women's glimmering breasts, and as soon as his wife's breasts begin to bore him, he compares them to glimmering snow.... He is capable of turning everything into anything—snow into skin, skin into blossoms, blossoms into sugar, sugar into powder, and powder back into little drifts of snow—for all that matters to him, apparently, is to make things into what they are not. (*GW* 1:138; *MWQ* 1:160–61 [37])

Musil is doing more than underscoring the irony that the most deluded dreamer of all is the practical realist, gazing at a dot that shifts and recedes with every present horizon. He is making a metaphysical assertion, to the effect that "even ordinary life is of a Utopian nature." This answers Ulrich's question of "why all figurative [*uneigentlichen*] and (in the higher sense of the word) untrue utterances were so uncannily favoured by the world." No sooner are the structures of reality erected than they are resisted by the force of a dream. And the stronger the dream, the less willing is the dreamer to give it life. Is there anyone, Ulrich asks, "who would not be at a loss if whatever he had been passionately demanding all his life long were suddenly to happen? If for instance the Kingdom of God were suddenly to burst on the Catholics or the Utopian State on the Socialists? ... One gets used to demanding and isn't ready at a minute's notice for the realisation of it" (*GW* 2:363, 1:148, 288; *MWQ* 2:72, 1:172, 342 [84, 39, 69]). Regaining possession of unreality would simply mean taking this utopian compulsion to its practical conclusion, rectifying the fact that the development of reality "is at least one hundred years behind [that of] thought" (*LWW* 339). Like the Collateral Campaign, life should be made to provide "an opportunity ... for giving practical reality to the things one believed greatest and most important." It should bring "ideas into the domains of power," rather than banishing them to the realm of dream (*GW* 1:93, 109; *MWQ* 1:106, 125 [22, 26]).

What Musil has in mind with the appropriation of unreality involves not idealistically negating the objective order but liberating the idealization of facts; not turning "life into art" but turning art into life; not imposing arbitrary form on things but allowing their forms to develop less arbitrarily than usual.[37] If anything, Musil agrees with Lenin's and Lukács' critiques of the implicit idealism and subjectivism of Machian empiriocriticism on which he was nourished.[38] Beneath Ulrich's fantasy of reinventing reality lies essentially the same conception of the twofold responsibility of art by which Lukács presumed to call writers like Musil to task: to depict the "dynamic infinity" and "intensive inexhaustibility" of objective particulars; and to reorganize these particulars in a new extensive order.[39] Far from "abstracting reality out of existence," as Lukács claims, Musil is interested in rediscovering reality's intensive and extensive dynamic. What he asks of both art and life is that they formulate an "actual idealism" at equal remove from naturalistic acceptance and subjectivist wish. Naturalism, he writes in his essay on Spengler, had offered "reality without spirit, expressionism spirit without reality: both of them non-spirit [*Ungeist*]" (*GW* 8:1059; *PS* 149). Or, in the words of a discarded preface to *Nachlaß zu Lebzeiten*, poetry should "describe not what is, but what should be; or what could be as a partial solution to what should be" (*GW* 7:970).

And thus Musil transcends the mimetic aesthetics of orthodox Marxism in the same utopian direction as Theodor Adorno. Allowing for the "moment of unreality and nonexistence" in art, Adorno stresses that such a moment "is not independent of the existent, as though it were posited or invented by some arbitrary will." Aiming to undo "the conceptualization foisted on the real world," art must necessarily "slough off a repressive, external-empirical mode of experiencing the world." To achieve a synthesis of not this order but its *membra disiecta* (scattered members), art must dialectically negate the ruling metaphors of a historical existence and give voice to what they exclude. And, though it is impossible to bring it to any final fruition, such a synthesis represents nothing but a higher and more sophisticated operation of *Geist*, a development of the same "principle whereby spirit has dominated the world."[40]

If there is anything inadequate about the way this spirit has ruled the world, it lies not merely in the fact that spirit has shown insufficient motivation but also that it has consistently settled for a univocal, narrative order, a linear chronology, a slow conceptual progress, a one-way schema of agents and actions, and causes and effects (the order that critics like Lukács then ask artists to mime, demanding that they display the "stable" determinations of things in the greatest possible "purity, clarity, and typicality").[41] No doubt, the narrator of *The Man without Qualities* reflects, there are people who still experience the world in terms of these personal narratives, "saying 'we were at So-and-So's yesterday' or 'we'll do this or that today'" (*GW* 1:150; *MWQ* 1:175 [39]), but the schema is too limiting, unduly exclusive, and mechanically selective. Musil sees the need to replace this paradigm of personal, logical, and diachronic order—which is not the way things occur at all—with another based on more flexible and multiple functional relations. To grasp both the intensive and extensive determinations of things, one must suspend both "narrative order" and the world it has produced in deference to essayistic order. Essayistic order alone can allow for a constructive determination of potential.

NOTES

1. Robert Musil, *Die Verwirrungen des Zöglings Törless* (*GW* 6:24), trans. Eithne Wilkins and Ernst Kaiser with the title *Young Törless* (hereafter *YT*) (London: Panther Books, 1971), 33. I have often revised the Wilkins-Kaiser translation.

2. Musil began to write *Törless* one year before he enrolled in the doctoral program in philosophy under Carl Stumpf at the University of Berlin in 1903; he finished it in 1905. Wilhelm Dilthey, the philosopher of the *Geisteswissenschaften*, was the chair of Musil's department, and Georg Simmel was a regular guest lecturer. While Musil wrote his dissertation on the empiriocriticism of Ernst Mach (approved with initial resistance by Stumpf and the degree conferred in 1908), the philosophies most in vogue during the period of Musil's studies were the phenomenological return "to things themselves" of Stumpf's student Edmund Husserl and the neo-Kantian investigations of the Marburg school, focusing on the conditions for the possibility of understanding. At the same time, in Cambridge, Bertrand Russell and G.E. Moore were laying the foundations for what would turn into analytic philosophy and logical atomism. By 1913 Ludwig Wittgenstein was at work on the *Tractatus Logico-Philosophicus*. On links between *Törless* and contemporary investigations into the legitimacy of scientific method, see Jan Aler, "Als Zögling zwischen Maeterlinck und Mach: Robert Musils literarisch-philosophische Anfänge," in *Probleme des Erzählens in der Weltliteratur: Festschrift für Käte Hamburger*, ed. Fritz Martini (Stuttgart: Klett, 1971), 234–90.

3. As Renate von Heydebrand notes, the tie between epistemology and morality had been underscored for Musil not only by Mach but also Nietzsche. In both thinkers the "positivistic critique of knowledge and language ... leads [unavoidably] to a critique of morality" (*Die Reflexionen Ulrichs in Robert Musils Roman "Der Mann ohne Eigenschaften": Ihr Zusammenhang mit dem zeitgenössischen Denken* [Münster: Aschendorff, 1966], 25).

4. Ludwig Wittgenstein, *On Certainty*, ed. G.E.M. Anscombe and G.H. von Wright (New York: Harper & Row, 1972), sec. 113. On connections between Musil and Wittgenstein, see Gerhart Baumann, *Robert Musil: Zur Erkenntnis der Dichtung* (Bern: Francke, 1965), 170–206; Jean-Pierre Cometti, *Robert Musil ou l'alternative romanesque* (Paris: Presses Universitaires de France, 1985), 223–36, and passim; Karl Corino, "Der erlöste Tantalus," *Annali* (Naples) 23:2–3 (1980); Allan Janik and Stephen Toulmin, *Wittgenstein's Vienna* (New York: Simon & Schuster, 1973), 66, 118–19; J.-C. Nyíri, "Zwei geistige Leisterne: Musil und Wittgenstein," *Literatur und Kritik* 113 (1977): 167–79; Ernst Randak, "Über die Möglichkeit," *Wort in der Zeit* 9 (1963): 25–26; Marie-Louise Roth, *Robert Musil: Ethik und Ästhetik: Zum theoretischen Werk des Dichters* (Munich: P. List, 1972), 84, 229, 447; and Walter H. Sokel, "Kleist's Marquise of O., Kierkegaard's Abraham, and Musil's Tonka: Three Stages of the Absurd as the Touchstone of Faith," in *Festschrift für Bernhard Blume: Zaufsätze zur deutschen und europäischen Literatur*, ed. Egon Schwartz, Hannum, and Lohner (Göttingen: Vanderhöck & Ruprecht, 1967), 331.

5. Ernst Mach, *The History and Root of the Principle of Conservation of Energy* (1909), trans. Philip E.B. Jourdain (Chicago: Open Court Press, 1911), 92.

6. Ladislao Mittner, *La letteratura tedesca del Novecento e altri saggi* (Turin: Einaudi, 1960), 318. The Collateral Campaign is the focus of satire, a strategy crucial to Musil's critical, dismantling writing. On the satiric dimensions of *The Man without Qualities* and their epistemological implications, see Helmut Arntzen, *Satirischer Stil: Zur Satire Robert Musils im "Mann ohne Eigenschaften,"* 2d ed. (Bonn: Bouvier, 1970); as well as the objections to Arntzen raised by Lothar Huber in "Satire and Irony in Musil's *Der Mann ohne Eigenschaften*," in *Musil in Focus: Papers from a Centenary Symposium*, ed. Lothar Huber and John J. White (Leeds: Institute of Germanic Studies, University of London, 1982), 99–114. For a critical discussion of *The Man without Qualities* as a whole, see Philip Payne, *Robert Musil's The Man without Qualities: A Critical Study* (Cambridge: Cambridge University Press, 1988).

7. Nietzsche, *Gay Science*, sec. 125. Frederick G. Peters also calls attention to Nietzsche's parable in his reading of the self-dissolution of the man without qualities as a psychological corollary of the void left by the retreat of god (*Robert Musil: Master of the Hovering Life* [New York: Columbia University Press, 1978], 37). On relations between Nietzsche and Musil, see Wilhelm Bausinger, *Studien zu einer historisch-kritischen Ausgabe von Robert Musils Roman "Der Mann ohne Eigenschaften"* (Reinbek bei Hamburg: Rowohlt, 1964); Charlotte Dresler-Brumme, *Nietzsches Philosophie in Musils Roman "Der Mann ohne Eigenschaften"* (Frankfurt am Main: Athenäum, 1987); Lynda J. Jeanne King, "The Relationship between Clarisse and Nietzsche in Musil's *Der Mann ohne Eigenschaften*," *Musil-Forum* 4 (1978): 21–34; F.G. Peters, *Musil and Nietzsche* (Ph.D. diss., Cambridge University, 1974); Roberto Olmi, "La présence de Nietzsche," *L'Herne* 41 (1981): 153–66; Herbert W. Reichert, "Nietzschean Influences in *Der Mann ohne Eigenschaften*," *German Quarterly* 39 (1966): 12–28; Ingo Seidler, "Das Nietzschebild Robert Musils," *DVjS* 39 (1965): 329–49; and Aldo Venturelli, "Die Kunst als fröhliche Wissenschaft: Zum Verhältnis Musils zu Nietzsche," *Nietzsche Studien* 9 (1980): 302–37.

8. See David S. Luft, *Robert Musil and the Crisis of European Culture 1880–1942* (Berkeley: University of California Press, 1980), 18–23.

9. Like satire, Musilian irony tends to expose the relativity and arbitrariness of a fact or phenomenon by presenting it from a disinterested or unusual perspective. On Musilian irony, see Beda Allemann, *Ironie und Dichtung* (Pfullingen, 1956), 177–220; Maurice Blanchot, *Le livre à venir* (Paris: Gallimard, 1959), 165–84; Enrico De Angelis, *Robert Musil: Biografia e profilo critico* (Turin: Piccolo Biblioteca Einaudi, 1982), 175–214; Marike Finlay, *The Potential of Modern Discourse: Musil, Pierce, and Perturbation* (Bloomington: Indiana University Press, 1990), 14–18, 100–134; Dietrich Hochstätter, *Sprache des Möglichen: Stilistischer Perspektivismus in Robert Musils "Mann ohne Eigenschaften"* (Frankfurt am Main: Athenäum, 1972); Huber, "Satire and Irony"; and Payne, *Robert Musil*, 69–75.

10. The lexical resonances of Musil's passage are unmistakable. *Überzeugung, Vorurteil,* and even *Glaube* come already staggering from the blows Nietzsche had delivered them. The missing fourth is *Gewissen,* or conscience, but it is obvious why Musil failed to include it. Far from giving us a positive return, like beliefs and convictions, conscience holds us in debt; it is not a debtor but a creditor object. The findings are analogous in Freud's theory of the superego, in Heidegger's analyses of *Gewissen* and *Schuld* (*Being and Time,* sees. 54–69), and in Nietzsche's archaeology of guilt in *Genealogy of Morals.* For Nietzsche and Heidegger guilt is the very origin of debtor-objects.

11. Friedrich Nietzsche, *Human, All Too Human: A Book for Free Spirits,* trans. Marion Faber, with Stephen Lehmann (Lincoln: University of Nebraska Press, 1984), sees. 630, 18.

12. Louis Althusser, "Ideology and Ideological State Apparatuses," in *Lenin and Philosophy, and Other Essays,* trans. Ben Brewster (New York: New Left Books, 1971), 170.

13. Toward the end of 1899, inspired by figures of speech in Nietzsche's *Beyond Good and Evil* (sees. 186, 218, 229), and *The Genealogy of Morals* (1:1 and 3:4), Musil wrote sketches for a work to be entitled "Monsieur le vivisecteur." Recounting "the adventures and peregrinations of a vivisector of souls at the beginning of the twentieth century," this projected work prefigures *The Man without Qualities* (Robert Musil, *Tagebücher* [hereafter *TB*], ed. Adolf Frisé, 2 vols. [Hamburg: Rowohlt, 1983], 1:1–3, and passim). In years to come Musil continued to refer to his analyses and dismantling of cultural practices as vivisection.

14. Musil was a keen reader of the first volume of Husserl's *Logical Investigations,* transcribing and discussing its argument in his journals. On Musil's ties to Mach and Husserl, see Gerhart Baumann, "Robert Musil: Eine Vorstudie," *Germ.-Rom. Monatsschr.* 34 (1953): 292–316; Cometti, *Robert Musil,* 17–46; Hartmut Cellbrot, *Die Bewegung des Sinnes: Zur Phänomenologie Robert Musils in Hinblick auf Edmund Husserl* (Munich: Fink, 1988); Finlay, *Potential of Modern Discourse,* 26–30; Ulrich Karthaus, "Musil-Forschung und Musil-Deutung: Ein Literaturbericht," *DVjS* 39 (1965): 441–83; Karl Menges, "Robert Musil und Edmund Husserl: Über phänomenologische Strukturen im *Mann ohne Eigenschaften,*" *Modern Austrian Literature* 9 (1976): 131–54; Claudia Monti, *Musil: La metafora della scienza* (Naples: Tullio Pironti, 1983); Gerd Müller, *Dichtung und Wissenschaft: Studien zu Robert Musils Romanen "Die Verwirrungen des Zöglings Törless" und "Der Mann ohne Eigenschaften"* (Uppsala: Almqvist & Wiksells, 1971); Walter H. Sokel, "Musil et l'existentialisme," trans. Albert Fuchs, *L'Herne* 41 (1981): 191–93; and G. H. von Wright, "Introduction," Robert Musil, *On Mach's Theories* (hereafter *MT*), trans. Kevin Mulligan (Washington, D.C.: Catholic University of America Press, 1982).

15. Quoted in Robert Musil, *Beitrag zur Beurteilung der Lehren Machs* (hereafter *B*) (Berlin: Dissertationen-Verlag Carl Arnold, 1908), 98, 81; trans. as *MT*, 67, 58, 64. The translations are mine.

16. Ernst Mach, *The Science of Mechanics: A Critical and Historical Account of Its*

Development (1883), 6th ed. through 9th German ed., trans. Thomas J. McCormack (La Salle, Ill.: Open Court Press, 1960), 316.

17. Edmund Husserl, *Ideas: General introduction to Pure Phenomenology* (1913), trans. W. R. Boyce Gibson (New York: Collier, 1962), sees. 47, 50, 47.

18. Musil's interest in Gestalt psychology (which was itself of Machian inspiration and began to develop under the influence of Carl Stumpf in the years Musil attended the University of Berlin) is well documented. Musil possessed Wolfgang Köhler's *Die physischen Gestalten in Ruhe und im stationären Zustand* (1920) and referred to it constantly. See the entries on Köhler, Kurt Lewin, Erich Maria von Hornbostel, and Max Wertheimer in *TB* (esp. 1:801, 2:583–84, 1213–15) and references in his essays (esp. *GW* 8:1085, 1141). On Musil's work as the product of a theoretical conjunction of Machian empiriocriticism and Gestalt psychology, see Monti, *Musil*; Aldo Venturelli, "Il mondo come laboratorio: Musil e la psicologia della Gestalt di Wolfgang Köhler," in *Musil nostro contemporaneo*, ed. Paolo Chiarini (Rome: Istituto Italiano Studi Germanici, 1985).

19. Robert Musil, "Ansätze zu einer neuer Ästhetik: Bemerkungen über eine Dramaturgie des Films" (1925; "Cues for a New Aesthetic: Remarks on a Dramaturgy of Film") (hereafter "Cues") *GW* 8:1146; *PS* 201). Mach admits as much in *Science of Mechanics*: Knowledge of every sort is motivated "directly or indirectly by a practical interest," in short, by the adaptation of the animal to its environment (578).

20. Robert Musil, "Das hilflose Europa oder Reise vom Hundersten ins Tausendste" (1922; "Helpless Europe, or a Digressive Journey"), *GW* 8:1081; *PS* 122.

21. Hannah Hickman proposes two more colloquial translations of *Seinesgleichen geschieht*: "History repeats itself" and "There's nothing new under the sun" (*Robert Musil and the Culture of Vienna* [La Salle, Ill.: Open Court Press, 1984], 145).

22. Musil is obviously rejecting the distinction that Köhler draws between "a mere chance solution" and "a genuine solution," a distinction presented by Ernst Cassirer as emblematic of the difference between humans and animals, the latter presumably operating only on the basis of practical intelligence, the former on the basis of a symbolic one. The example of the dog underscores the extent to which Mach himself already acknowledges this "other," form-taking necessity in history, for it was he who first utilized the example to substantiate his claim that experimentation underlies even "instinctive" and unreflected action. The trial and error of the dog is identical in procedure to the intellectual experimentation of scientific research; both end up assuming what only appear to be "necessary" forms. See Ernst Cassirer, *An Essay on Man* (New Haven, Conn.: Yale University Press, 1965), 33; Wolfgang Köhler, *The Mentality of Apes* (New York: Harcourt Brace, & Company, 1925), 192–234 (esp. 201); and Ernst Mach, *Knowledge and Error: Sketches on the Psychology of Inquiry* (1905), trans. Thomas J. McCormack and Paul Foulkes (Dordrecht: D. Reidel, 1976).

23. See Jakob Johann von Uexküll, *Theoretical Biology* (1920), trans. A. L. MacKinnan (London: Kegan Paul, 1926); and *Umwelt und Innenwelt der Tiere* (Berlin: Springer, 1909). While the connection between Musil and Uexküll is merely incidental, it attests to Musil's tight and uneasy relation to the various mechanistic, functionalist, and behaviorist approaches to experience developed at the turn of the century (among which one might also recall Jacques Loeb's "theory of tropism" in his 1918 work, *Forced Movements, Tropisms, and Animal Conduct* [New York: Dover, 1971]).

24. Even so, the yearning for an "authentic" or "real" reality that is so characteristic of Ulrich and his contemporaries leads *The Man without Qualities* to research, with increasing ardor, the possibility of a *unio mystico* with a plenary Being underlying the mechanistic structures of history. In the wake of the debates inspired by Kaiser and

Wilkin's reading of the novel in precisely this key, most scholars have agreed that Musil never succeeds in discovering a satisfactory articulation for either this intuition of plenary Being or the ethical program that it might entail. Mystical union remains only the desideratum of his essayistic quest. On the mystical goal toward which Musil and his protagonist Ulrich are working, see Dietmar Goltschnigg, *Mystische Tradition im Roman Robert Musils: Martin Bubers "Ekstatische Konfessionen" im "Mann ohne Eigenschaften"* (Heidelberg: Stiehm, 1974); Ernst Kaiser and Eithne Wilkins, *Robert Musil: Eine Einführung in das Werk* (Stuttgart: Kohlhammer, 1962); and the exchange between Cesare Cases and Walter Boehlich in *Merkur* 18 (1964): 266–74, 696–99, 897–900.

25. Cf. Oswald Spengler's cyclical account of history in terms of this same opposition between culture and civilization. In a lengthy review Musil criticizes Spengler but remains sympathetic to the basic distinction. See Robert Musil, "Geist und Erfahrung: Anmerkungen für Leser, welche den Untergand des Abendlandes entronnen sind" (1921; "Spirit and Experience: Notes for Readers Who Have Escaped the Decline of the West"), *GW* 8:1042–59; *PS* 134–49. For similar treatments of generative versus degenerative history in Musil's time, see Nicolas Berdyaev, *The Meaning of History* (1923), trans. George Reavey (London: Geoffrey Bles, 1936), esp. 207–24; René Guénon, *La crise du monde moderne* (Paris: Bossard, 1927); and Paul Valéry, "La crise de l'esprit" (1919), *Varieté I et II* (Paris: Gallimard, 1978), 13–51.

26. Cf. Siegfried Kracauer, "Time and History," *Zeugnisse: Theodor W. Adorno zum sechzigsten Geburtstag*, ed. Max Horkheimer (Frankfurt am Main: Europäische Verlangstalt, 1963), 50–64; "General History and The Aesthetic Approach," *Die nicht mehr schönen Künste: Grenzphänomene des Aesthetischen (Poetik und Hermeneutik 3)*, ed. H. R. Jauss (Munich: Wilhelm Fink, 1968), 111–27.

27. On "volatization," see Heidegger, *Being and Time*, sec. 18; on simulation, see Jean Baudrillard, *Simulations*, trans. Paul Foss, Paul Patton, and Philip Beitchman (New York: Semiotexte, 1983).

28. On the automatism of perception, see the Russian Formalists, esp. Victor Shklovsky, "Art as Technique" (1917), in *Russian Formalist Criticism: Four Essays*, trans. Lee T. Lemon and Marion J. Reis (Lincoln: University of Nebraska Press, 1965), 3–24.

29. Husserl, *Ideas*, sec. 55.

30. On an analogous distinction between "fluid" and "static" morality, see Musil's "Skizze der Erkenntnis des Dichters" (1918; "Sketch of Scriptorial Knowledge"), *GW* 8:1025–30; *PS* 61–65.

31. Husserl, *Ideas*, sec. 46.

32. Husserl, *Ideas*, sec. 47.

33. On Musil's constructive use of analogy, see Dorrit Cohn, "Psycho-Analogies: A Means for Rendering Consciousness," in Martini, ed., *Probleme des Erzählens*, 291–302; Dieter Kühn, *Analogie und Variation: Zur Analyze von Robert Musils Roman "Der Mann ohne Eigenschaften"* (Bonn: Bouvier, 1965); Ulrich Schelling, "Das analogische Denken bei Robert Musil," in *Robert Musil: Studien zu seinem Werk*, ed. Karl Dinklage, Elisabeth Albertson, and Karl Corino (Reinbek bei Hamburg: Rowohlt, 1970), 170–99; as well as the studies by Roth, *Robert Musil*, and Monti, *Musil*.

34. Friedrich Nietzsche, *The Will to Power*, ed. Walter Kaufmann (New York: Random House, 1968), sec. 853. Cf. also his *Birth of Tragedy*, in *Basic Writings of Nietzsche*, ed. and trans. Walter Kaufmann (New York: Modern Library, 1968), "Attempt at a Self-Criticism," sec. 5.

35. This is the position taken by Georg Lukács against Musil and other modernists in

"The Ideology of Modernism," *The Meaning of Contemporary Realism*, trans. John and Necke Mander (London: Merlin Press, 1963), 17–46.

36. Wilhelm Worringer, *Abstraction and Empathy: A Contribution to the Psychology of Style* (1907), trans. Michael Bullock (New York: International Universities Press, 1980), 15–16.

37. For a thorough study of Musil's attempt to "potentiate reality," see Roth, *Robert Musil*, 185–266.

38. See Vladimir Lenin, *Materialism and Empirio-Criticism: Critical Comments on a Reactionary Philosophy* (1909) (New York: International Publishers, 1970). Like Max Planck, Lenin took issue with what he read as Mach's advocacy of the purely subjective validity of the relations expressed by the laws of physics. Of course, Husserl had already accused Mach of a "psychologization of logic" in 1900 (*Logical Investigations*, vol. 1). It is interesting that the young Albert Einstein defended Mach against both accusations in a letter of 1913. See Alfonsina D'Elia, *Ernst Mach* (Florence: La Nuova Italia, 1971).

39. Georg Lukács, "Art and Objective Truth," *Writer and Critic and Other Essays*, ed. and trans. Arthur D. Kahn (New York: Grosset & Dunlap, 1970), 38–39. On Musil's writing as executing Lukács's dictum that irony constitutes the "objectivity of the novel," see Frank Trömmler, *Roman und Wirklichkeit: Eine Ortsbestimmung am Beispiel von Musil, Broch, Roth, Doderer and Gütersloh* (Stuttgart: Kohlhammer, 1966), 68–100.

40. Adorno, *Aesthetic Theory*, 10. In a similar vein Manfred Sera argues that the simultaneously utopian and parodic intentions of *The Man without Qualities* establish a dialectic in which narrated reality begins to border on unreality, making it the task of the novel to overcome the discrepancy between life without spirit and spirit without life. See his *Utopie und Parodie bei Musil, Broch and Thomas Mann: Der Mann ohne Eigenschaften; Die Schlafwandler; Der Zauberberg* (Bonn: Bouvier, 1969). On Musil's (pre-Adornian) critique of the Enlightenment faith in the "trinity of nature, reason, and freedom," see *GW* 8:1123; and Jacques Bouveresse's commentary in "Robert Musil ou l'anti-Spengler," *L'Herne* 41 (1981): 170. For a critical reading of Musil from the standpoint of the Frankfurt school and Freudian psychoanalysis, see Klaus Laermann, *Eigenschaftslosigkeit: Reflexionen zu Musils Roman "Der Mann ohne Eigenschaften"* (Stuttgart: Metzler, 1970).

41. Lukács, *Writer and Critic*, 47.

ERIC WHITE

Chance and Narrative in Musil and Buñuel

"All moral propositions," Ulrich confirmed, "refer to a sort of dream condition that's long ago taken flight and flown away out of the cage of rules in which we try to hold it fast."
—Robert Musil, *The Man without Qualities*

For my part, I see liberty as a ghost that we try to grasp ... and ... we embrace a misty shape that leaves us with only a wisp of vapor in our hands.
—Luis Buñuel, in an interview

Suppose the concept of "chance" as an ontological first principle. Suppose events come to pass very largely by chance from the fortuitous convergence of indeterminately many factors. Suppose history consequently follows a wayward and errant path as a succession of contingencies with neither an origin to define its direction nor a destination to guide its course. Suppose, further, that the predictable routine of everyday life may be interrupted at any time by intrusions from an ineluctable "outside" endowed with a seemingly limitless capacity for producing surprise, an outside whose unforeseeable agency insures that knowledge and belief will always be in medias res, in the middle of a "chaosmos" where lawful regularity and purposeful design mingle with purely random developments in complex confusion. Finally, if chance decides what befalls individuals and groups in

From *Chance, Culture and the Literary Text*, edited by Thomas M. Kavanagh. ©1994 by Michigan Romance Studies.

the sense of good luck or misfortune, suppose that contingent circumstance presents as well the hazardous or risk-filled opportunity to take a chance, the chance to think and do otherwise.

In the following essay, I am going to argue that suppositions such as these provide crucial beginning premises for Robert Musil's unfinished magnum opus *The Man without Qualities* (1930–32) and Luis Buñuel's late film *The Phantom of Liberty* (1974), each of which elaborates an ethos or fundamental orientation toward the world in which chance is assigned a paramount role. Responsiveness to the sudden and unexpected promptings of emergent situations in fact connotes vital fullness and abundance in both works. Buñuel and Musil affirm chance, in other words, as the promise of release from compulsive repetition. They therefore set out in *The Phantom of Liberty* and *The Man without Qualities* to programmatically delegitimate the various forms of closure—psychological, social, ideological, and including the aesthetic closure of narrative form itself—by means of which, in their shared view, European culture has sought to abolish contingency and the unlimited openness of becoming in favor of some putatively final state of affairs. Foregoing settled structures and normative truths, in their pursuit of the "dream condition" of "liberty" Musil and Buñuel instead propose to make the most of metamorphosis by trusting, precisely, to chance.

The Man without Qualities offers numerous figurations of the cultural realm as a chance-driven spectacle or happening. Reflecting on the dynamic of historical process, Musil's protagonist Ulrich makes this point:

> World history ... evolved not from a centre, but from the periphery, from minor causes ... The course of history was therefore not that of a billiard-ball, which, once it had been hit, ran along a definite course; on the contrary, it was like the passage of clouds, like the way of a man sauntering through the streets— diverted here by a shadow, there by a little crowd of people, or by an unusual way one building jutted out and the next stood back from the street—finally arriving at a place that he had neither known of nor meant to reach. (II:70)[1]

An idler out for a stroll, seeking diversion in trivial amusements and curiosities; the shapeshifting vagaries of cloud formations; the amplification to macroscopic effect of minute fluctuations, as in the case of the Lucretian clinamen whose unaccountable swerving ensues in the genesis of material form: such are the tropes Musil offers for the waywardness of history. From the very beginning of *The Man without Qualities*, which famously opens with a weather report and the implicit suggestion that images of turbulent flow enjoy a certain privilege as metaphors for historical process, Musil emphasizes the constitutive role chance plays in the unfolding of human affairs. So haphazardly various a procession of events does not lend itself to narrative representation except in the form of the simplest chronicle whose organizing principle is bare successiveness, or one thing after another without an overarching purpose or meaning.

According to Musil, this spectacle of contingency becomes all the more pronounced as history in effect accelerates over the course of the nineteenth and into the twentieth centuries, giving rise to that unsettled and volatile conjuncture now commonly referred to as Postmodernity. Postmodernity entails a narrative crisis: no "grand narrative," to borrow Lyotard's phrase, can any longer effectively serve as a universal point of reference implicitly orienting all of cultural life.[2]

Ulrich speculates along these lines in this remarkable passage:

> And what occurred to him then was one of those seemingly out-of-the-way and abstract thoughts that so often in his life took on such immediate significance, namely that the law of this life, for which one yearns, overburdened as one is and at the same time dreaming of simplicity, was none other than that of narrative order [*erzählerischen Ordnung*].... What puts our mind at rest is the simple sequence, the overwhelming variegation of life now represented in, as a mathematician would say, a unidimensional order.... [I]n their basic relation to themselves most people are narrators. They do not like the lyrical, or at best ... only for moments at a time.... What they like is the orderly sequence of facts, because it has the look of a necessity, and by means of the impression that their life has a 'course' they manage to feel somehow sheltered in the midst of chaos. And now Ulrich observed that he seemed to have lost this elementary narrative element to which private life still holds fast, although in public life everything has now become non-narrative, no longer following a 'thread', but spreading out as an infinitely interwoven surface [*in einer unendlichen verwobenen Fläche*]. (II:435–36)

Instead of an orderly progression whose linear continuity insures comprehensive understanding, both public and private life now transpire within an all-encompassing field of ever ramifying complexity that can never be grasped as a whole. Postmodernity can be defined, in other words, as the absence of an organizing center or shared frame of reference. The world is now awash with the noise of competing, exclusive centers of meaning. To borrow an allusion Frank Zappa once derisively made to the music of the spheres, a sea of dissonance henceforth drowns out the cosmic "Big Note" with which every other sound ought to resonate in harmony. What Musil calls the "great rhythmic throb" of the traditionally dominant powers is perpetually beset by the "discord and dislocation of ... opposing rhythms" (I:4). And this condition is inescapable, or comprises the unsurpassable horizon of life in the contemporary metropolis as a spectacle of incoherent "rambling about in a multitude of things, from a hundred possibilities to yet a thousand others, and always without a basic unity" (I:17).

The Man without Qualities takes place on the eve of the First World War in Vienna, capital of the Austro-Hungarian Empire, a complex multi-ethnic industrialized state that Musil regarded as representative of European culture in general during a period of transformation and crisis. The novel investigates an already complicated civil society becoming even more finely articulated along numerous axes: a highly differentiated division of labor; a market economy that actively incites demand for ever more various goods and services; a multiplication of branches of knowledge into specialized academic disciplines; experimentalism and rapid stylistic turnover in the fine arts alongside a burgeoning so-called mass culture; movements for women's emancipation, workers' rights, self-determination on the part of emergent nationalities; and so on.[3] What principally engages Musil, however, is the proliferation of outlooks on life that accompanies this social transformation. That is, as irreducible heterogeneity increasingly characterizes the social sphere, hitherto dominant belief systems begin to lose their authority. Any claim for a shared cultural ethos or collective narrative framing of the meaning of existence becomes less and less plausible. Moreover, the likelihood of even an individually cohesive subject position is threatened. The absence of a center in the public realm has its precise corollary in every subject's psychic structure:

> For the inhabitant of a country has at least nine characters: a professional one, a national one, a civic one, a class one, a geographical one, a sex one, a conscious, an unconscious and perhaps even too a private one; he combines them all in himself, but they dissolve him, and he is really nothing but a little channel washed out by all these trickling streams, which flow into it and drain out of it again in order to join other little streams filling another channel. Hence every dweller on earth also has a tenth character, which is nothing more or less than the passive illusion of spaces unfilled; it permits a man everything with one exception: he may not take seriously what his at least nine other

characters do and what happens to them, in other words, the very
thing that ought to be the filling of him. (I:34)

The overdetermination of personal identity in a world in which "tailors,
fashions, and chance" shape and continually reshape putatively
transtemporal human nature from the outside in thus produces an anguished
sense of inner vacuity and fragmentation (II:126). As Ulrich earlier observed,
most people do not like the "lyrical," do not like to regard their personal
histories as chance concatenations of unconnected moments or themselves as
cobbled-together assemblages of social roles and poses. If psychic
equilibrium traditionally depends upon identification with some one or at
most a few unchanging images of interior essence, then the individual in
early twentieth-century Austria-Hungary suffers acutely from what many of
the characters refer to as a loss of "integral" being. This troubled awareness
that there "is no longer a whole man confronting a whole world, but a human
something floating about in a universal culture-medium" (I:257) typically
produces by way of compensation an aggressive insistence on paranoiacally
rigid dogmas and overheated enthusiasms in order to center cognitive and
affective life. Musil's consummately ironic narrator remarks in this
connection that "in his potentialities, plans, and emotions, man must first of
all be hedged in by prejudices, traditions, difficulties and limitations of every
kind, like a lunatic in a strait-jacket," if he is to "keep vertical in the flux" of
contemporary city-life (I:7, 17). A great portion of *The Man without Qualities*
is consequently devoted to an anatomy of the cultural pathologies of
Postmodernity.

Musil pursues this investigation by way of a story-line that recounts the
planning stages for a state-sponsored celebration of "True Austria"'s cultural
preeminence and world historical mission. The goal is for the Austro-
Hungarian Empire, representing all of humanity, to provide a "mirror for the
world to gaze into and blush. And not only blush, but, as in the fairy-tale, see
its true face and never be able to forget it again" (I:209). The planners in fact
hope to articulate a worldview sufficiently capacious to encompass the
divergent ideologies of contemporary social life and thus achieve "a human
unity embracing humanity's extremely varied activities" (I:115). The futility of
this attempt to inaugurate a new human unity with reference to the example
of Austro-Hungarian society is evident from the start. First of all, the project's
real inspiration is hardly ecumenical in character, deriving instead from a
context of great power rivalry. Dubbed the Collateral Campaign (*die
Parallelaktion*), its architects' not too hidden agenda involves displacing
attention from a similar event scheduled to take place in the German Empire,
which had already by the beginning of the twentieth-century succeeded

Austria-Hungary as the dominant power in Central Europe. It therefore comes as no surprise when this supposed celebration of common humanity is later coopted by the worldly-wise emissaries of Realpolitik for whom "the State was the power of self-assertion in the [Darwinian] struggle of the nations" (II:18). Secondly, the campaign's planning is in the charge of a social elite drawn from the feudal aristocracy and more recently empowered bourgeoisie who evidently believe that every interest can be happily reconciled within the scope of an altogether improbable synthesis of Catholic monarchism (expressing aristocratic nostalgia for a time "when people grew naturally into the conditions they found waiting for them"; II:367) and Enlightenment progressivism (according to which "nothing irrational happens in the history of the world"; I:204).

The committee's oversight in this regard becomes abundantly clear when a prying journalist makes public their intention to elaborate a comprehensive definition of Austro-Hungarian cultural identity. The Collateral Campaign finds itself deluged with suggestions from every quarter of society and quickly becomes what amounts to a collective Rorschach test, eliciting the most various and discrepant proposals for celebrating "The Austrian Year." The truly unforgettable face of Austria-Hungary now emerges as a chaotic jumble of incompatible standpoints:

> The Superman was adored, and the Subman was adored; health and the sun were worshipped, and the delicacy of consumptive girls was worshipped; people were enthusiastic hero-worshippers and enthusiastic adherents of the social creed of the Man in the Street; one had faith and was skeptical, one was naturalistic and precious, robust and morbid; one dreamed of ancient castles and shady avenues, autumnal gardens, glassy ponds, jewels, hashish, disease and demonism, but also of prairies, vast horizons, forges and rolling-mills, naked wrestlers, the uprisings of the slaves of toil, man and woman in the primeval Garden, and the destruction of society. (I:59)

A range of fixations and one-sided affirmations is thus brought to light propelled by energies far too volatile and urgent to be dismissed with reference to the complacent belief that "old Austria" has always been able to accommodate conflicting points of view by "muddling through" (fortwursteln). Each of these putatively definitive solutions to the problem of living in the twentieth century not only excludes other strategies but assumes a paranoiac posture according to which persecutorial rivals surround it on every side.

According to some proposals, contemporary society can once more produce "good, whole, integral human beings [*gute, ganze und einheitliche Menschen*]" (I:252) by reviving the cultures of "great and integral times [*großer, ungebrochener Zeiten*]" (I:167), as in the supposed "unity of religious feeling in all human activities that has been lost" either since the Middle Ages (I:115) or, further back, since the disappearance of an archaic Aryan culture whose social life was organized around magical "symbols" (the precise significance of which, Musil's narrator mockingly observes, will forever remain mysterious, "first because symbols cannot be expressed in sober words, secondly because Aryans must not be sober;" II:10). Other scenarios for a unified social order are fringed with millenarian yearnings: "the present time was expectant, impatient, turbulent and unhappy, but the Messiah for whom it was hoping and waiting was not yet in sight" (II:121). Still others propose neither a restoration of a prior cultural order nor a leap into some hitherto unimaginable beyond but instead embrace the present on the condition that it be purged of the corrupting elements responsible for its characteristically fragmented or dissociated sensibility. A "surge of hostility toward Jews" thus wells up, who are now scapegoated as a "destructively analytical-minded alien race" (I:239) whose attitude of disbelief regarding salvationist absolutes reinforces Postmodernity's unwelcome cultural heterogeneity.

But no matter what their specific content—be it steadfast adherence to a redemptive Idea, or the augmentation of State-power and social discipline, or a hundred other panaceas—these divergent and frequently contradictory solutions all posit "something inevitable to hold on to" (I:67), an unquestionable truth that renders every other expedient redundant. In their aggregate effect, they therefore contribute to the "state of vague atmospheric hostility with which the air is laden in this epoch of ours" (I:24). On the one hand, that is, Austro-Hungarian society constantly invents ever-new perspectives and experiences. On the other, it remains determined to settle upon a unique and unalterable way of life. These conflicting motives produce a condition of mounting psychic distress whose eventual outcome can only be "a demand for bloodshed" (II:197). The multifarious world salvationist schemes that look to the Collateral Campaign for their practical implementation, each a self-anointed orthodoxy contesting a field of heretic rivals in what Ulrich terms the "Millennial War of Religion" (III:441), are in fact sustained, it turns out, by frustrated desires for ultimacy that find their apotheosis in literally psychotic fantasies of apocalyptic "world conflagration" (I:168–69).[4]

Unlike his deluded contemporaries who have so heavily invested in fantasies of unchanging essence, Musil's protagonist Ulrich resists the temptation to turn away from history's unpredictable openness. Trained in the natural sciences and a mathematician by profession, he approaches reality on the basis of a skeptical materialism that has dispensed with the hypothesis of a providential design in favor of a view of the universe as a Heraclitean flux. The present "order of things is not as solid as it pretends to be; nothing, no ego, no form, no principle, is safe, everything is in a process of invisible but never-ceasing transformation" (I:296). This orientation toward experience, stressing the contingency of every element in life including "human nature" (henceforth a transitional moment in a suite of aimless transformations) and the self's presence to itself as a resolved whole, is precisely what renders Ulrich the "man without qualities" or essential attributes, a "possibilitarian" (*Möglichkeitsmensch*) who looks forward to the chance to become other instead of compulsively recycling a limited set of characterological automatisms. In the eyes of his contemporaries, Ulrich's availability to emergent circumstances renders him suspect. The fact that "every one of his answers is a part-answer, every one of his feelings only a point of view" implies that his personality is so metamorphic, so without definition, that he "isn't really human at all!" [*So ein Mensch ist doch kein Mensch!*] (I:71–72). But although Ulrich in many respects embodies Musil's own outlook, *The Man without Qualities* is hardly an idolatrous celebration of an ideally post-human subject-in-process who is miraculously immune to the folly of his culture.

During the period in his youth when he first seriously addressed the only "question worth thinking about … the question of right living" (I:303), Ulrich had proposed to follow the example of scientific practice by organizing his life as a series of deliberate experiments in thought, feeling, and action. According to this "Utopian idea of exact living," the one "whose imagination is geared for change [*dessen Phantasie auf Veränderungen gerichtet ist*]" (I:293) must maintain an attitude of inventive openness toward experience, proceeding experimentally—or "lyrically"—from one situation to another without prejudgment or the retrospective imposition of some explanatory design that resolves heterogeneous events into a unity. But "exact living" depends as well, Ulrich claims, upon devaluing one's involvement in everyday life or refusing to be distracted by quotidian affairs to the point that the self's exclusive objects of attention will henceforth be those privileged moments when new forms of thinking, feeling, and doing reveal themselves: one must remain "indifferent wherever one has not had that ineffable sensation of spreading one's arms and being borne upward on a wave of creativeness" (I:291). In this latter respect, Ulrich reveals the extent to which he has himself been imprinted with his culture's characteristic craving for an end to history. That is, Ulrich's intention to so concentrate himself upon those crucial occasions of unprecedented emergence that his life would come to resemble a "primordial fire" affiliates him with an aestheticist philosophy (propounded, for instance, in Walter Pater's *Studies in the History of the Renaissance* [1873]) that was able to affirm becoming only by reducing multiplicity to a few peak experiences of exquisite perfection. An essentializing impulse thus underlies the utopian idea of exact living very like what Oscar Wilde critiques in *The Picture of Dorian Gray* (1891) when—moving beyond Pateresque aestheticism—he foregrounds the contradiction between Dorian Gray's appetite for variety and his ultimately fatal wish for a condition of self-possession wholly invulnerable to historical process.

Ulrich's somewhat later adoption of the "Utopian idea of essayism" (*die Utopie des Essayismus*), his dream of joining the ranks of "essayists and masters of the floating life within [*Essayisten and Meister des innerlich schwebenden Lebens*]" (I:301) might seem to mark a genuine departure in so far as an essayistic ethos, resistant in principle to conclusiveness, can be understood to entail an affirmation of life's wayward and contingent character. But when the story opens in 1913 with Ulrich now in his early thirties, he finds himself "in the worst state of emergency in his life [*in dem schlimmsten Notstand seines Lebens*]" (I:304). Far from practically implementing essayism as an exemplary approach to the world, he "hesitates to become anything. A character, a profession, a definite mode of existence—for him these are notions through which the skeleton is already peering, the skeleton that is all that will be left of him in the end" (I:296). Ulrich's reluctance to commit to a definite path of development is motivated, in other words, less by apprehension over entrapment in cultural convention than by his inability to consent to the restriction of possibility inevitably imposed by the specific conditions of anyone's life. He would rather enjoy the breath-taking prospect of an infinite number of potentially available options—in other words, fantasmatically swallow up the totality of past and future existence in an eternal instant—than accede to the finitude of a particular course.

He thus fundamentally misconstrues the nature of essayism from the very moment he seeks to put it into practice. Although his personality contains "something" that works against "logical systematization, against the one-track will, against the definitely directed urges of ambition" (I:300), he has eliminated this "something"—precisely, a responsiveness to contingent circumstance—from his understanding of the concept of essayism. He defines the term in a manner that recalls his earlier enthusiasm for exact living. The essayist's goal is precisely an essentialization of experience: "an essay is the unique and unalterable form that a man's inner life assumes in a decisive thought. Nothing is more alien to it than that irresponsibility and semi-finishedness of mental images known as subjectivity ..." (I:300). While this formulation does usefully highlight the fact that an essay is irreducibly the product of its occasion, the repugnance Ulrich evidently feels toward the "irresponsible" vagaries of subjectivity suggests that rather than participating in the metamorphosis of the world his ambition is to preside over experience as the master of his own becoming.

His confused affirmation of historical process testifies to the continuing influence of a libidinal orientation internalized at an early age, a desiring economy whose workings are such that the self must occupy a commanding height before it can enjoy its transactions with otherness, precisely, a conventionally masculinist erotics that confuses pleasure with power:

> Associated with [Ulrich's] intellectual suppleness, which was based simply on a great variety of gifts, there was, in him, a certain bellicosity too. He was of a masculine turn of mind.... It might even be said that he himself had wanted to become something like a dominant spirit and master-mind. And who, after all, would not? It is so natural for the mind to be considered the highest of all things, ruling over all things. That is what we are taught. (I:176–77)

All of Ulrich's speculations concerning a circumstantially improvisational perspective on reality as an exemplary standpoint from which to engage with the cultural condition of Postmodernity covertly share this aspiration for mastery and transcendence. The "urge to make an onslaught on life, and so to dominate it, had always been very marked in him.... And everything that, as time went on, he had called Essayism and the Sense of Possibility ... —all these terms" (II:360) served merely to disguise an underlying propensity for aggression against the world.

Musil offers plentiful evidence for a psychoanalytic interpretation of Ulrich's inability to encounter difference from any position other than one of dominance, suggesting that this quite definite "quality" or personal characteristic has its prototype in the infant's ambivalent relationship with its mother. In conversation with his cousin Diotima, whose salon provides the meeting place for the planning of the Collateral Campaign, Ulrich is irritated when she reveals an acute insight into his own thinking:

> 'So it's come to this, has it,' he said to himself, 'that this giant hen has begun talking exactly like me?' Before his mental eye he again saw Diotima in the shape of a colossal hen that was about to peck

at a little worm, which was his soul. The childish terror of old,
the dread of the Tall Lady, reached out to him.... (II:327)

On the basis of this evidence, Ulrich's alienation from phenomenal
experience and ambition to become a "dominant spirit and mastermind"
could be said to originate in the infant's paranoiac fears concerning a
devouring (or castrating) maternal figure.

Musil's narrator goes on to argue, however, that Ulrich's "dread of the
Tall Lady" should not be understood to provide a definitive revelation of his
unconscious psychic constitution. To the contrary, in the course of his
struggles to surmount his present impasse, Ulrich's "inner attitude, which
had always been that of an attacker, was gradually loosening up" (II:328).
Diotima notices the change as well, remarking that he no longer voices
adherence to "precision of feeling" but instead affirms a life of "taking things
as they came" (II:338). Pertinent in this connection is Ulrich's subsequent
recollection of a time in his childhood when his mind was filled with fantasies
of becoming a woman himself. He thus remembers a costume party and the
appearance there of his sister Agathe: "Although he was himself menacingly
encased in knightly armour"—representing the protective self-enclosure of
the putatively autonomous masculine ego—at the sight of her he suddenly
felt an indescribable longing ... to be a girl himself" (III:26). On the one
hand, this fantasy of the female body as a self-delighting erotic plenum
merely reiterates Ulrich's ingrained aspiration for self-sufficiency (this time
in the register of pleasure rather than of power); but on the other, it testifies
to the potential in him for another orientation toward experience, an
alternative desiring economy.

The possibility of genuinely consenting to history's unforeseeable
eventfulness depends crucially, in Ulrich's view, upon reviving "some primal
memory of a childlike relationship to the world, all trustfulness and
abandonment" (II:360). That is, he hopes for the recurrence of a psychic
condition comparable to what Julia Kristeva refers to under the rubric of the
"semiotic chora," a condition of relatively unstructured libidinal flow in which
drive energy spends itself polymorphically and at random in relation to the
maternal body that is the infant's original environment.[5] Only an orientation
toward the subject's immediate surroundings such as this could provide the basis
for a desiring economy free from the compulsion to control, no longer fearfully
alienated from material reality, ready instead to chance the fortune of the
moment, to respond to opportunities as they unpredictably present themselves.

Ulrich does not, of course, merely succumb at this point to nostalgia for
the polymorphous perversity of infancy. Drawing upon adult experience, he
proposes rather to test the hypothesis that the royal road to the re-enchantment

of the Earth has for its point of departure the libidinal intensity conventionally associated with romance and lovemaking. In other words, among the repertoire of inherited practices available to an early twentieth-century European, the tradition of romantic love offers the best chance for elaborating a cultural ethos able to say yes to the flux of matter in motion. Ulrich thus describes an affair he had as a young man in the immediate aftermath of which he entered into a sort of erotic communion with phenomena as such:

> He had drifted into the very heart of the world. From him to the distant beloved was as far as the next tree. Inscape [*Ingefühl*] had linked the living beings where space was no more, as in dreams two living beings can pass through each other without intermingling; and this altered all their relations. Otherwise, however, this state of mind had nothing in common with dream. It was clear, and abounding in thoughts. Only nothing in it moved according to cause, purpose and physical desire, but everything went rippling out in circle upon circle, as when a continuous jet plays upon a pool of water.... It was an utterly changed form of life.... If, for instance, a beetle ran past the hand of the man sunk in thought, it was not a coming nearer, a passing by and a disappearing, and it was not beetle and man; it was a happening ineffably touching the heart, and yet not even a happening but, although it happened, a state. (I:144)

Ulrich's passion for his lover here overflows its object, bringing about an interlude of paradisal immanence in which *jouissance* everywhere permeates contingent circumstance. The state of libidinal intensity that she evokes in Ulrich ensues not in the obsessive interpretation of every new element in experience as her metaphorical representative but in a displacement or metonymic scattering of desire over the entire sensory field. The world is eroticized in its heterogeneous suchness rather than as a graspable totality. Later in the novel, Agathe finds herself in a similar situation:

> Everything that came her way was expanded into a limitless Now [*zu einer grenzenlosen Gegenwart*]. Even when she did anything, all that happened was that a dividing-line disappeared from between herself the doer and the thing done.... On all sides she was in some kind of suspension where she felt at once exalted and as though vanished. She might have said, I am in love, but I don't know with whom. (III:226)

For Ulrich and Agathe both, the received cultural apparatus that customarily defines the nature of reality prior to any encounter with particular situations is placed on hold for the duration of their sojourn in the Eternal Present. Such seemingly inescapable categories as self and other, past and future, cause and effect, being and becoming (not to forget, human and insect) coalesce in paradoxical undecidability. The desiring excess of romantic love thus occasions an imponderable "happening" (that is simultaneously a "state") in which the normative version of the Real is replaced by what Gilles Deleuze and Felix Guattari, following Gregory Bateson, call a "plateau of intensity" that can be imagined as a flat surface suffused with drive energy— in other words, the phenomenal realm cathected in its pre-categorical specificity—across which a nomadic subject migrates from one contingent site of erotic bliss to another, from one provisional "center" to another, seeking neither to organize this infinite expanse into a lasting unity nor arrive finally at some culminating terminus.[6]

Ulrich names this experience of paradisal immanence to which he and Agathe are intermittently privy the Other Condition (*der andere Zustand*) and attributes to it an ontological significance. Over the course of human history, he says, many routes have been found to the Other Condition besides the tradition of romance, especially among the mystical teachings of the world. "Christian, Judaic, Indian and Chinese" forms of mysticism furnish plentiful evidence for its existence as "a highly important condition that man is capable of entering into and which has deeper origins" (III:117) than the various creeds engaged in the Millennial War of Religion that effectively prohibit anyone's passage there when they enshrine and thus reduce Utopia to a concept in their respective doctrinal edifices. In this "strange, unqualified, incredible and unforgettable state of mind" (III:189), the subject is able to assume an affirmative orientation toward phenomena without recourse to defensive illusions of redemptive totality because experience now unfolds as a movement from partial object to partial object, each of which comprises a situationally satisfying plenum. The Other Condition implies a responsiveness to the world that seeks not control (it entails giving up "personal greed toward one's experiences" [II:74]) but rather a sort of erotic proximity in which "one is linked with everything and at the same time can't get *to* anything" in the sense of acquisition or possession. Instead "you float like the fish in the water or the bird in the air, but there simply is no bank and no branch but this floating" (III:99) as subject and object henceforth swirl together in a vortex of mutual transformation.

For Ulrich, the ontological reality of the Other Condition guarantees the viability of his essayistic ideal, his aspiration to follow a path of circumstantial shapeshifting. His commitment to an ethos of occasionality and improvisation need not, in other words, provoke a melancholic effort to impose upon the wayward flow of events some overarching form. Notwithstanding the undeniable longing for continuance evoked in even the most situational subject when faced with certain death—for instance, the replicant Roy Batty, whose dying words at the end of Ridley Scott's 1982 film *Bladerunner* as he looks back on a life composed of intense episodes are "all those moments will be lost in time, like tears in rain"—from the perspective of the Other Condition, the present is enough. Permanent residence in this zone would therefore enable Ulrich to fulfill his promise as a possibilitiarian "born to change ... surrounded by a world created for change" (I:325). Greeting each encounter with, the world as an occasion for invention, his psychic economy, attuned now to the promptings of emergent phenomena, would continually vary from predictable routine, or fluctuate in response to its ever-mutating surroundings.

But for the duration of the novel, Ulrich never enjoys more than intermittent and fleeting access to the Other Condition. His dream of extending the feeling-state characteristic of romantic involvement to experience in general remains compromised by a contrary inclination that would substitute for the unforeseeable vicissitudes of becoming the imperturbable equilibrium of a blissful self-enclosure. Thus, when he first realizes the predatory nature of his past amorous relationships, Ulrich resolves to treat any future romantic partner in a "sisterly" fashion, implying mutuality and a foregoing of manipulation. The new partner with whom he becomes emotionally (if not physically) intimate, however, is his actual sister Agathe. Musil's narrator makes the inevitable inference:

> Anyone who has not already picked up the clues to what was going on between this brother and sister had better now lay this account aside, for what is narrated is an adventure he will never be able to approve of, a journey to the furthest limits of the possible, skirting the dangers of the impossible and the unnatural, even of the repulsive, and perhaps not quite avoiding them. (III:111)

The narrator here evokes the spectre of incest in order to imply the difficulty Ulrich and, for that matter, Agathe experience in genuinely embracing difference. Each sees in the other the promise of a state of plenitude and completeness so fulfilling as to render moot the question of the world's desirability. As Ulrich puts it in a moment of acute self-insight:

> It goes back a very long way, this desire for a *doppelgänger* of the opposite sex, this craving for the love of a being that will be

entirely the same as oneself and yet another, distinct from oneself.... This old, old dream of the essence of love meeting, unhampered by the limitations of the corporeal world, in two identical-distinct figures [*zwei gleichverschiedenen Gestalten*]—it's conjured up innumerable times through the ages by the solitary alchemistic processes that go on inside the alembic of the human skull.... Even under the most ordinary everyday conditions in which love occurs one does still find traces of this: one finds it ... in the significance of correspondences between oneself and the other, the repetition of oneself in the other [*die Bedeutung der Übereinstimmung und Ichwiederholung im anderen*]. (III:282)

Even as they seek to enter "the Millenium," then, the self-proclaimed "Siamese twins" are entangled in a narcissistic conspiracy of two, a dyadic relationship of specularity that causes the Other Condition, at the very moment when its advent is most palpably and tantalizingly imminent, to recede ineluctably before them over the horizon.

In thus qualifying what has hitherto been presented as the most likely way to achieve permanent residence in the Other Condition and thereby leaving open the question of how an unalienated stance toward experience can be brought about, Musil exemplifies his own commitment to an essayistic approach that in fact everywhere characterizes his writing practice. *The Man without Qualities* anatomizes the heterogeneous religious, scientific, aesthetic, philosophic, political, legal, and economic discourses with reference to which diverse groups in turn-of-the-century Austria-Hungary articulate their respective worldviews. As he traverses this field of divergent and conflicting perspectives—a virtual babel of mutually incomprehensible outlooks—the Musilian narrator caricatures, mocks, and at the very least, withholds assent from each in turn without, however, implying his own adherence to an alternative normative scheme. That is, he resists the temptation to insist on his own version of the truth by remaining perpetually in motion, subversively miming one complex of attitudes and beliefs after another in an endless round of parodic citations. The narrator of *The Man without Qualities* would sooner speak in tongues than make a claim for the incontestable authority of his own voice, the irrefutable finality of his personal point of view. In this connection, Musil's failure to complete the concluding volume of his unfinished magnum opus amounts to an entirely appropriate gesture on the part of a writer who can find no warrant, precisely, for conclusiveness. Notwithstanding the personal hardships that he suffered in the last decade of his life, the fact that his novel never settles upon a definitive answer to the "question of right living" can be interpreted as the implementation in narrative form of a philosophical essayism according to which every solution is at best provisional and contingent.

Yet the effect of *The Man without Qualities* is not simply one of demystification, as if Musil had meant to pursue a radical *via negativa* that excludes every affirmation in principle. To the contrary, the novel's protagonist Ulrich exemplifies, albeit approximately, an ethos able to respond to an unpredictably metamorphic reality in an improvisationally inventive or "essayistic" manner thanks, first of all, to its freedom from psychologically internalized cultural coding, or the "qualities" that insure stereotyped behavior; and, secondly, to the libidinal mobility that access to the "Other Condition" confers. The subject-position Ulrich imperfectly incarnates is offered, so to speak, in the sense of a Kantian Idea that orients without limiting conduct to a particular course because it constitutes a horizon of indeterminately many possibilities; or in another parlance, a rhetorical topos pragmatically invoked as a point of departure for circumstantial improvisation; or even further afield, a chaotic attractor in complex dynamics whose self-similarity in the midst of seemingly infinite variability portends a middle way between strict repetition and pure chance.[7] In other words, Musil accomplishes a rapprochement with the Imaginary, zone of illusory presences and putatively unchanging truths, by adopting an ironic stance toward the identity that any subject must assume in order to pursue a particular course in life. The ethos of the libidinally mobile skeptical essayist is affirmed with the understanding that even a standpoint as programmatically open to experience as this will inevitably be revised in the course of its encounters with the always unforeseeable Real.

As this essay nears its own provisional conclusion, I am going to turn now to Luis Buñuel's 1974 film *The Phantom of Liberty* for a contrasting perspective on the prospects for reconciling cultural life with the unlimited openness of becoming.[8] On the one hand, Buñuel can be said to adhere to an Epicurean view of chance as the material basis of liberty. He would have agreed with Lucretius' observation in *De rerum natura* that "what keeps the mind itself from having necessity within it in all [its] actions ... is the minute [aleatory] swerving of the [atoms] at no fixed place and at no fixed time."[9] But on the other hand, he maintains as well that "necessity"—understood here as an ineluctable desire for a culminating state of affairs—ordinarily prevails to such an extent as to effectively foreclose the emancipatory potential of chance. The faith traditionally vested by Surrealism in the irrational spontaneity of the Id should not obscure the fact, he says, that "the truly gratuitous act doesn't exist: it would always have some obscure motive," or bear the traces of unconscious compulsion.[10] Liberty is therefore a phantom, an ungraspable "misty shape" that haunts the dissident imagination. Less optimistic than Musil regarding the possibility of contriving an ethos that could be relied upon to facilitate inventive improvisationality, Buñuel's strategy in *The Phantom of Liberty* suggests an uncompromising suspicion of the entire cultural repertoire. From this point of view, even Musil remains implicated in a traditionally teleological interpretation of human being-in-the-world in so far as he posits as a normative goal the "essayistic" practice of an agent "without qualities" whose proper residence is the eroticized suchness of the "Other Condition."

Where Musil invites his readers to internalize as their ego-ideal a speculatively tentative representation of an improvisational shapeshifter responsive to the flux of the drives and the specificity of contingent circumstance, Buñuel pursues a contrary strategy of disrupting the process of psychological identification itself. To achieve this end, he presents a series of vignettes, each featuring a different cast of characters, conjoined in a purely fortuitous manner as a succession of discrete happenings. In the consequent absence of any teleological imperative, *The Phantom of Liberty* could in principle be prolonged indefinitely. As Buñuel himself remarks, "each episode gives way to another, each character to another, and thus we could go on *ad infinitum*. If we were faithful to its spirit, the film would never end."[11] This subversion of closure is replicated within many of the film's episodes by inconsistencies, contradictions, and violations of verisimilitude that render them interpretively ambiguous. Moreover, Buñuel terminates most narrative sequences in mid-course without even the pretense of a formal conclusion.

The protagonist of an episode early on in the film, for instance, awakens one morning from uneasy dreams. Over the course of the night, he has been the recipient of a stream of uncanny visitations. A rooster, a hooded figure who shows him a clock, a postman on a bicycle who delivers a letter, and finally, an ostrich have all paraded past the foot of his bed. Sufficiently concerned to consult his family physician, he is dismayed when his doctor, no specialist in the interpretation of dreams, advises him to see a psychoanalyst, "for months, years if necessary." But in a small *coup de théâtre*, he triumphantly produces the very letter the nocturnal postman had delivered. His visitors were not unconsciously motivated apparitions after all but emissaries from a world other than this one. Before the contents of the mysterious message from beyond can be disclosed, however, the doctor's nurse produces her own letter, this one summoning her home to the countryside to tend her gravely ill father, at which point the film departs with her for the family farm.[12]

Buñuel first promises a tale transpiring in a psychological register that is evidently meant to deliver a derisive comment on psychoanalysis; he then complicates this possibility with the dreamtime missive's continued existence by the light of day and the attendant implication that the sequence should be read as a species of fantastic allegory, an expression, say, of renewed faith in the existence of the "Other Side" on the part of a lapsed Surrealist; and finally, at precisely the moment when suspense is at its most intense for his audience, he abandons this story-line altogether, as if the medical condition of a hitherto peripheral character's parent were of greater significance than a bizarre violation of the laws governing the known universe. The audience of *The Phantom of Liberty* no sooner becomes engrossed in unravelling the enigma of one sequence of events than the film swerves in an entirely unexpected direction, recounting a new anecdote that in similar fashion will never be allowed to get to the point. By thus constantly changing the subject, as prospective interpretations accumulate and one story fragment follows another, Buñuel intends precisely to *change the subject* in the sense of the subject of desire, the viewing subject who is offered in *The Phantom of Liberty* what amounts to a crash course in evading immobilizing identifications. For Buñuel, liberty is not a state and cannot be resumed in an image, no matter how, ineffably figurative, or a concept, no matter how ironically provisional. Liberty is, rather, a form of movement, the arbitrary, even capricious passage from one particular to another that formal logic labels non sequitur.

The nonsensical waywardness of narrative development in *The Phantom of Liberty* does not, however, prevent Buñuel from pursuing a surprisingly comprehensive disquisition on the vicissitudes of desire. Over the course of the film, he submits to alternately comic derision and satiric critique diverse avatars of an obsessively repeated aspiration for permanence and plenitude that he, like Musil, regards as symptomatic of psychic resistance to an understanding of reality as a spectacle of eternal change. Buñuel is particularly interested in showing how even the most promising emancipatory projects can become unwitting instruments of the Death Drive's never-ending quest for finality.[13] *The Phantom of Liberty*, whose 1974 release coincidentally commemorates the fiftieth anniversary of the publication of the first *Manifesto of Surrealism*, thus focuses on two prototypical Surrealist strategies: *transgression*, according to which a condition of cognitive and affective mobility can be achieved by violating social norms and conventions; and *becoming-animal*, which proposes to step outside the cultural realm entirely, discovering an experience of vital intensity in the swarming immediacy of the biosphere.

Given a Symbolic Order that articulates the cultural universe by means of diacritical contrasts, an exemplary transgressive practice would follow a nomadic itinerary, moving unforeseeably from one temporarily privileged position to another across a decentered expanse in which every element emerges in relation to indeterminately many other possibilities. Transgression would ideally serve, in other words, as a modality of invention and discovery, a strategy for renewing cultural life by putting it into endless variation. But in the examples of failed emancipation from routine that Buñuel presents satirically in *The Phantom of Liberty*, this potentially unlimited freeplay is constrained to interminable oscillation between the twin poles of a fixed binary opposition, an oscillation, that is, between a socially dominant orthodoxy and its taboo or abjected contrary. Respectively transgressive and normative realms of experience are thus constituted as symmetrical inversions of each other in what amounts to a compromise-formation that seeks to reconcile differential articulation (which permanently defers presence and totality) with the fantasy, precisely, of a condition of surpassing consummation. The result is a restricted economy in which libidinal energy, instead of following an aleatory path, merely shuttles back and forth between contradictory versions of ultimacy. Even as the everyday world complacently proclaims its exclusive legitimacy, it is tempted by forbidden objects of desire. Meanwhile, the pleasures of transgression depend in turn on covert identification with the prevailing normative perspective in the absence of which the transgressive act could not be apprehended as such.

Consider, first of all, the cultural standpoint of normality. At a provincial police academy, a group of gendarmes (representing those powers most invested in enforcing social order) farcically invert their customary mode of comportment as they sing, dance, blow trumpets, and shoot out light bulbs with their revolvers. A professor then arrives to deliver a lecture on the topic of "the relativity of customs and of laws." He begins his talk by remarking that legal codes are not historically and culturally constant but "change from one country or period to another. They're only conventions, as are customs and mores." Mentioning polygamy as a practice that "is the rule, in some societies, [but] taboo in ours," he advises his students to consult in this connection the works of Margaret Mead on sexual, practices in Melanesia which, he says, "will help you better understand the relativity of customs and consequently of laws." The professor would thus have his audience perceive him as an incarnation of humane moderation: when "you compare one culture with another, it becomes a matter of point of view—one is always someone else's barbarian." That is, he counsels an audience charged with the task of maintaining law and order to adopt a stance of sceptical detachment and pragmatic flexibility where putatively universal values are concerned.

But in a reversal that is typical of the way Buñuel confounds narrative logic and audience expectation throughout *The Phantom of Liberty*, this befuddled academic fails to draw the appropriate inference from his discourse on cultural relativism: "as you know," he continues, "the question of changing laws is often considered. We also hear about some sort of evolution that would tend to change customs and mores.... Some people even hope for a general upheaval. But the consequences of such an upheaval would be unbearable, and even monstrous." By way of example, he then proceeds to recount an imaginary social engagement to which he and his wife are invited. This affair is not a dinner party, however, for although the guests are gathered around a large table, they are seated upon commodes and engage in polite conversation on the daily global production of human excrement. To complete this inversion of the cultural coding that customarily associates ingestion with sociability while consigning excretion to a private, taboo space, he concludes his edifying fable with a brief account of his own withdrawal to a small room in the rear of the apartment where he proceeds to dine in seclusion. The professor maintains that this ostensibly repulsive tale self-evidently justifies his insistence on compelling allegiance to currently prevailing customs and mores. But the undeniable enthusiasm he manifests in elaborating his hypothetical scenario suggests he is less repelled than excited by the prospect of just such a carnivalesque overturning of quotidian life. Moreover, his discussion in the first part of the lecture of Margaret Mead's anthropological research on sexual practices in Melanesia—a gratuitous reference in the context of an audience concerned with law enforcement—bespeaks once again a desiring interest in transgressing convention. He reads Mead's works, in other words, not for their ethnographic value but in order to stimulate erotic fantasy. Like his misbehaving gendarme students, the professor operates from within an economy of law and its transgression according to which normative strictness alternates with interludes of festive release. Though culturally illicit practices are always condemned and adherence to the norm officially avowed, the two sides of the opposition mutually constitute and ratify one another.

Buñuel presents the symmetrical inverse of the professor's affirmation of a normative standpoint that is tempted constantly by the prospect of transgression in *The Phantom of Liberty*'s immediately preceding episode. One night at a roadside inn, a veritable carnival of transgressions takes place whose principal participants include: a group of dissolute monks (instancing Buñuel's habitual anti-clericalism); an Oedipally-fixated young man with incestuous designs on his maiden aunt (certainly, no more explicit allusion could be made than this to the motive for transgression as a desire for *the* "lost object"); and a sado-masochistic couple whose exhibitionist antics constitute the episode's centerpiece.[14] The sado-masochistic couple lure the other guests into their room with the following invitation: "Let's celebrate chance which has brought us together in this place." But though they profess to "love the unexpected," their idea of celebrating chance is to stage a stereotypical (though appealingly ludicrous) psychodrama in which the sadist, now dressed in the customary black leather attire of a dominatrix, lashes the masochist with a whip while he shouts "I am a pig! I am filth! Hit me!" As the assembled guests hastily clear the room, the masochist forlornly cries out, "Wait! Don't leave! At least let the monks stay!" For his suffering and humiliation to ensue in ecstasy, he requires an audience of onlookers whose presumably cold contempt and emotionless self-mastery would throw into relief his own intense affectivity. This supposed cultural outlaw thus remains fixated on the norm as the condition of possibility for his transgressive *jouissance*. More generally put, the Symbolic Order as delineated in *The Phantom* of *Liberty* precludes the possibility of genuine emancipation by recuperating every putatively transgressive gesture as the binary opposite of a term already existing in the cultural repertoire.

The character I referred to earlier as the recipient of a stream of uncanny nocturnal visitations vents his distress with this apparent ineffectuality of transgression as an emancipatory strategy by exclaiming that he's "fed up with symmetry," or with entrapment in a mazeway of dualisms. He then signals his intention to assay becoming-animal as an alternative approach by placing a large tarantula mounted in a glass viewing box on the mantelpiece in his apartment. The giant spider evidently represents for him the utopian possibility of an irrecuperably non-human form of vitality. His experience of arachnid life is, however, strictly vicarious. Instead of implementing his desire to escape the human condition by becoming-tarantula himself, his relationship with the world of spiders is merely that of a hobbyist intent upon mastering the classificatory names of diverse arachnid species. His fascination with spiders remains a compensatory fantasy. An alienated object of knowledge safely locked inside its viewing case, the tarantula does not portend the sort of merging with an arthropod other enjoyed by the man without qualities in his interlude of paradisal immanence. Buñuel thus qualifies becoming-animal by emphasizing the extent to which non-human forms of life are always already culturally coded. In this connection, he confronts his audience with their own inclination to invest in stereotyped versions of the natural world by next presenting a fox, traditionally a figure for subversive guile and craftiness. That is, he entices viewers of *The Phantom of Liberty* to identify with the fox and consequently compliment themselves on their own cunning intelligence. This pleasant self-conception is then disrupted, and the identificatory process that sustains it made plainly visible, at the very end of the film. As the sounds of police suppressing an attempt to liberate the animals at the zoo from their cages are heard from off-screen, the camera focuses on the head of a seemingly bewildered ostrich, a less than promising emancipatory ideal, especially in the context of Freud's well-known remark in *The Interpretation of Dreams* regarding the ego's ostrich policy of shutting out whatever threatens its narcissistic self-enclosure.

As transgression loses its capacity to make a difference when it becomes merely the affirmation of a counter-norm, so becoming-animal lends itself to fantasies of transcending the cultural realm once and for all. Trusting to chance would therefore seem to offer the one sure route to liberation from obsessional routine and stereotyped response. But even "chance," after all, is a relatively defined term; and *The Phantom of Liberty* is hardly void of aesthetic artifice and intentionality, as Buñuel himself implies by means of elaborate structural repetitions that formally pattern the film throughout. In other words, although he is convinced that "chance, coincidence governs our lives.... Nevertheless, *The Phantom of Liberty* only imitates the mechanisms of chance."[15] Moreover, even if the film were a truly aleatory spectacle, its emancipatory aspirations could easily be neutralized, as when the genuinely chance-derived verbal and musical compositions of John Cage are returned to the realm of doxic cliché by attributing them to the wise folly of a Zen master. In this sense, the difference between the respective approaches of Musil and Buñuel need not entail making a choice between them. On the one hand, an aura of ironic disclaimer halos the Utopian countenance, of Musil's libidinally mobile skeptical essayist; on the other, Buñuel artfully *dissembles* an activity of sense-making open to the wayward drive energy of the unconscious that is ceasingly provoked in the subject in the course of its transactions with the world. Their respective experiments should therefore be received, not as unfailing strategies for bringing about a genuinely affirmative orientation toward reality's unforeseeably metamorphic flux, but as contributions to a reserve of rhetorical commonplaces that anyone might invoke in the never certain enterprise of promoting mobility in self-definition and inventive ingenuity in relation to circumstances.

NOTES

1. Musil quotations can be found in: *The Man without Qualities*, translated by Eithne Wilkins and Ernst Kaiser, 3 volumes (London: Picador Classics, 1988). Where the German is given, I am quoting from *Der Mann ohne Eigenschaften*, edited by Adolf Frisé, 2 volumes (Reinbek bei Hamburg: Rowohlt, 1978).

2. Although the term "Postmodernity" was not, of course, available to Musil, I have nevertheless decided to employ it as a descriptive label for the social world depicted in *The Man without Qualities* which anticipates with surprising prescience recent discussions of the postmodern condition. For an overview of Lyotard's writings that addresses many of the issues taken up in this essay, see my review article "Lyotard's Neo-Sophistic Philosophy of Phrases," *Poetics Today* 15:3 (Fall 1994).

3. Robert Luft makes this point: Musil regarded "old Austria" as "a model for the larger theme of the transition from traditional bourgeois society to modern, pluralistic, mass culture." See *Robert Musil and the Crisis of European Culture 1880–1942* (Berkeley, University of California Press, 1980), p. 214.

4. As Luft observes, the characters in *The Man without Qualities* are searching for order "in the chaos of a culture which has broken down into competing partial ideologies." Their quest is in vain until they discover, finally, a "reassuring totality" in "the emotional union of war" Luft, 234).

5. For a concise description of the "semiotic chora," see *The Kristeva Reader*, edited by Toril Moi (New York: Columbia University Press, 1986), pp. 93–98.

6. Gilles Deleuze and Félix Guattari, *A Thousand Plateaus: Capitalism and Schizophrenia*, translated by Brian Massumi (Minneapolis: University of Minnesota Press, 1987); see pp. 21–22.

7. Along these lines, Thomas Harrison suggests that Ulrich's privileged terms—"possibilitarianism," "essayism," and so on—should be received as "heuristic anticipatory logics and paradigms for action.... Such metaphors enact Musil's own principle of constructing scaffoldings for ethical direction"; see his *Essayism: Conrad, Musil and Pirandello* (Baltimore: Johns Hopkins University Press, 1992), p. 174.

8. *The Phantom of Liberty/Le fantôme de la liberté*; screenplay by Luis Buñuel and Jean Claude Carrière; produced by Serge Silberman and Twentieth-Century Fox (France, 1974).

9. Lucretius, *De rerum natura*, translated by W.H.D. Rouse, revised by Martin Ferguson, 2nd edition (Cambridge, Massachusetts: Harvard University Press, 1982), p. 119.

10. See José de la Colina and Tomás Pérez Turrent, *Objects of Desire: Conversations with Luis Buñuel*, edited and translated by Paul Lenti (New York: Marsilio Publishers, 1992), p. 222.

11. Ibid., p. 218; in this connection, Susan Suleiman says that *The Phantom of Liberty* is a "narrative film that does not 'tell a story.' It is narrative, for it consists of a combination of contiguous narrative sequences; but it does not tell a story, for there is no narrative logic that can *connect* the first sequence to the last one." See her "Freedom and Necessity: Narrative Structure in *The Phantom of Liberty*," *Quarterly Review of Film Studies* 3 (Summer, 1978), p. 287.

12. Buñuel thus creates a picaresque effect by correlating narrative development, in Linda Williams' words, with the "physical trajectory" of each of the principal characters: "the restless generative force that propel's the film's narrative cannot resist the impulse to follow a physical movement, even—or especially—if that movement leads us away from the primary story." In other words, "where there is movement there goes the story" (*The Figures of Desire: A Theory and Analysis of Surrealist Film* [Urbana: University of Illinois Press, 1981], pp. 162, 170.)

13. Buñuel touches explicitly on this issue in *Objects of Desire* when one of his interlocutors suggests that an appropriate ending for *The Phantom of Liberty* would be for it to "close itself into a circle." He responds: "No, if it closes itself into a circle, it's not liberty, it's death. Completing the vital circle: the end." See *Objects of Desire: Conversations with Luis Buñuel*, p. 218.

14. According to Williams, Buñuel suggests that the search for the "original 'lost object'" provides the basis for "not only political ideals and erotic pursuits but human identity itself." See *The Figures of Desire*, p. 175.

15. *Objects of Desire: Conversations With Luis Buñuel*, pp. 224, 217.

BURTON PIKE

Robert Musil:
Literature as Experience

Robert Musil was a trained scientist with a formidable intellect, an expert in behavioral psychology, mathematics, and engineering who was also widely and deeply read in philosophy.[1] Science and philosophy were the quarters from which, with Nietzschean fervor and intent, he approached his mission as a writer. He was impelled by the desire to create through imaginative writing, by experimental means, a new morality that would reflect the new world brought about by the discoveries of the physical and human sciences, a morality that would replace the tattered set of outmoded ethics whose hollowness Nietzsche and the industrial, scientific, and technological revolutions of the nineteenth century had so pitilessly exposed. He unremittingly worked toward the goal of achieving in his writing a new synthesis of spiritual and moral values with the utmost scientific precision.

One major strand of Musil's enterprise was his attitude toward experience and language as it developed out of his early training in the discipline of behavioral psychology and philosophy associated with William James, Husserl, and Mach, thinkers who were attempting to synthesize empirical scientific progress and cultural values. This theme is particularly interesting in light of our century's enduring obsession with language and its role in constituting or mediating or inhibiting our experience of the world.

Too often in discussing the complex web of ideas behind a writer's work

From *Studies in Twentieth-Century Literature* 18, no. 2 (Summer 1994). © 1994 by *Studies in Twentieth-Century Literature*.

we forage in the work for the ideas, without pausing to think that the processes of fiction are radically different from those of intellectual discourse, and that the two cannot be equated. What makes Musil so interesting is that he had the scientific training and ability to engage thoroughly in intellectual discourse, but spent his life trying to reinvent this discourse in prose fiction, creating a new kind of literature in the process.

In this century philosophy and literary criticism and theory have followed two general orientations. One gives priority to language as mediating our knowledge of the world, the other subordinates language to sensory and perceptual experience, which language serves to mediate. The first view holds that language precedes experience "logically, ontologically, and genetically, and modifies and distorts experience." The second gives priority to "the logical and ontological primacy of experience over language" (Koestenbaum xii). These orientations are by no means mutually exclusive, but serve to indicate a primary emphasis on one or the other aspect. The orientation favoring language describes a general line from Nietzsche, Wittgenstein, Mauthner, Saussure, and Heidegger through structuralism, post-structuralism, and deconstruction; the second, originating in the philosophy of Husserl, reaches generally through phenomenology to existentialism and to the group of phenomenologist critics Sarah Lawall has called "the critics of consciousness."

The approach based on the primacy of language over experience assumes, as one commentator has put it, "that at least some, and perhaps all philosophical problems are the logical consequences of quasi-grammatical errors or ambiguities in the use of language." Husserl, on the other hand, "assumes that language reflects the structure of experience, or, if it does not, that we can examine experience independently of language" (Koestenbaum xii). Today this latter notion, which disregards language as the vehicle through which experience is rendered, seems naive. But for the purpose of my argument, I would like to maintain a distinction between the emphasis on language and the emphasis on experience, even while recognizing that it is not absolute. ("Experience" is taken here to refer to perceptual and sensory experience and its cognitive effects.)

My general argument is that writers of the early modernist generation, and certainly Musil, were not blocked by language's presumed inability to represent experience, but on the contrary were struggling to develop a new kind of literary language that would adequately represent experience as a cognitive process as it was then coming to be understood. Musil's extraordinary enterprise, in particular, does not seem amenable to structuralist or post-structuralist theoretical generalizations. He was a writer of fiction who was attempting to forge with the greatest possible precision a language of images that would portray the inexact process by which a character proceeds through life within the envelope of his individual perceptions, sensations, thoughts, and experiences. In *The Man without Qualities* Musil pushed this further, attempting to reconcile this process of individual perception with the utopian goal of a world in which social institutions would be morally and ethically revitalized. The work of art was to point the way to this revitalization.

Musil's was an experiment at once literary, scientific, and moral, and the language of fiction was for him the means to craft the revaluation and reintegration of values that Nietzsche and Mach had called for. He was not interested in discovering the relation of mind to world from an abstract point of view, but in experimentally integrating mind and world through the images and situations of the surrogate reality of fiction.

Where, aside from Nietzsche and Mach, was Musil coming from? His teachers and those who influenced him when he was young, the pre- and early phenomenologists Brentano, Mach, Stumpf, Husserl, and William James, were engaged in trying to counter the Newtonian and Cartesian reduction of the world to impersonal elements and mechanical processes, as expressed in the mid-nineteenth century by means of the reigning scientific paradigm of positivism. Positivism admitted as evidence only those things that could be measured and quantified; Dickens grotesquely caricatured it in the figure of Mr. Gradgrind in *Hard Times*. The direction the early phenomenologists took was the result of new insights into cognition and an ardent desire to unify human understanding on the basis furnished by idealistic philosophy. Their basic criticism was directed at what seemed to them a too narrow notion of science.[2] They were not out to reject positivism, but rather sought to broaden this then prevailing scientific paradigm by including among its empirical concepts a fluid continuum of reason plus sensation and feelings and not simply discrete measurable data alone, as constituting the totality of data on which scientific hypotheses should be based. As Alfred North Whitehead put it in 1925, "The disadvantage of exclusive attention to a group of abstractions, however well-founded, is that, by the nature of the case, you have abstracted from the remainder of things. In so far as the excluded things are important in your experience, your modes of thought are not fitted to deal with them" (Whitehead 59).[3]

Musil offers the interesting case of a writer trained as a scientist for whom literature operates primarily on the basis of empirical perception and sensory experience and for whom language serves as the vehicle to represent experience. This argument implicitly rejects the idea that what literature conveys is graspable only through an analytic procedure that reduces it to rational or rationalized elements of language such as narrative and discourse.

A writer, even an analytic writer like Musil, might be interested in pursuing other goals: in his case, as Philip Payne notes, this includes the winning back of the ground of the subject. This ground "has been lost," Payne says, "in the field of ideas, to the march of a militant objectivity which is both superficial and insensitive; it has been lost in the field of morals with the sense that principles are written on tablets of stone rather than in the human heart; it has been lost in the field of science with the disappearance of the observer from the scope of what he observes" (Payne 210–11). It might also be said of modernist literature generally that it resists the attempts of theory to reduce literary expression to the problem of language alone. This kind of literature uses language to project images that incorporate action in an envelope of sensory experience rather than using it descriptively or discursively. The senses, emotions, affects, moods, and subliminal effects involved in perception and experience are considered essential. It is too reductive, as some critics would have it, to consider literary language as merely a doomed attempt at some kind of rational discourse that eludes both writer and reader, a fruitless butting one's head against the walls of the "prison-house of language."

The anchoring of modernist literature in perceptual and sensory images possibly illustrates what Wittgenstein meant when he wrote in the *Philosophical Investigations* that "a *picture* held us captive. And we could not get outside it, for it lay in our language and language seemed to repeat it to us inexorably" (Wittgenstein 48, ¶115). Suzanne Langer expressed something similar when she said that the artist's way of knowing feelings and emotions "is not expressible in ordinary discourse [because] ... the forms of feeling and the forms of discursive expression are logically incommensurate, so that any exact concepts of feeling and emotion cannot be projected into the logical form of literal language" (Langer 91).[4]

As a series of cognitive images, this kind of literature is primarily based on and appeals to an expanded notion of experience, using language as its vehicle. The writer seeks to engage the reader in the experience by creating verbal images that attempt to re-evoke the perceptual and sensory aura of the experience for the reader. Writers as ambitious as Proust or Musil will further seek ways to raise experience, understood in this fashion, to the level of the generally representative, so that it might serve a socially representative function as well—become cultural experience, as it were. The overwhelming focus of literary theory on language as discourse in recent times has not been very helpful in comprehending this notion. Language-based critics or theorists generally operate by positing or assuming language as the exclusive field of operations and then excerpting linguistic micro-features such as metaphors, metonyms, or discourses from a work and analyzing them narrowly within a structural, quasi-philosophical, political, ideological, or sociological context, without paying particular attention to other aspects or to the work as a whole.

All this is perhaps simply another way of maintaining that literature as an art is essentially empirical and descriptive rather than abstract and analytical: Flannery O'Connor called art a virtue of the practical intellect. Broadly speaking, the phenomenological perspective offers a foundation for the premise that modernist literature, using language as its vehicle, functions primarily as a mediator of experience as perceived by an experiencing consciousness. My thesis is that when writers call upon philosophers, they do so not to grasp and argue the philosophical system, but to define an experimental and necessarily *ad hoc* field for their own fictional representations. So although Musil's thought was largely formed by a specifically phenomenological environment, his many quarrels with phenomenological theory are marks of the questing and questioning writer rather than the concerns of a developing psychologist or philosopher. It is therefore not my purpose to summarize or criticize Husserl's philosophy; Musil did both in some detail in his *Tagebücher* (*Diaries*). My focus is rather on how Musil's way of projecting the world in literature, strongly formed by phenomenological ideas, provided a base and framework for his experimental writing.

This said, Musil's connection with the early phenomenologists was a direct one: he was thoroughly grounded in empirical phenomenology as well as empirical science. Carl Stumpf, to whom Husserl dedicated the *Logical Investigations*, was Musil's *Doktorvater* in Berlin; he wrote his controversial doctoral dissertation on Ernst Mach under Stumpf's direction (*Toward an Evaluation of Mach's Theories*, 1908). Musil's goal as a writer of uniting precision with soul, as he put it in the *Man without Qualities*, arose out of this background.

For the writer as well as for phenomenology and empirical science, "precision" was a tough problem. In Husserl's view, in one critic's words, "there is no absolute criterion of precision. Precision is a function of context and subject-matter.... [In order] to accept Husserl's analyses we must grant that *vague* experiences are legitimate objects of philosophic scrutiny. We cannot restrict our efforts to the simple, the clear, and the distinct.... [What is to be analyzed] consists of obscure, fuzzy, and cloudy clusters of experience.... The fact that the experiences analyzed are often vague does not diminish their *certainty*" (Koestenbaum xiii). Scientific rationality and precision—still upheld as a primary value, but enlarged—is therefore to be seen as a variable that is a function of different contexts rather than a categorical summation of fixed points. Musil's self-imposed task as a writer was to find a literary language able to render with precision these "obscure, fuzzy, and cloudy clusters of experience."

Musil was born in 1880, the year Husserl turned twenty-one. This was the year in which Zola, in the conclusion to his essay "*Le Roman expérimental*," called for a new kind of novel, one that would embody the unfolding discoveries of empirical science about the workings of mind and body in relation to the world. This new empirical method would replace the traditional conventions that reach back to classical drama and rhetoric with a new, experimental method, the triumph of which, Zola wrote, "is an inevitable evolution. Literature ...," Zola goes on to say, "does not depend merely upon the author; it is influenced by the nature it depicts and by the man whom it studies. Now if the savants change their ideas of nature, if they find the true mechanism of life, they force us to follow them, to precede them even, so as to play our role in the new hypotheses. The metaphysical man is dead; our whole territory is transformed by the advent of the physiological man. No doubt," Zola continues, "'Achilles' anger,' 'Dido's love,' will last forever on account of their beauty; but today we feel the necessity of analyzing anger and love, of discovering exactly how such passions work in the human being ...: we have become experimentalists instead of philosophers" (Zola 598–99).[5]

As a novelist and a firm believer in positivism, Zola tried to follow this program by combining affect and intellect in his construction of character and in his passages of narrative description. Zola's successors, although less confident about positivism than he was, attempted to fashion images in a new way that would reflect the complexities of cognition as it was then coming to be understood, and—still "scientific" in the experimental sense—would use art to expand knowledge. (The example of Zola figures in Musil's diaries.) This new way of fashioning literary images, founded on a more inclusive concept of precise science than the mere gathering of data, would make serious fiction itself a branch of knowledge, giving it a social, "scientific" function. Art as knowledge (*Erkenntnis*), as projected by Nietzsche and his literary followers (Musil, Kafka, Rilke, and Thomas Mann, among others), would be both scientific and moral and could serve as a principal means of restoring unity (but a new kind of unity, not an old one) to the rapidly fragmenting values of Western culture. (Here we see the considerable influence of Mach, whose vision is inscribed in the works of many of these writers.)

By the turn of the twentieth century positivism was fading as the leading paradigm of basic scientific thinking. Rather than attempting to uncover a few basic, material laws, scientific thought was turning to less rigid notions. It was becoming a process, as John Weiss has noted, of "pragmatic, hypothetical analysis, revealing tentative, if highly probable, generalizations." With the new physics that was developing, the natural sciences "ceased to be the ally and main support of the materialistic metaphysics which had seemed unassailable since the eighteen-fifties. If matter in motion was not the ultimate reality but merely a useful hypothesis for explaining some natural phenomena, one could legitimately reestablish equality of status for man's values, ideals, and emotional responses to his environment" (Weiss 12–13). Karl R. Popper put this new footing of scientific investigation succinctly: "I think that we shall have to get accustomed to the idea that we must not look upon science as a 'body of knowledge,' but rather as a system of hypotheses, that is to say, as a system of guesses or anticipations which in principle cannot be justified, but with which we work as long as they stand up to tests, and of which we are never justified in saying that we know that they are 'true' or 'more or less certain' or even 'probable'" (Popper 317, quoted in Holton 20). Musil, in the course of a detailed series of notes and comments in his diaries in 1904 or 1905 discussing Husserl's *Logical Investigations*, notes that "... there remains only a scale of degrees of probability, and it is conceivable that a certain level of probability is what we call certainty" (*Tagebücher* 119; translation mine). Bergson, with his emphasis on experience as flux, also contributed to undermining the notion of a fixed rhetorical literary language used to depict defined characters in defined situations, and William James called his influential study *The Varieties of Religious Experience*.[6]

It was this paradigmatic change in the assumptions of scientific thought that gave Musil the impetus for his experimental search to communicate with precision, through fiction, an expanded notion of experience. In a Machian context science and literature could be thought of as aspects of a unitary process with different emphases but the same goal, the increase of knowledge through a process of rigorous experimentation: knowledge not for its own sake, but knowledge that would lead to a higher and more humane morality while still passing the test of experimental rigor. Although outside the scope of this discussion, Musil's overriding purpose was a moral one; his passion and his intellect were both fueled by his specifically equating ethics with aesthetics—an equation that seems to have had its roots in Schopenhauer, Kierkegaard, and Nietzsche, and which is also found in many other writers around the turn of the century.[7]

Throughout his fiction Musil stresses both the inadequacy of received metaphysical notions and the inadequacy of traditional rhetoric and conventions of narrative literature to explain the world. He put hypotheses he derived from the phenomenologists' view of experience into the testing crucible of fictional situations. As a writer he was concerned with image-making, but he wanted to construct fictional situations that, in accord with the Husserlian approach, would be consonant with empirical scientific verification. Art as knowledge in fiction could thus become, as Zola had prophesied, part of science, although Zola's empiricism had been totally positivistic, while Musil's was more thoroughly scientific and experimental. In Musil's view, the chief function of language as it is used in literature is to mediate experience as projected by the author. These experiences and feelings are not the author's own, at least in primal form: there is a distinction between autobiography and fiction. They are rather material the writer can work with. (Suzanne Langer notes that "every work of art expresses ... not feelings and emotions which the artist *has*, but feelings and emotions which the artist *knows*; his *insight* into the nature of sentience, his picture of vital experience, physical and emotive and fantastic" [Langer 91]).

The burden of language as Musil understands it is not to mystify, but to analyze and order experience without reducing it. He makes his characters, within their immediate fictional situations, attempt to relate to each other and the world through their changing perceptual and sensory envelopes in terms of the experiences he tries out on them. What we can know, according to Husserl, is not the actual physical world but only our experience of it. Unlike Husserl, Musil is quite rigorous in making this process experimental and in developing a literary language that can express it with great precision. He puts all his major characters in this same experimental stance.

This is a tough enterprise for a writer, for not only is representing the complexity of experience thus understood a boundless task, but it rejects as impossibly artificial (not "true to life") the traditional literary notions of plot, dramatic action, and characterization that normally provide a guiding structure for readers as well as writers. The results are contradictory and paradoxical: self and world, as Musil treats them, dissolve into a flow of endless "possibilities," of the kind so lovingly developed in *The Man without Qualities*.[8] The only way to temporarily arrest this flow, Musil postulates, is for an individual to attain an attenuated, tentative, ineffable, and quite transitory mystical state that he calls the "other condition," an ecstatic state of heightened awareness similar to that advocated by Walter Pater.[9]

The problem with regarding thoughts and sensations as a stream or flow with intermittent stases is, to quote William James, "introspectively, to see the transitive parts for what they really are. If they are but flights to conclusions, stopping them to look at them before a conclusion is reached is really annihilating them.... Let anyone try to cut a thought across the middle and get a look at its section, and he will see now difficult the introspective observation of the transitive tract is.... Or if our purpose is nimble enough and we do arrest it, it ceases forthwith to be itself.... The attempt at introspective analysis in these cases is in fact like ... trying to turn up the light quickly enough to see how the darkness looks" (quoted in Holton 124).

Musil, who was quite familiar with James's work, understood this dilemma very well: throughout his diaries, essays, and interviews he worries endlessly about the technical problems this posed for him as a writer. Rejecting narrative in the traditional sense, he relies on a narrator external to the action to frame and control the experimental process as it unfolds. But since each scene is limited to representing the envelope of perceptions, sensations, actions, and experiences of the characters who are perceiving, sensing, acting, and experiencing within it, each scene tends to become a hermetic unit and *mise-en-abyme*. No extended dramatic narrative (for which characters must be defined as consistent types or counters) is possible. Musil's "non-narrative narrative" consists of a sequence of quasi-independent micro-narratives, each of which could be extended at will in any direction or interspersed with other micro-narratives. Like Husserl, Musil believed in building up and analyzing *all* the data that hypothetically constitute experience. He did not, like Thomas Mann or Hermann Broch, for example, begin with an *a priori* set of values or literary notions.

This might explain why Musil had trouble finishing anything, notably *The Man without Qualities* and his essays: the experimental path he set up, "the path of the smallest steps" as he called it, that would ultimately reconcile the potential of probability with the reality of what actually happens, can never end. This is a negative consequence of his dedication to a hypothetical approach that gives primacy to "a scale of degrees of probability," and that defines certainty as only the closest approach to the greatest achievable degree of probability—a kind of Zeno's arrow of probability suspended in its flight toward certainty.

Of course language as well as experience may be looked at as also constituting an amalgam of emotions and ideas, especially in the sequences of cognitive images that are a major feature of much modernist literature. Something of Musil's sophisticated awareness of this interdependence—in this respect he is unlike Husserl—can be indicated by an argument of Mary Hesse's that is very close to Musil's conception. Hesse claims that meanings are not fixed in relation to universals or types, but "grow in dynamic interaction with culture and experience." If the meaning of words is thus changeable rather than fixed, the way to get beyond individual uses of each word is, Hesse argues, "to replace the Aristotelian model of 'intuition of the universal,' which goes from particulars 'up' to the universal and 'down again' to its other realizations, by a model that goes 'horizontally' from particulars to particulars. Members of a class ...... she argues, "are loosely grouped by relations of similarity and difference into fuzzy, overlapping, and temporarily defined classes whose boundaries change with experience and cultural convention" (Hesse 38). This last statement is related to Husserl's inclusive notion of experience and indicates the principal way that Musil, like William James, sees language as mediating the ever-shifting boundaries of perceptual and sensory experience, relying on constantly changing contextual determinations of meaning rather than on fixed ones. The narrator of *The Man without Qualities*, for instance, says at one point that everything that the central character, Ulrich, and his sister Agathe "encountered on the plane of ideas had the tensed, tightrope-walking nature of the once-and-never-again, and whenever they talked about it they did so in the awareness that no single word could be used twice without changing its meaning" (Musil, *GW* 4:1400).[10]

Pity the poor writer! The conflicts and paradoxes inherent in this approach to fiction are set out at the very beginning of *The Man without Qualities*. A scientist and mathematician, Ulrich is unable to fix any actual or potential moment in the flow of experience as definitive, or to fashion a language that could mediate the flow of experience in any reliable fashion, such as empirical science demands. In his very first appearance in the novel, Ulrich is standing behind a window in his house with a stopwatch in his hand, trying without success to freeze the flow of traffic and pedestrians on the street outside in a statistical measurement.

Representation, and the language that is its vehicle, can only be valid in Musil's view if rendered with the utmost precision. *The Man without Qualities* contains a veritable catalog of the ways people talk, write, and interact in their lives, and these ways are considered unsatisfactory and insufficient. Each social class, profession, and individual in the novel is given his/her/its/their own hermetic vocabularies and grammars. Musil included mystic, philosophical, and scientific language, as well as the everyday conversational idiolects of each of the characters in the novel. (Each character speaks in his or her own style, idiom, vocabulary, and syntax, crossing but rarely intersecting with the others.[11]) Musil even includes body language, as well as the inner, unrealized language of the inarticulate and the insane! The problem, as he saw it, lay in somehow fashioning a language that would overcome these obstacles and permit objective communication of the whole complex flow of experience from person to person and within society as a whole, and thus make *true* communication possible.

I would disagree with Marike Finlay, who sees Musil's *oeuvre* exclusively in terms of discourse, that is, narrative considered solely as a problem of discursive language. Finlay says that *The Man without Qualities* "is the discursive practice which is, par excellence, built up of the pragmatic material interaction of infinitely expanding fields of other discursive practices." *The Man without Qualities*, she says, "is not narrative; it is a constant narration made up of other narrations, a discourse of and with other discourses. Herein lies the major transformation that Musil's discursive practice effects on the procedures of the classical episteme, thus heralding the opening of the modern episteme" (Finlay 133–34).

It is quite true that the problem of narrative was a central one for Musil, but it is misleading to focus on this *only* as a problem of discourse, in the current fashion, as Finlay and others have done. If a writer envisions experience as a complex floating membrane of thoughts, feelings, memories, and sensations that changes at every moment, and language likewise, then conventional techniques of narrative, and even some not so conventional, will appear reductive and impossibly simplistic, but discursive analysis alone is not capable of encompassing the phenomenon. A recurring image in Musil's fiction is that of puffy white clouds continually forming and reforming as the invisible force of the air moves them along against the background of a remote, unattainable blue sky. These moving clouds are non-narrative and non-discursive, but they figure the billowing reality of experience that Musil is trying to encompass and express.

In his novella *Tonka* an impatient young middle-class scientist, whose understanding of the world is exclusively scientific and empirical, has an affair with a silent, uneducated working-class girl. Tonka, the girl in question, has a powerful intuitive understanding of the world, but cannot express herself at all through language. He is totally articulate, she is totally inarticulate. Musil's problem was how to present their relationship as a flow of solipsistically individualized experience. At one point they are sitting at the edge of some woods, "and he was simply gazing into space though half-shut eyelids, not talking, letting his thoughts roam. Tonka began to be afraid she had offended him again. Several times she took a deep breath, as if about to speak, but then shyness held her back. So for a long time there was no sound but the woodland murmur that is so tormenting, rising and sinking away in a different place at every instant. Once a brown butterfly fluttered past them and settled on a long-stemmed flower, which quivered under the touch, swaying to and fro and then quite suddenly being quite still again, like a conversation broken off. Tonka pressed her fingers hard into the moss on which they were sitting, but after a while the tiny blades stood up again, one after the other, row on row, until there was finally no more trace of the hand that had lain there. It was enough to make one weep, without knowing why. If she had been trained to think, like her companion, at that moment Tonka would have realized that Nature consists of nothing but ugly little things that one hardly notices and which live as sadly far apart from each other as the stars in the night sky. The beauties of Nature.... A wasp was crawling over his shoe. Its head was like a lantern. He watched it, contemplating his shoe, which was sticking up broad and black, oblique against the brown of the earth" (Musil, "Tonka" 275 [ellipsis in original]).

This passage presents the disparate flow of stimulation and response in two mismatched lovers in a natural setting. The setting provides an external unity—it is the same for both—but the characters' responses to it place them in different worlds. The man observes nature strictly as an empirical scientist would, noting only objective data and apparently decrying feeling—but in doing so he exhibits feelings he refuses to acknowledge. Tonka, without his education or ability to articulate her thoughts in words, shrinks from nature because of her feelings for the man. She is able to *feel* the world directly but not to conceptualize or judge it (hence her experience can only be indirectly pointed at); the man conceptualizes and judges the world but cannot feel it, at least directly. The setting is a screen on which the characters project what each is experiencing but cannot express, and of which, at some level of consciousness, they are only dimly aware. It is these subliminal feelings that shape the experience and that Musil is trying to shape into a story.

Here, then, Musil is experimenting with how language can be made to convey the flow of experience in a way that is inaccessible to the conventional languages of literature and science. By his ingenious use of language, he draws the reader into re-feeling what the characters are feeling. This ability to evoke with great precision in the reader the complex web of feelings associated with the situation and thoughts of the character is perhaps Musil's greatest achievement as a writer.

This technique is far more skillfully developed in *The Man without Qualities*. At one point Ulrich and his sister Agathe, who is living with him, are "changing to go out for the evening. There was no one in the house to help Agathe aside from Ulrich; they had started late and had thus been in the greatest haste for a quarter of an hour when a short pause intervened. Piece by piece, nearly all the ornaments of war a woman puts on for such occasions were strewn on the chairbacks and surfaces of the room, and Agathe was in the act of bending over her' foot with all the concentration called for by the pulling on of a thin silk stocking. Ulrich was standing behind her. He saw her head, her neck, her shoulders, and this nearly naked back; her body was curved over her raised knees, slightly to the side, and the tension of this process sent three folds around her neck, shooting slender and merry through her clear skin like three arrows: the charming physicality of this painting, escaped from the instantaneously spreading stillness, seemed to have lost its frame, and passed so abruptly and directly into Ulrich's body that he left the place he was standing and, not so entirely without consciousness as a banner being unfurled by the wind, but also not with deliberate reflection, crept closer on tiptoe, surprised the bent-over figure, and with gentle ferocity bit into one of those arrows, while his arm closed tightly around his sister. Then Ulrich's teeth just as cautiously released his overpowered victim; his right hand had grabbed her knee, and while with his left arm he pressed her body to his, he pulled her upright with him on upward-bounding tendons. Agathe cried out in fright."

"Up to this point everything had taken place as playfully and jokingly as much that had gone on before, and even if it was tinged with the colors of love, it was only with the really shy intention of concealing love's unwonted dangerous nature beneath such cheerfully intimate dress. But when Agathe got over her fright, and felt herself not so much flying though the air as rather resting in it, suddenly liberated from all heaviness and directed in its stead by the gentle force of the gradually decelerating motion, it brought about one of those accidents which no one has in his power, that she seemed to herself in this state strangely soothed, indeed carried away from all earthly unrest; with a movement changing the balance of her body that she could never have repeated she also brushed away the last silken thread of compulsion, turned in falling to her brother, continued, so to speak, her rise as she fell, and lay, sinking down, as a cloud of happiness in his arms" (Musil, *GW* 4:1081–82).[12]

Musil's notion that the task of literature is to represent with precision the fuzzy wholeness of experience was but one of many analogous attempts by modernist writers to try to find new and more accurate forms of expression. Even Henry James had written in 1888 that "experience is never limited, and it is never complete; it is an immense sensibility, a kind of huge spider-web of the finest silken threads suspended in the chamber of consciousness, and catching every air-borne particle on its tissue. It is the very atmosphere of the mind" (H. James 52).

The problem raised by many modernist writers is one central to phenomenological theory: a view of "consciousness" and "experience" such as Musil's presupposes a subjective consciousness, that is, an individual mind—whether the character's, narrator's, author's, or some combination of them—that is doing the perceiving and experiencing. What is the nature of the world independently of being perceived, Husserl had wondered. This was a question that intensely preoccupied Musil. How can a bridge (a utopian, hence idealistic bridge) be built from this isolated subjective mind to the social, moral, and ethical concerns of society at large? Does not this approach to perception and experience, so radically centered on the subjective mind, commit a writer to a mode of fiction centered on solipsistic characters? (Virginia Woolf's and D.H. Lawrence's fiction, Rilke's novel *Malte Laurids Brigge*, and Joyce's two major novels also raise the question.) In much of fiction written in the last few decades, on the other hand, characters are frequently counters or stereotypes, actors in social situations rather than perceiving consciousnesses. Does this "post-modern" fiction rest on or appeal to sensation, perception, and experience at all, in the phenomenological or modernist sense?

There would seem to have been in the early phenomenologists and in Musil an underlying idealism that has since been lost, a belief that in spite of the increasing solipsism and dehumanizing specialization of modern life there is some sphere or some level—one hardly knows what to call it—in or on which all the conflicting and apparently unrelated fragments, self and world, feeling and intellect, science and society, skepticism and belief, could somehow be melded into a coherent, ethical whole. This might explain why the phenomenological basis is no longer fashionable in literary criticism and theory, and why language-based criticism, with its entrenched skepticism about idealist assumptions, has become dominant—it suits the temper of our time, which is disillusioned about any form of larger unity in the world. In the tradition of idealistic philosophy, phenomenology conceived experience as the experience of an individual person, but underlying the phenomenological enterprise was the intention of bringing about moral and ethical reform on the level of the larger community, and the belief that this could be done through an awakened subjectivity that would somehow expand outwards from the individual to the social and cultural world. Our time, however—as Musil himself trenchantly observed many times in his essays and in *The Man without Qualities*—has moved instead to a collectivist mode of thinking in which political, ideological, ethnic, and tribal thought and behavior rather than the individual's subjectivity have become the framework for social thought, and in which literary characters, no longer the anchoring centers of the world they had been since Romanticism, have become in extreme cases cartoon characters. In collectivist fashion the contemporary human sciences, psychology, medicine, and sociology approach the individual only as a statistical manifestation of generalized and abstracted characteristics. (Thus the disease is more important than the patient, who represents for the medical profession only a manifestation of it, a "case.")

Musil found reason enough to despair of himself and the world around him, of which he was a strenuous, acute, and untiring critic; but he still believed, as did many of his modernist contemporaries, that there was a way forward, if only it could be found, and that a bridge had to be built from the individual person equipped with a new and heightened awareness to a new society in which ethics would assume a central place. This was the matrix of his experimental struggle to forge a language that would truly represent and communicate experience.

NOTES

1. I am indebted to Vincent Crapanzano and to E.J. Baylis Thomas for their helpful comments and suggestions in the preparation of this article. A broad and invaluable picture of the importance of the psychology of perception in late nineteenth and early twentieth century European and American culture can be found in Judith Ryan, *The Vanishing Subject: Early Psychology and Literary Modernism* (Chicago: U of Chicago P, 1991). Ryan is more concerned with the broader picture of empiricist psychology as a cultural phenomenon at the turn of the century. She focusses on Musil more narrowly in relation to empirical thought, whereas my focus is on the problems that arise at the experimental boundary between theory and fictional technique, as Musil tried to construct a world-view in his fiction that was inspired but not explained by empiricist philosophy. Another, much broader, contextualization of the cultural phenomenon is in Stephen Toulmin, *Cosmopolis: The Hidden Agenda of Modernity* (Chicago: U Chicago P, 1992 [1990]). Also valuable but more technical is Hartmut Cellbrot, *Die Bewegung des Sinnes: Zur Phänomenologie Robert Musils im Hinblick auf Edmund Husserl*, Musil-Studien Bd. 17 (Munich: Fink, 1988). See, too, Karl Menges, "Robert Musil and Edmund Husserl: Über phänomenlogische Stukturen im *Mann ohne Eigenschaften*," *Modern Austrian Literature* 9.3–4 (1976): 131–54.

2. "The incapacity and unwillingness of science to face problems of value and meaning because of its confinement to mere positive facts seems to [Husserl] to be at the very root of the crisis of science and of mankind itself. In contrast to the science of the Renaissance, which had been part of a comprehensive philosophical scheme, a positivist science of mere facts appeared as a truncated science endangering man, and in fact endangering itself, by a 'decapitation.'" Herbert Spiegelberg, *The Phenomenological Movement: A Historical Introduction*, 2nd ed. (The Hague: Martinus Nijhoff, 1971) 1:80.

3. William James had voiced a similar thought in *The Principles of Psychology*: "Science ... must be constantly reminded that her purposes are not the only purposes, and that the order of uniform causation which she has use for, and is therefore right in postulating, may be enveloped in a wider order, on which she has no claims at all." (Authorized Edition in Two Volumes. New York: Dover, 1950 [1890]) 2:576.

4. To discuss the central importance of the emotions in relation to perception and sensation for Musil and the phenomenologists is beyond the scope of this paper. There is a good exposition in Cellbrot, and in the chapter in the *Nachlaß* of *The Man without Qualities* titled "Agathe stößt zu ihrem Mißvergnügen auf einen geschichtlichen Abriß der Gefühlspsychologie" (*GW* 4:1138–46). See also William James, *Principles of Psychology*, chapter 2, "The Emotions," and Heydebrand 117–33.

5. Musil offers a short but penetrating analysis of Zola's essay in a 1927 tribute on the sixtieth birthday of the critic Alfred Kerr. Musil notes that while Zola had misapprehended the nature of science he had framed the problem correctly, "for literature can not be spared having to conform to the scientific depiction of the world, and a great part of contemporary literature's lack of objective referentiality [*Gegenstandslosigkeit*] comes about because it has been behind the times." (*GW* 8:1183. Translation mine).

6. For Musil's relation to Bergson see Heydebrand 213–16.

7. See also Musil's *Tagebücher* and Thomas Mann's essay, "Nietzsche's Philosophy in the Light of Our Experience."

8. "In *Ideas* ¶47 [Husserl] talks of possible worlds. His notion of possible worlds is very heavily constrained, however. Since for him the world is not the world transcendent of us, not the actual physical world, that is, but only our experience of it, what is possible for Husserl means what is experienceable. And experienceability, he says, '*never betokens*

any empty logical possibility, but one that has its *motive* in the system of experience.'" Samuel R. Levin, *Metaphoric Worlds: Conceptions of a Romantic Nature* (New Haven: Yale UP, 1988) 59.

    9. See Ryan, chapter 2. There is a mention of Pater in Musil's diaries.

    10. Translation mine (copyright Alfred A. Knopf, Inc.).

    11. Language as Babel is used in a similar way in Hofmannsthal's 1921 play *Der Schwierige*. Walter Moser has treated this topic in Musil in an excellent article, "La Mise à l'essai des discours dans *L'Homme sans qualités* de Robert Musil," *Canadian Review of Comparative Literature* 12.1 (1985): 12–45.

    12. Translation mine (copyright Alfred A. Knopf, Inc.).

Works Cited

Finlay, Marike. *The Potential of Modern Discourse. Musil, Peirce, and Perturbation.* Bloomington: Indiana UP, 1990.

Hesse, Mary. "Texts without Types and Lumps without Laws." *New Literary History* 17.1 (1985): 31–47.

Heydebrand, Renate von. *Die Reflexionen Ulrichs in Robert Musils Roman 'Der Mann ohne Eigenschaften.'* Münster: Aschendorff, 1966.

Holton, Gerald. *Thematic Origins of Scientific Thought: Kepler to Einstein.* Cambridge: Harvard UP, 1988.

James, Henry. "The Art of Fiction." *Henry James: Literary Criticism: Essays on Literature, American Writers. English Writers* New York: Library of America, 1984.

James, William. *Principles of Psychology.* 1890. New York: Dover, 1950. 2 vols.

Koestenbaum, Peter. "Introductory Essay," *The Paris Lectures.* By Edmund Husserl. Trans. Peter Koestenbaum. The Hague: Nijhoff, 1970. ix–lxxvii.

Langer, Suzanne. *Problems of Art.* New York: Charles Scribner and Sons, 1957.

Lawall, Sarah. *Critics of Consciousness: The Existential Structures of Literature.* Cambridge: Harvard UP, 1968.

Musil, Robert. *Essays. Gesammelte Werke in neun Bänden.* Ed. Adolf Frisé. Reinbek: Rowohlt, 1981. Vol. B.

———. *Der Mann ohne Eigenschaften. Gesammelte Werke in neun Bänden.* Ed. Adolf Frisé. Reinbek: Rowohlt, 1981. Vol. 1–5.

———. *Precision and Soul, Essays and Addresses.* Ed. and trans. Burton Pike and David S. Luft. Chicago: U Chicago P, 1990.

———. *Tagebücher.* Ed. Adolf Frisé. Reinbek: Rowohlt, 1976.

———. "*Tonka*." Trans. Eithne Wilkins and Ernst Kaiser. *Robert Musil: Selected Writings.* Ed. Burton Pike. The German Library 72. New York: Continuum, 1986.

Payne, Philip. *Robert Musil's 'The Man without Qualities': A Critical Study.* Cambridge, England: Cambridge UP, 1988.

Popper, Karl R. *The Logic of Scientific Discovery.* London: Hutchinson, 1959.

Ryan, Judith. *The Vanishing Subject: Early Psychology and Literary Modernism.* Chicago: U Chicago P, 1991.

Weiss, John, ed., *Modern Consciousness.* Detroit: Wayne State UP, 1965.

Whitehead, Alfred North. *Science and the Modern World: Lowell Lectures*. New York: Macmillan, 1967.

Wittgenstein, Ludwig. *Philosophical Investigations*. Trans. G.E.M. Anscombe. 2nd bilingual ed. New York: Macmillan, 1958.

Zola, Emile. *The Experimental Novel*. Trans. Belle M. Sherman. *Literary Criticism: Pope to Croce*. Eds. Gay Wilson Allen and Harry Hayden Clark. Detroit: Wayne State UP, 1962.

ROBERT ZALLER

Robert Musil and the Novel of Metastasis

As Susan Sontag has pointed out, cancer has become the reigning metaphor of late twentieth-century culture. It serves to describe so many phenomena of recent and contemporary life: imperialism (forcible acts of colonization), capitalism (reckless, random growth), culture (the Disneyization of taste). But illness has long been a Romantic badge of honor. What cancer and AIDS are to the end of the millennium, tuberculosis was— before Koch's vaccine drove it from the scene of the respectable classes—for the nineteenth and early twentieth centuries. We can date the transition with some precision. Thomas Mann's *The Magic Mountain*, published in 1924, was the definitive "tubercular" novel. That same year, Robert Musil began serious work on the epic novel, *The Man without Qualities*.[1] Musil nowhere mentions cancer in his novel, though the action pivots around a death whose description is compatible with it; after Mann, any specification would only have been vulgar. Rather, Musil's book takes metastasis as its structural principle: an inexhaustibly extensive growth incapable of reaching term without self-extinction.

There is, of course, every difference between a work that resists completion because of inadequate vision or stamina, and one whose very conception precludes it. Musil had a powerful organizing intelligence, and *The Man without Qualities* shows a symphonic grasp of form that in terms of scope

From *Boulevard* 13, no. 3 (Spring 1998). © 1998 by Opojaz, Inc.

and ambition can perhaps only be compared to Wagner's *Ring* cycle. The comparison is not inadvertent, since Wagner's music is itself a leitmotif of the novel, and Wagner's great theme—the quest for redemption in an era of dissolution—is Musil's own. Musil's project might indeed be described in shorthand as Wagner plus irony, except that irony is the one quality not only lacking in but incompatible with Wagner. It was this absence that turned Nietzsche, the other presiding genius of Musil's work, from Wagner, and it is in juxtaposing the two men that Musil's own irony takes flight. To put it somewhat reductively, if the Wagnerian hero's quest ends in Christian bathos and the Nietzschean superman begins with the demand for a clean sweep of it, Musil's hero—post-Wagnerian, post-Nietzschean, and, from a compositional perspective, postwar—exemplifies the dilemma of the intellectual who rides the cusp of his age without being able either to transcend or transform it.

Like Siegfried and Zarathustra, Musil's hero is known to us only by a single name, Ulrich. Ulrich does not lack a family name, of course, being a properly registered subject of the Austro-Hungarian empire and the son of an eminent *Hofrat* and jurist. We are discreetly informed, however, that this name "must be suppressed out of consideration for his father"—a presentiment of scandal that does not in fact befall Ulrich in either the text published in Musil's lifetime or the surviving manuscript material, although its possible outlines are suggested. Thus, when Ulrich must be referred to by more than his Christian name, he is Ulrich What's-His-Name or Ulrich von So-and-So, or, to use the sobriquet bestowed by his friends, the Man without Qualities.

The implied question in this is what kind of name a Man without Qualities deserves. A name is simultaneously a family heirloom, a set of nonsense syllables, and the sheet anchor of one's identity ("Ulrich" is a good German name; "von" is indicative of noble status: we already know a good deal about our hero just in that). To withhold a part of someone's name is therefore to suggest a social if not an ontological deficit; when Joseph K. first appears to us in *The Trial*, the reduction of his surname to an initial foreshadows the slow; torturous deprivation of his juridical identity, and when Samuel Beckett presents us with "The Unnameable," we know that we are in the presence of one for whom all surrounding context has vanished, so that to give him a name would be literally to offer us only nonsense.

In a sense, then, Ulrich's scandal is already specified, and will not depend on any contingencies of plot. Unlike Siegfried and Zarathustra, whose single predicates denote fullness and self-sufficiency, Ulrich's "absent" surname indicates his deficiency as a social being. But which are the qualities he lacks? Musil offers us a possible explanation:

The inhabitant of a country has at least nine characters: a professional, a national, a civic, a class, a geographical, a sexual, a conscious, an unconscious, and possibly even a private character to boot. He unites them in himself, but they dissolve him, so that he is really nothing more than a small basin hollowed out by these many streamlets that trickle into it and drain out of it again, to join other such rills in filling some other such basin. Which is why every inhabitant of the earth also has a tenth character that is nothing else than the passive fantasy of spaces yet unfilled.

This permits a person all but one thing: to take seriously what his at least nine other characters do and what happens to them; in other words, it prevents precisely what should be his true fulfillment. This interior space—admittedly hard to describe—is of a different shade and shape in Italy from what it is in England, because everything that stands out in relief against it is of a different shade and shape; and yet it is in both places the same: an empty, invisible space, with reality standing inside it like a child's toy town deserted by the imagination. [30]

What Ulrich attempts to do is to give content to this "tenth character," which functions in Musil's universe rather like the *primum mobile* in the Ptolemaic one, the invisible axis on which the visible cosmos rotates. This cannot be done without holding his other nine characters in suspension, or in Husserl's term "bracketing" them; in practical terms, this means subjecting them to experiment, or leading what Ulrich calls from time to time the experimental life.

Musil's account of character has further implications, however. The picaresque hero of early modern European fiction, reflected in Lockean and associationist psychology, was the passive receptor of experience, a transparency through which the reader could project his own fantasies. Even the most famous counterexample, Don Quixote, only makes the point more forcibly, for the rebuffs his chivalric fantasies receive from an unaccommodating reality only emphasize the hero's situation as the product rather than the shaper of his environment. As nineteenth-century bourgeois society imposed its own codes, however, the hero became once again, as in medieval romance, the exemplar of a dominant value system, exhibited this time not in terms of virtuous action (rescue, pilgrimage, crusade) but in the display of virtuous traits (steadfastness, honesty, thrift). These traits, or qualities, in their sum constituted character, and the individual personage or "character" of a novel was in turn an entity exhibiting the qualities of which it was composed.

This model, already under attack by naturalism and modernism, is simultaneously caricatured and complicated—but not entirely rejected—by Musil. Instead of a single output, character, resulting from the interplay of qualities, we have a galaxy of characters within the individual, each itself presumably complex. These are "united" in the self, conceived again in Ptolemaic fashion as a *primum mobile* or balance wheel; at the same time, they also negate that very self, conceived as a mere basin or receptacle, like a riverbed that takes its shape entirely from the currents that flow over it. This conceit in turn derives from quantum physics (or magic), with its assumption that the same entity can manifest itself in different shapes or appear simultaneously in different places.

Musil is of course using scientific analogy to deconstruct received concepts of character and self, already in such disarray by the early twentieth century that they could only be handled ironically. The Homeric catalogue of "characters"—some overlapping, some implicitly contradictory—could be extended (and refined) indefinitely: they are laid out only to indicate their arbitrary, conventional nature, and merely to name them is to indicate their absurdity. On the other hand, they are real in precisely the same way all conventions are, in binding us to the extent we accept them. To be an Englishman is to accept a certain set of stipulations; to be an Italian is to accept another set. We can (and, Musil suggests, almost do) accept such conventions as a self, for they provide us with the civilized equivalent of instincts, the patterns of response that define for us hunger and satisfaction, danger and safety. They offer us everything we need to negotiate an ordinary human life except conviction.

Of course, we do not accept or reject the elements that constitute what we might call the social self, for they are imposed on us imperatively from birth. Nor are we free to dispense with them at any time; the alternative to being an Englishman is not to be an Italian but a traitor. It is unsafe to wander abroad even for an hour without the buckler of one's identity, as Ulrich discovers in the opening pages of the novel when in trying to decide whether the three muggers who surprise him on the street are truly thieves or mere manifestations of the *Zeitgeist* he is not only robbed but beaten senseless.

Musil comments that his hero had "apparently indulged in too much thinking," but it soon becomes apparent that Ulrich is confronting a nervous crisis. At the age of thirty-two, a bachelor without responsibilities and a scholar without affiliation, credit-worthy and connected at the highest social levels, he has decided to take a year's sabbatical to explore his life and determine, if he can, how he should live it. He has no clear idea how to undertake this task except to suspend his customary activities (a mathematical problem he is working on) and to discard his mistress (who is, however, immediately replaced by another, equally distracting one). What he has promised himself is that if he does not satisfy his somewhat nebulously formulated quest in the allotted period, he will commit suicide.

The moment at which we meet Ulrich is precisely dated: August 1913. He will be thirty-three when his self-imposed deadline expires, the age of Christ's sacrifice (it goes without saying that Ulrich, a man of his time, is a freethinker). It will also be August 1914, the month when Europe plunged into the Great War: the collective suicide attempt of a civilization, and fatal to Austria-Hungary, which would dissolve in its aftermath. Whether Ulrich will live or die (or simply change his mind) is undetermined; what will die is the nation of which he is a part, and which is, as Musil reminds us, a part of him. For Ulrich is neither English nor Italian; he is an Austrian mandarin, which in the world of Freud, Wittgenstein, and Carnap was a high estate indeed. One can imagine Ulrich surviving the war (Musil considered portraying this), but not the consciousness that staked itself on exploring its own farthest margins, like a receding galaxy trying to catch up with the space it was creating. That was a question that could only have been asked before the universe of European imperial civilization collapsed back on itself.

Ulrich's story, then, is bound up with the last days of the Austro-Hungarian Empire, or Kakania, in the locution Musil sometimes substitutes for it. This locution, as he explains, derived from the description of all things official in the empire as *kaiserlich-koniglich* (Imperial-Royal) or *kaiserlich und koniglich* (Imperial *and* Royal), a distinction reflecting the constitutional arcana of the Dual Monarchy itself (an Austria-Hungary that was both an Austria and a Hungary, among other things). Musil's happy sobriquet had overtones of perpetual discord (the cacophony of its subject peoples as well as that of its two recognized master races), not to mention of scatology. An anachronism if not an absurdity in a world of nation-states, it was also a model (alas, unrepeatable) for containing the ethnic tribalism that so unexpectedly succeeded it.

The head of this precarious enterprise was the Emperor Franz Josef, at the beginning of the novel eighty-three years old and, having been installed in the revolutionary year 1848, already the third longest reigning monarch in history. It was Musil's inspiration to remember that the seventieth anniversary of Franz Josef's accession was to have coincided with the thirtieth anniversary of that of Emperor Wilhelm II of Germany in 1918, a date that saw not the celebration but the collapse of both empires. On that simple fact he constructed the loom of his plot. The Austrians, though formally allied with their upstart German neighbors, were for good historic reasons competitive with them. What more natural than that they should fear being upstaged on the occasion of their Emperor's jubilee by that of Wilhelm's? And what more logical a consequence than that some farsighted imperial minister, anticipating such a denouement, should move to head it off by devising a pageant that would not only celebrate Franz Josef's superior longevity but Kakania's unique contribution to world culture: a Year of Austria, in fact?

Thus is born the Parallel Campaign.

It will not escape the reader that the delicious and just-sufficiently plausible absurdity of the Parallel Campaign, the quest to define the soul of a nation that exists only as a tissue of exquisitely poised contradictions, itself parallels and in the gentlest way parodies Ulrich's personal campaign to define himself. By a further elegant step, Ulrich is co-opted into the Campaign at the insistence of his father, whose wishes he is not (having need of an allowance to pursue his meditations) in a position to ignore. This paternal intervention is the first of two occasions, separated by an arch of more than six hundred pages, on which Ulrich finds the course of his life diverted by a note from his father.

The Parallel Campaign introduces us to a gallery of new figures: Count Leinsdorf, whose brainchild it is; Diotima, whose salon serves as its general headquarters; Tuzzi, her skeptical and long-suffering husband; General Stumm von Bordwehr, the military's man on the scene; and Paul Arnheim, the German entrepreneur who goes slumming in it for purposes of his own. The endless soirees at which the Campaign tries, like a dinosaur that is all tail but dreams of a head, to envisage its theme, is political satire of the highest order.

As always in Musil, however, the comic serves a sober purpose. The Parallel Campaign is an exercise in stupidity, and stupidity—a subject Musil made the focus of a public lecture in 1937[2]—is, for him, one of the enabling devices of civilization, and almost a category of perception. Stupidity is, in brief, the decision to make sense of the world (as opposed to the always indecisive process of doing so to which we are all subject at every moment). By veiling consciousness, it converts the infinitely complex calibrations of will and energy required for the simplest act into the blithe conditioned responses of the workaday nervous system. If, however, by some infirmity one is unable to lower this veil, paralysis will result. This was precisely the condition of Ulrich, confronted by the three muggers and, in general, by life as such.

Stupidity is not an automatic process; it requires the service of ideas. The ultimate product of stupidity's ideas, in Musil's terms, is genius. Genius, as he describes it, is the faculty in any culture for expressing exactly what everyone knows. This collective content is stupidity itself, but to illuminate it in such a way that each individual can experience the shock of recognition for himself and thereby affirm with everyone else the common wisdom, is a faculty that elicits the highest gratitude. Thus honored, the genius becomes an institution, the Great Man; and since institutions, once created, abhor a vacuum, it follows that each epoch will produce exactly the number of Great Men it requires.

At this point, Austria is one short of its quota. The Parallel Campaign, with its search for the great unifying idea that will express the essence of Kakania, is obviously on stupidity's errand. The Great Man it attracts is Arnheim, a personage as effortlessly in motion as Ulrich is painfully at rest. Arnheim is the scion of an industrial magnate. Like many such he has developed *bienpensant* aspirations. While retreating annually to his estates to dictate the meditations that have won him an international reputation, he remains the consummate man of power, ruthless in the boardroom, persuasive in diplomacy, masterful in the salon. He has what only unembarrassed wealth and will to use it can command, the ability to view society from the heights and to act on it at will. This has led him to the concept of the Business King. The Business King is he who understands that while money is both the creator of the modern world and the most potent instrument for controlling it, it is by this very duality "most delicately involved with everything it controls." The businessman who thinks of money only in terms of profit— like Arnheim's father, a troglodytic capitalist who still runs the family business—is like a painter who thinks of his palette only as a means of sealing cracks against the rain. The true businessman understands money as the fusion of matter and spirit, and himself as its alchemist:

> Because he understood this subtle interdependence of all the forms of life ... Arnheim came to see the regal man of business as the synthesis of change and permanence, power and civility, sensible risk-taking and strong-minded reliance on information, but essentially as the symbolic figure of democracy-in-the-making. By the persistent and disciplined honing of his own personality, by his intellectual grasp of the economic and social complexes at hand, and by giving thought to the leadership and structure of the state as a whole, he hoped to help bring the new era to birth.... Objectively put, he had brought about the fusion of interests between business and soul ... and that feeling of love that had once taught him the unity of all things now formed the nucleus of his conviction that culture and all human interests formed a harmonious whole. [421–22]

This wonderful Weberian hybrid (based on the real-life figure of Walter Rathenau, the prewar industrialist and later Weimar foreign minister) is the ideal candidate to serve as resident genius to the Parallel Campaign but for two disabling handicaps: he is a Jew, and a Prussian. The Austrian idea, whatever else it may be, is certainly Catholic, and definitely not Hohenzollern. Arnheim, however, is so magisterial a figure, so clearly a world-bestriding colossus of finance and culture, that minor details such as citizenship and confessional origins hardly seem to matter, at least to the awestruck Diotima, who receives him as Danae received the shower of gold. Diotima does not know much about the nature of Arnheim's business or the ramifications of his interests; it suffices that she recognizes in him the New Man destined to synthesize the life of the mind and monopoly capital, and she is giddy at her coup.

Diotima is also Ulrich's cousin, although they are barely acquainted. Through the mild barrier of consanguinity they too are viscerally attracted to each other: "They both undoubtedly felt some aversion, and yet it occurred to them that they might nevertheless fuse to the point of extinction." This attraction appears destined to remain unconsummated, even unacknowledged on a conscious level, because their antipathy of mind is more fundamental. Like all of Musil's women but more so than most, Diotima is erotically activated by ambition, and ambition, in any conventional sense, is precisely what Ulrich has forsworn. This is masked by the fact that, as Count Leinsdorf's personal representative, Ulrich is presumably an interested party in the progress of the Campaign and a regular at Diotima's salon. Diotima senses his indolence, but this only draws her closer to him as an intimate with whom she can share the mounting frustration of her passion for Arnheim and the secret misgivings about the Campaign that accompany it.

Thus Musil sets up one of the most important of his triadic structures, that of Ulrich–Diotima–Arnheim. These triads are composed of dyadic relationships that, like free radicals, combine and separate nimbly and form in turn the basis of complex though unstable molecules: Diotima's salon; the Parallel Campaign; Austria itself. Although it is Diotima who binds the triad together, the crucial dyad in it is Ulrich–Arnheim. Ulrich is content for the most part to observe Arnheim as a phenomenon; their imparity is too great, their spheres and aims too separate for rivalry. But Arnheim correctly perceives Ulrich as a threat, less to any concrete interest than to the whole solid imposture of his life. He warns Diotima against Ulrich's skepticism, all the more pernicious because of its affable charm. Arnheim himself is not immune to this charm; "I could almost say I love him," he allows, "for something that is extraordinarily free and independent in his nature" (351).

It is just that something that Arnheim must capture and tame, for it is intolerable to him that anything so free should swim into his ken and remain beyond his control.

Ulrich himself is not indifferent to Arnheim's influence, which brings out the feminine side in his nature. He has long, gossipy conversations with the afflicted Diotima about her relationship, with Arnheim, which itself consists of conversations, albeit very long, intense, and exalted ones. After mature consideration, Diotima decides that adultery would do less harm to all concerned than divorce from Tuzzi. For the lordly Arnheim such bourgeois compromises will not do, but marriage, too, will require more than he can prudently invest in it. The result is impasse. Ulrich half-jokingly suggests that he and Diotima try their luck with each other, but this sally too is lost in clouds of Jamesian equivocation. What remains is the real crux of the business: Arnheim's seduction of Ulrich.

The weakness Ulrich has probed in Arnheim is the problem of bridging the gap between a material world ruled by the iron hand of money and the realm of spirit whose infusions it awaits. Arnheim has put off this problem in the way all modern persons put off inconvenient questions, by compartmentalizing his thought. Ulrich, however, has borne it home to him by insisting on the provisional, experimental nature of all values, a constraint which would seem to nullify all prospects for the happy integration of business and soul. Arnheim demands that Ulrich explain this position in a nonfrivolous manner, because the demands of the business world are incompatible with indeterminacy.

This conversation takes place at Diotima's house but in her absence, as crowds denouncing the Parallel Campaign demonstrate outside. Predictably, the Campaign has degenerated into ethnic contention and bureaucratic infighting, and as Diotima's relationship with Arnheim slowly unravels, her faith too in the Austrian Idea has begun to waver. This failure to infuse "soul" into the unstable composite of Kakania obviously parallels the fatuity of Arnheim's grander schemes, but, gazing at the crowd with "Caesar-like calm," he does not appear to notice it. In any case, he has compartmentalized his investment in the Parallel Campaign as well, using the contacts it offers to gain access to oil fields in Galicia and (possibly) to stir up pacifist sentiment on behalf of the Tsar. When Ulrich, rejecting Arnheim's gambit, taxes him with leading Diotima on, the latter rebukes him for his naivete. What Arnheim does, however, is far more impulsive than anything he has permitted himself with Diotima: he offers Ulrich a job as his executive secretary, promising to remedy the defects of his worldly education and, incidentally, enabling him to become very rich.

Arnheim's motives in this are mixed: the desire to captivate and neutralize Ulrich; to keep a pet conscience by his side; to challenge himself with a recalcitrant son. No sooner has he spoken than he regrets the offer, realizing how vastly he has overestimated Ulrich's importance (or the threat he represents). At the same time, however, he cannot resist the urge to dominate, and he lays an arm across Ulrich's shoulder in a manner that precisely balances cajolery and intimidation:

> That arm on his shoulder made Ulrich unsure of himself. To stand there in this quasi-embrace was ridiculous and unpleasant, a miserable feeling, in fact. Still, it was a long time since Ulrich had known a friend, and perhaps this added an element of bewilderment. He would have liked to shake off the arm, and he instinctively tried to do so, even while Arnheim, for his part, noticed these little signals of Ulrich's restiveness and did his utmost to ignore them.
>
> Ulrich, realizing the awkwardness of Arnheim's position, was too polite to move away and forced himself to put up with this physical contact, which felt increasingly like a heavy weight sinking into a loosely mounded dam and breaking it apart. Without meaning to, Ulrich had built up a wall of loneliness around himself, and now life, by way of another man's pulse beat, came pouring in through the breach in that wall, and silly as it was, ridiculous, really, he felt a touch of excitement. [700]

Thus divided, Ulrich reacts in two radically opposed (but not disconnected) ways: part of him wants to accept Arnheim's Faustian offer, and to respond to the sexual invitation it casually proffers; and part of him wants to seize a weapon and kill this monstrous predator on the spot. In the event, Ulrich merely says he will think things over—the only commitment he seems seriously capable of making to anyone.

Another powerful triadic relationship involves Ulrich, his childhood friend Walter, and Walter's young wife Clarisse. Walter is a genius *manqué*, the kind of polymorphous child prodigy who never settles on a specific talent; he is employed as an arts factotum and burns off energy with Clarisse by playing reckless duets of Wagner. In a way Walter is Ulrich's opposite, tormented by flights of ambition he cannot realize in any project, and bitterly resentful of his friend's irony toward all that is high and holy. Clarisse, whose "Himalayan" romance with Walter was founded on their joint belief in his greatness, punishes him relentlessly for the mediocrity he has become. When he vents his jealousy of Ulrich, she dares him to kill him; in a later scene, however, she decides to have Ulrich's child and makes a disastrous attempt to seduce him.

Clarisse is in fact unbalanced, and in his unhurried fashion Musil traces her descent from eccentricity to madness over more than a thousand pages. The most visible manifestation of this is her obsession with Moosbrugger, a notorious sex murderer in whom she sees a combination of martyr and seer. Serial killers are a staple of contemporary fiction, but just as Arnheim represented one of the first portraits of a modern capitalist, so Christian Moosbrugger is the first madman of modern literature. Moosbrugger is attached to no one, and so he is the free-floating nightmare of all; he is the most famous man in Austria other than the Emperor, and as suitably remote.

Moosbrugger is far more than a symbol of the irrational or a harbinger of the war to come, however. In portraying him, Musil represents *in extremis* a condition found in passional relationships, mystical vision, and "experimental" living: the contesting of boundaries between the inner and outer realms of experience. It is only by such means, Ulrich argues, that a fruitful tension can be maintained between self and world; the alternative is the hectoring confusion of modern life, in which "There's no longer a whole man confronting a whole world, only a human something moving about in a general culture-medium" (234). The price of failing to contest boundaries is, paradoxically, the loss of all proper demarcation, and with it of personal identity. Moosbrugger's case is extreme because, for him, what occurs is neither the volitional projection of self into world (the Nietzschean paradigm, which Musil sometimes calls "essayism") nor the willing engulfment of self by world ("one day," Ulrich suggests, "the horizon will begin to flow and come roaring at us"); rather, the distinction between inner and outer is involuntarily flipped, so that Moosbrugger finds the world literally and horribly inside himself in the person of the women who cross his path: he kills to eject it. This persuades him into the unshakeable conviction of his own normality, for in his own mind he is simply seeking the most elemental of all human rights, the right to be let alone. Apparently the voices he heard in his head were a unique gift, but

> That wasn't the important thing. Often he could not have described exactly what he saw, heard, and felt, but he knew what it was. It could be very blurred; the visions came from outside, but a shimmer of observation told him at the same time that they were really something inside himself. The important thing was that it is not at all important whether something is inside or outside; in his condition, it was like clear water on both sides of a transparent sheet of glass. [258]

Language, too, is Moosbrugger's enemy, because it taught one to signify the world, and then allowed it to slide back into chaos again: "Moosbrugger's experience and conviction were that no thing could be singled out by itself, because things hang together. It had happened that he said to a girl, 'Your sweet rose lips,' but suddenly the words gave way at their seams and something upsetting happened: her face went gray, like earth veiled in a mist, there was a rose sticking out of it on a long stem, and the temptation to take a knife and cut it off, or punch it back into the face, was overwhelming" (259). Words just occurred, singly at first like faces, but then in combinations that possessed the magical power to transform reality; and that reality had to be dealt with. It was better when words melted down into nonsense syllables, as they did in prison, where inside and outside coincided, and Moosbrugger was free because the order imposed on him clearly emanated from himself:

> The words he did have were: hm-hm, uh-uh.
> The table was Moosbrugger.
> The chair was Moosbrugger.
> The barred window and the bolted door were himself.
> [428]

What Moosbrugger achieves artlessly, Ulrich seeks through an act of will, a will that induces illness and self-loathing, that threatens itself with suicide, and approaches (without being able to enter) madness. On the verge of breakdown, Ulrich walks into his garden on a winter evening in his pajamas and has a vision of the abyss: "the darkness suddenly, fantastically, reminded him of Moosbrugger, and the naked trees looked strangely corporeal, ugly and wet like worms and yet somehow inviting him to embrace them and sink down with them in tears" (277). Even as he is tempted, however, Ulrich is revolted at the "sentimentality" of his impulse, and returns indoors; the kingdom of psychosis is not to be entered with the false papers of *Weltschmerz*.

What hope remains, then, for the hopelessly sane? The Ulrich of Volume I is striving for an ethic of moral economy, as befits a neurotic mathematician. There are too many superfluous acts in the world, Ulrich thinks, which is why he has decided to forgo his own quota, and above all too many words: "Human activities," he reflects, "might be graded by the quantity of words required: the more words, the worse their character" (264). Ulrich firmly eschews writing (other than scientific papers, presumably), although there is a casual reference to a book of his on poetics later on, as well as the diary we encounter in Volume II. This ideal taciturnity is contrasted with the loquaciousness of Arnheim, whose treatises include words on:

> algebraic series, benzol rings, the materialist as well as the
> universalist philosophy of history, bridge supports, the evolution
> of music, the essence of the automobile, Hata 606, the theory of
> relativity, Bohr's atomic theory, autogeneous welding, the flora of
> the Himalayas, psychoanalysis ... [230]

Arnheim's writings, whatever their subject, are invariably "soothing," that is to say vulgarizing. From complexity they yield simplicity, just as the affairs of the capitalist, however ramified, always tend toward the single result of profit. For Ulrich, any "result," except as a springboard for further complication, is calcifying. For this reason, "a character, a profession, a fixed mode of being," in short everything conjured up by the word bourgeois, is anathema to him. Ulrich is certainly no socialist—as a parasitic intellectual (the unkindest but also the most lapidary description of his socioeconomic status) he is a thoroughly characteristic product of the bourgeois order—but his notion of essayism is interestingly close to Marx's concept of the liberated worker who is free to "hunt in the morning, fish in the afternoon, rear cattle in the evening, (and) criticize after dinner ... without ever becoming hunter, fisherman, cowherd, or critic.[3] Taken to its logical extreme, Ulrich's program would make capitalism impossible. That this is the least of his concerns does not make him a less threatening and subversive figure; hence Arnheim's profound if misconceived desire to co-opt him.

Throughout Volume I, Ulrich's project remains negatively defined; it is what he refuses to do or to be. When after months of idleness he solves the mathematical problem on which he had been working he takes no satisfaction in it, for he reflects that someone else would have solved the problem sooner or later if he had not, and that he had thus merely served an "impersonal" destiny (784). From this perspective, Ulrich's refusal of all proferred roles, occupations, and "qualities" is a search for the indelibly and uniquely individual, in short, for personal assertion. This is an illusory quest, however, because the belief in individual distinctiveness is merely the category error of subjectivity. The individual in the modern world is at most a statistical aberration, reconciled in the mass, and "it is not oneself that matters but only this mass of faces, these movements wrenched loose from the body to become armies of arms, legs, or teeth," the social monster to which "the future belongs" (785). This monster has a language of its own, that of the statistical norm, in terms of which all particular deviations are necessarily expressed. As a scientist with a well-honed contempt for the woolly Nietzscheanism of his age, Ulrich above all understands that individuals no longer exist because the language through which they could be represented is now otiose. Musil remarks at one point that the Austro-Hungarian empire was to perish finally of "inexpressibility"; clearly, this is the fate of the individual in the modern world as well. He must die because he can no longer be described.

The consequence of this for Ulrich is paralyzing depression, "a state of mind without goal or ambition." Ulrich refuses to act unless his act is necessary (as opposed to merely useful). In the collective, all acts are useful that promote the social result; none are indispensable. The very terms "necessary" and "superfluous" belong to an obsolete language, an extinct mode of being. Ulrich, of course, continues to *function*: as a lover, as a solver of mathematical problems, as General Secretary to the Parallel Campaign, as a potential suicide. But none of this behavior is volitional. Ulrich is seduced by the women he lacks sufficient energy to repel and drifts into an enterprise he regards as absurd. His last resort is an irony that only closes the circle of his isolation.

Volume I ends in this cul-de-sac, but also with a telegram that announces his father's death. This event sets in motion the principal action of Volume II. Ulrich is obliged to arrange his father's funeral and settle his estate. He is also reintroduced to his younger sister Agathe, whom he has hardly seen in almost twenty years and of whose existence the reader has heard nothing up to now—to be precise, until Page 731. Even in a narrative as leisurely as Musil's, this is a long time to await the arrival of the second most important personage of the novel, if "second" she is.

When Ulrich and Agathe meet in their father's parlor they are dressed in almost identical lounging outfits, and Agathe's first words are, "I had no idea we were twins!" Ulrich notices they are of equal height and similar coloring; even their body scent (almost the defining physical element in a Musil character) is similar. Agathe's features alone are unfamiliar, but in a way that suggests a kinship far deeper than physical resemblance: they are "expressive" without conveying any particular expression, or indeed suggesting any "traits of character" at all. Agathe is thus Ulrich's feminine complement, a woman without qualities, though she lacks the exacerbated sense of self that has led him to go on strike against the world. Nonetheless, she is at her own point of crisis, and her father's death leads her to take two very determined steps: she decides to divorce her husband, the academician Hagauer, whom she has come to detest; and to cheat Hagauer of his legal share in the family estate by altering her father's will.

These acts and their consequences are still in progress at the end of Volume II; they remain unresolved in the chapters that Musil drafted in the last years of his life. We know only that Hagauer, after putting the most face-saving construction on his wife's behavior, resorts to the law to enforce his marital and financial rights. Agathe's actions, inexplicable on a rational level, display the impulsiveness of those timid spirits whose first plunge into will is self-immolating. They also represent a challenge to Ulrich to follow her into the thickets of uncharted experience where, possibly, his own salvation lies.

Agathe is strongly associated with fire; she burns her childhood dolls although she had loved them "more fiercely than I have ever loved a man" (978), and suggests that one must be willing to sacrifice everything and leap "naked into the fire" to be worthy of one's life (937). She has already been refined by the experience of a near-fatal childhood illness that has left her, even in adulthood, with the feeling of living always close to death, and she keeps a capsule of poison by her as a charm. This "did not at all mean," Musil tells us, "that Agathe at this time already intended to kill herself" (929)—another foreshadowing of plot that is never developed—but signifies rather a romantic attachment to life that is energized by the contemplation of death. Moreover, although Agathe's life up to this point has been characterized by an acute dissociation from experience—even the lovers she has taken to spite Hagauer (or herself) have left no mark on her—her passivity is that of someone who awaits her destiny and not, like Ulrich's, that of someone who has lost the motive for action. Thus, her impulse to suicide is easily turned into aggression against others: she tells Ulrich that she would like to kill Hagauer (806), and her scheme to defraud him is a kind of civil murder. The secret compact with death that brother and sister share, however different for each of them, is one of the things that draws them ineluctably together.

For Agathe, Ulrich appears in the shape of her density, although a destiny she greets with a certain skepticism and sibling reserve. For him, she is his unsuspected complement, the mirror image that not only completes him narcissistically but makes permeable the boundary between the inner and the outer world that too easily dissolves for Moosbrugger but has become Ulrich's prison. Ulrich discovers with an astonishment clearly disproportionate to the novelty of the observation that "the human being comes in twos," and that the sexes are united at a level far deeper and more aboriginal than their gender differentiation. In this musing condition he remembers the long-buried memory of his childhood yearning for a female playmate, or more precisely an ego-ideal. Now, looking intently at his sister, he senses in her a hint of sexual ambivalence, as if she too lacked completeness in herself. Later she appears to him as a doppelganger, "a dreamlike variant and repetition of himself," and although that uncanny intuition vanishes, it leaves behind its trace: Ulrich has discovered in the world his feminized simulacrum, the proof and validation of his own existence (754).

At the same time, the flesh and blood Agathe is right beside Ulrich, not merely a projection but a partner. Almost without thinking about it, and freed by Agathe's decision to divorce Hagauer, they decide to live together. The question they will attempt to resolve, each according to his own nature, is *how* to live; that is, in Ulrich's terms, how to reconcile an ineradicable sense of subjectivity with a world defined in terms of its exclusion.

To live subjectively in the world is to live ethically, that is in a free state of obligation to oneself and others, but in a purely instrumental world the relation of freedom (and therefore the relation to oneself) is suppressed, leaving only rules to be obeyed. This cuts one off in turn from the natural world, because without a free relation to oneself one cannot be oriented in nature, morality in this sense being, as Musil remarks, "nothing more than an ordering that embraces both the soul [*Geist*] and things" (811). The result, familiar enough to us today, is that the world is reduced to the pictures we make of it and the uses we put it to, while our relations with others are reduced to duty. The alternative to this (since life will seek an outlet) is the search for pleasure or the lapse into violence; as General Stumm puts it in his soldierly way, "Somehow or other, order, once it reaches a certain stage, calls for bloodshed" (505).

For the individual, escape from the instrumental world can come only through transgression or beatitude, the forcing or the fusion of the inner and outer realms. Transgression—the liberating criminal act—has of course a long literary history that goes back to Sade. For Agathe, the essence of transgression is its impulsiveness rather than its specific character or consequence; something new is created, something unanticipated, and when it is over there is, as Ulrich puts it, "something more besides me" (806). Agathe's complaint about Ulrich—"You always take everything back!"—suggests his incapacity for such action (*vide* his aborted impulse to kill Arnheim), but he too is lured by the "balsamic scent of freedom" into abetting her scheme against Hagauer.

If to act ethically is to act freely (and vice versa), the paradox of morality, as Musil defines it, is that it decays as it is codified. Thus a good act conscientiously performed turns into its opposite, and the "good person" is the enemy of the good. The problem goes deeper, however, and relates to the fundamental distinction between inner and outer, self and world; as Ulrich notes, "One might almost say that our evil desires are the dark side of the life we lead in reality, and the life we lead in reality is the dark side of our good desires" (807).

This general condition transcends the individual will; it is the sickness of a civilization that is approaching its term. In such a condition, the "complications" of morality become overwhelming, the personal act (such as Agathe's) engenders its opposite no less fatefully than the impersonal, conventional one, and any attempt to resolve the paradox of morality only enmeshes one more deeply in it. Ulrich concludes that all efforts to effect a Nietzschean transvaluation of values must fail, because "no civilization has so far been capable of replacing its lost inner elasticity" nor of countering "the weakening of the significance of all actions" that accompanies it (896).

If transgression thus cannot renew either the individual or his society, beatitude—the unmediated relation to the nonhuman world—remains. Ulrich wonders if such a state, the state of grace attested by mystics, might not still be attained even by an unbeliever, and whether it would not be possible to rest in it as in a "boundless opulence of light." Such a condition would hold the distinction between inner and outer in ecstatic suspension while intensifying the experience of each:

> I would say [Ulrich speaks] that it's like looking out over a wide shimmering sheet of water—so bright it seems like darkness to the eye, and on the far bank things don't seem to be standing on solid ground but float in the air with a delicately exaggerated distinctness that's almost painful and hallucinatory. The impression one gets is as much of intensification as of loss. One feels linked with everything but can't get close to anything. You stand here, and the world stands there, overly subjective and overly objective, but both almost painfully clear, and what separates and unites these normally fused elements is a blazing darkness, an overflowing and extinction, a swinging in and out. You swim like a fish in water or a bird in air, but there's no riverbank and no branch, only this floating! [816]

It is questionable whether such a state could be sustained without the anchor of God, the pull of a supersensual attraction toward the world. Yet even under the most favoring circumstances, Ulrich opines, "faith could not live more than an hour" (826), and the vulgarized nature mysticism of modern culture, "that unmistakable vacuousness of the elevated gaze one experiences on a mountaintop .... [that] sublimity [of] solitude, pretty little flowers, and murmuring little brooks," all but doomed the effort.

Musil does not drop this subject; there are notes for a theory of the emotions in the withdrawn chapters of Volume III that pursue the relation of inner and outer reality further (1240ff.). At the same time, however, the *Gestalt* that Ulrich appears to be aiming at cannot be reached by any mere heightening or intensifying of the emotions, the limit case of such a condition being neither the saint nor the transgressor but Moosbrugger, whose berserker fits are merely "a rampant metaphor of order" (712).

This leaves one other possibility: the encounter of Self and Other. Agathe and Ulrich fall quickly into that heightened state of receptivity toward one another characteristic of lovers. They are immediately taken for such by a farm couple who give them hospitality on a country outing, and Musil describes their relationship as "hovering" between that of sister and wife. At the same time the very indeterminacy of that relationship permits them to live experimentally with each other, in Ulrich's term. The rules of consanguinity are suspended rather than abrogated; nothing is forbidden, but what is most available is precisely what is not chosen. Trying to describe what this condition might be, Ulrich calls it "the Millennium,"[4] defining it as "the desire to live, with the aid of mutual love, in a secular condition so transcendent that one could only feel and do whatever heightened that condition" (949). This does not mean living for another, which was merely "egoism going bankrupt," but rather taking the Other as a compass, and being so taken in turn. The seal of such a relationship was a morally spontaneous act, which, because by definition it defied convention (whether or not it actually violated some legal code) was necessarily a "crime", hence the overall name which Musil gave to Volume II, "Into the Millennium (The Criminals)."

Superficially, the relationship between Ulrich and Agathe that is the heart of Volume II bears no little resemblance to that between Diotima and Arnheim in Volume I. Both entail long and fervent talks, and neither is consummated physically. Whereas Diotima and Arnheim are separated by a divergence of worldly interest and a failure of erotic nerve, however, Ulrich and Agathe approach each other without preconditions, and sex is not so much renounced as deferred, as perhaps the one "crime" that would be too obvious to commit. If Volume I is in this sense the story of an inauthentic relationship, Volume II suggests what the—admittedly utopian—basis for an authentic one might be, or more precisely might have been, in the complex twilight of a society on the verge of extinction.

Extinction: the unreachable terminus of Musil's novel was the war that brought about the dissolution of the Austro-Hungarian empire and thus the fictive world in which his imagination was embedded. *The Man without Qualities* is the great novel of the subjunctive, an act of retrospection that is also, like the adventure of Ulrich and Agathe, a journey in suspension toward a shore not to be reached.[5] The Great War is alluded to only a handful of times in the text, less as a means of acknowledgment than as a kind of alienation effect, but its shadow, for reader and author alike, is omnipresent. As Musil remarked in a worknote, "The immanent depiction of the period that led to the catastrophe [i.e., the war] must be the real substance of the story, the context to which it can always retreat as well as the thought that is

implicit in everything" (1748). This was the intended connection between
Ulrich and Agathe, whose story was in the last analysis, as Musil noted, "an
attempt at anarchy in love," and the Parallel Campaign, whose machinations,
culminating in a projected Congress for World Peace, were to have helped
precipitate the war. Certain characters too, such as the anti-Semite Hans
Sepp and the irrationalist philosopher Meingast, were clearly intended to
adumbrate the rise of fascism. Far then from being an exercise in nostalgia
or historical pathology, Musil's vast fresco was an attempt to understand the
convulsed landscape of the postwar world and the second great war to which
it would lead in his own lifetime. By looking resolutely over his shoulder, he
showed as few artists of his century have the path ahead. The extraordinary
freshness of his vision suggests that the issues he grappled with—the
obsolescence of the individual, the desiccation of moral vision, and the
rationalized anarchy of the global order—are, under the guise of
postmodernism, no less urgent for us.[6]

NOTES

1. All textual references (indicated by bracketed numbers in the text) are to the
English translation by Sophie Wilkins and Burton Pike (New York: Knopf). This edition
is in two volumes, with the first volume breaking at p. 725; pagination however is
continuous, so that no volume number will be indicated. The translation is based on the
1978 German edition edited by Adolf Frisé which supersedes the 1951 edition on which
the previous translation by Ernst Kaiser and Eithne Wilkins was based. The Frisé edition
does not however contain all the extant manuscript material relating to the novel, which
has been available on CD-ROM since 1990. Readers interested in the extensive critical
literature on Musil are referred to Christian Rogowski's *Distinguished Outsider: Robert Musil
and His Critics* (Columbia, S.C.: Camden House, 1994).

2. "On Stupidity," in Robert Musil, *Precision and Soul: Essays and Addresses*, edited and
translated by Burton Pike and David S. Luft (Chicago: University of Chicago Press, 1990):
268–286.

3. *The German Ideology*, in *Karl Marx. Selected Writings*, ed. David McLellan (Oxford:
Oxford University Press, 1977), 169.

4. In other drafts and sketches called "the Other Condition."

5. Musil's sketch for the end of the novel—far from reached, even in draft form—
was for the Parallel Campaign to end in the outbreak of the war and for Ulrich to enlist
despite Agathe's entreaty that they go on living "as if nothing were happening" (1756,
1758). At the same time, Ulrich experiences regret for "the fascinating moment that
never quite happened between himself and Agathe," presumably the sexual one. Musil
also considered an Afterword by Ulrich from the vantage point of the Second World War.
But these ideas can only be regarded as tentative in the highest degree; given the open
form of the novel, the continual evolution of Musil's ideas and conceptions, fed by a
constant stream of reading and reflection, the stubborn perfectionism of his style, and
above all the gulf of the Great War itself, the idea of final closure could only have been a
spur to further revision.

6. By printing not only the text of the novel published in Musil's lifetime but the chapters he withdrew in press and the mass of other rejected drafts and sketches, the Frisé edition (and now the Wilkins-Pike translation) has created a postmodern text in which the "authorized" version exists side by side with variants in which, for example, Ulrich and Agathe consummate an incestuous relationship and Ulrich makes love both to Diotima and Clarisse. In a sense, Musil's open and contingent form invites us to incorporate these alternate narratives in our reading, and many will doubtless be inclined to conflate the authorized text and the *Nachlass*. It seems nonetheless essential to distinguish between the creative process and the created work, i.e., the text licensed for publication by Musil. *The Man without Qualities* is not Cortazar's *Hopscotch*.

ALEXANDER HONOLD

Endings and Beginnings:
Musil's Invention of Austrian History

In the beginning there is the ticking of a mechanical clock. What does it sound like? What does it say? The clock says "tick-tock," sure, but what is the problem with that? The problem is that there is no reason at all, considering the physical experience, to distinguish between two different sounds produced by the pinion of the watch. Nevertheless we do not perceive its sound as a monotonous "tock-tock-tock," which would correspond to the real acoustical phenomenon. Instead of hearing what is to be heard, we insist on having the impression of a tick-tock, tick-tock, a repetition of two alternate sounds. This phenomenon, if my reading of Frank Kermode's book on narrative endings is right, must be considered as a decisive element for the rise of what we are still used to calling "literature." "Of course," he says, "it is we who provide the fictional difference between the two sounds; *tick* is our word for a physical beginning, *tock* our word for an end.... The fact that we call the second of the two related sounds *tock* is evidence that we use fictions to enable the end to confer organization and form on the temporal structure."[1]

Rethinking Kermode's argument now, this example offers many observations that can help us to understand how narration works, and that is, how beginnings and endings are used and what they are needed for. Auditory sensations like the ticking of a clock appear almost meaningless on their own,

From *Austria in Literature*, edited by Donald G. Daviau. © 2000 by Ariadne Press.

without any semantic structure. So we humanize them with fictions; and this happens not only with such simple perceptions, but even to the most complicated events. What we do is organize them, restructure them temporally. Just as we possess a spatial coordinate system that tells us what is right or left, above and below, we need a temporal scanner system that tells us what is going on subsequently. I am still with Kermode with my first thesis: To understand things that happen, we have to put a certain beginning and an ending to them.

Thus, beginnings and endings are not "the real thing," they are ours, they emerge when we face and interpret the world outside. This idea of temporal scanning probably somehow reminds you of Immanuel Kant, especially of his intention to find what he called "the transcendental conditions of perception," that is, preexisting structures that determine our daily experience. What I termed scanning, Kant called "Schematismus" (a pattern). It is not from experience, Kant argued, that we are given the notions of space and time. As these organize everything that man is able to perceive, they must precede our experience. The only thing that experience can do is to apply and confirm the patterns it was generated by. So far, all that does not sound exceedingly dramatic, and we learned to live as Kantian beings long ago; so let us simply take Kant's conceptualizations of time and space for granted, and the narrative patterns of beginning and ending along with them.

But things look different if we take a critical case, that of the principle of causality. From eighteenth-century Empiricism to the early twentieth century, causality was regarded as a linkage of two events as cause and effect: A causes B. This assertion can at least include two different propositions. The first one is the assertion of what we could call "weak" causality, and it says: B would not have happened if A had not happened before. For example: "The king died and then the queen married again." Weak causality just argues that things occur one after the other and that you cannot change the order of a given time sequence. Now, the alternative concept, as you might have guessed, is that of "strong" causality, in which B follows A necessarily. If we have any given A, we are able to predict its B. This concept of strong causality was valid first and foremost in empirical science, at least until Einstein and Heisenberg came along. The course of a billiard ball, for example, is strictly determined by the way it was struck. The impulse at the beginning already provides all the necessary information to predict the final results. In this case, the relation between cause and effect can be proved, and, what is even more, the whole arrangement can be repeated and controlled anywhere at any time. Operating with this notion of strong causality, we presume a closed artificial system, with totally known initial conditions, and its final results perfectly conforming with the expectations. Of course, things do not work this way, and whoever has played billiards, knows that not even that game does. What scientists try to omit, and in fact have to omit, is the influence of any disturbing element of uncertainty and singularity. In this sense, causality tries to eliminate blind chance, while history and our methods of producing historical knowledge are based on matters of contingency. History positively depends on the intervention of new, disturbing elements that can change the whole story; and so does narrative.

Nevertheless our approach to history has also to do with the desire for explanations and reasons, for causes and effects. To explain events of the past, means to search for initial conditions and final results. When we are trying to understand what is going on we have to find out: When did it start? And, to what end? So we are asking for a narrative that explains to us how our billiard ball of history finds its way through. Thus, my second observation is: Science and history offer singular models of actions and happenings that lead from a beginning to an end, and both of these models have been "disenchanted" as fictions or sheer arrangements—and, by the way, this is where "Postmodernism" gets into it. Causality, in the strict sense of necessity, came to its limits with Heisenberg's principle of indeterminacy, whereas our understanding of history was questioned by the discovery of its basic narrative or rhetorical ingredients. Although these fictions and narratives are still more or less useful, they cannot claim objectivity or absolute validity anymore.

It is important to keep in mind the trivial fact that whatever we can experience hardly fits into those patterns, be it a scientific one or a narrative one, because "reality" is an open signifier for something without beginning or end. We are just part of a chain of circumstances that is causeless and unpredictable. I dare say: as human beings we are not able to experience origins or last things at all, and that is exactly why we are so desperately trying to fix them or manipulate them. Transforming reality into a text is like following a modest thread entangled in an always-already existing web. But we are tempted anyway to identify the text's limits with those of history itself, as the Bible does: whatever happens in history, be it human or divine, happens between the beginning and end of the book of books, that is, within the limits of time defined by Genesis and Revelation. The A and O, Alpha and Omega, were regarded for a long time as symbolic demarcations, because all that can be written and read is confined by the limits of the alphabet.

I would like to sum up what we have seen so far. The patterns of beginning and ending provide a narrative framework that transforms the eternal flux of disparate events into something that deserves being called a plot. Thus, plotting works as a chaining together of events that can achieve different degrees of intensity, ranging from mere chronological order to the assertion of strong causality.

With these questions in mind, it is time to begin, or to begin again, or perhaps I should better say: to put an end to these tiring and exaggerated preliminary remarks, passing over to the realm of literature. Let us enter Musil's invention of Austrian history—in fact, we already stepped into it some time ago. It is precisely Musil's occupation with causality and contingency that I have tried to sketch so far; and when we talk about Musil's philosophy, we do not deal with a particular theoretical or ideological approach, but with problems located in the triangle of science, history, and literature.

The beginning and ending of a novel can be determined on at least two different levels: first, they are defined by the interval that covers writing time, and in this case, a great deal of a lifetime as well; second, there is another interval that covers the area of written text, framed by its first and last words. To examine the endings of *Der Mann ohne Eigenschaften* (*The Man without Qualities*) seems easy and difficult at the same time, for the simple and sad reason that when Musil's writing was interrupted by death, there was no final chapter authorized by the writer's hand. For a long time, scholarship and publishing efforts were mainly dedicated to the purpose of posthumously bringing this immense fragment to an end. Musil critics spent thousands of pages discussing whether the love story of Ulrich and Agathe would have come to an unhappy ending or not, and whether a showdown of violence and anarchism would have been privileged on the very last pages or, on the contrary, a sign of utopian hope. But even the posthumous papers published in the second volume of Frisé's edition could not put an end to such speculation. The only thing that can supply some indications for that nonexistent ending, is to study those parts of the narrative framework Musil himself had finished and published in his lifetime. All that we know about the novel's mysterious ending, we know by its beginning and we know it from the beginning.

When did Musil start writing *The Man without Qualities?* A few short fragments date from the very beginning of the century, outlining some of the characters we meet again in the final version, such as Moosbrugger, Clarisse and Walter, and the protagonist himself. Nevertheless, Musil's project took shape only when he was confronted with the experience of the First World War and the collapse of the Austro-Hungarian Empire.

I think we cannot understand the novel's basic structure unless we take into account its deep addiction to the world of ancient Austria, or "Kakanien," to fin-de-siècle Vienna and its culture of decadence. Two of the protagonists, Ulrich and his friend Walter, are introduced as having joined the fin-de-siècle generation and its glorification of youth. On the other hand, that youth of the century's first decade was surrounded by an atmosphere of historicism and eclecticism. In spite of intellectuals like Freud, Ernst Mach, Otto Wagner or Ludwig Boltzmann, Vienna was not exactly a place of modernity, but a fortress of traditionalism, the old-fashioned capital of an Empire that showed undeniable symptoms of decline. The outbreak of World War I in August 1914 only accelerated this decline, which culminated in the emperor's death in 1916 and at last in the military defeat in 1918. Finally, Vienna ceased to be the "Imperial Capital and Royal City," as it is called in the first chapter of *The Man without Qualities*.[2]

Therefore August 1914 is a crucial point for the creation of Musil's novel as well as in history itself. For Musil, the beginning of war is regarded first and foremost as an ending, as a symbol of social and cultural change. To understand what exactly enabled most people to affirm the declaration of war enthusiastically, historians as well as novelists have tried to analyze its preceding circumstances. When interviewed by Oskar Maurus Fontana in 1926 about his work in progress, Musil emphasized that the central issue he wanted to focus on in his novel was the outbreak of war, because that event provided a key to his understanding of the prewar period. As he declared in that interview, his purpose was a genealogical one, he intended to demonstrate the different and even contradictory tendencies that finally resulted in war.

And again we get stuck in the predicament of causality. "Die Frage nach der Ursache," that is, to be in search of a first cause that could be made responsible for the whole process; as Musil puts it, this is an absolutely useless undertaking. It is simply everybody and everything, he says, that has to be taken into account, so that you cannot isolate one single man or one single nation as being decisive. And that is why his novel of prewar Viennese society disperses, splitting into dozens of places and sequences, often interrupted by reflections and digressions which demonstrate the author's analytical—and satirical!—capacity.

There is a chapter (Chapter 83), one of the famous ones, which is entitled: "Seinesgleichen geschieht oder warum erfindet man nicht Geschichte?" In the recent translation by Sophie Wilkins and Burton Pike, it says the following: "Pseudoreality prevails, or: Why don't we make history up as we go along?"[3] (And I have to admit that it sounds even more precise than the original.) It seems to be one of Musil's special tics to show us his hero most extensively whenever he is on his way home. In this chapter we meet Ulrich after a visit to Clarisse's house, returning slowly to the inner sections of town. The chapter starts when he leaves the tram for a little walk, rethinking the argument he had with Clarisse. It has been her yearning for carrying out something really spectacular (actually she starts planning Moosbrugger's rescue), her being crazy, about great historic events which brings Ulrich to an attitude of radical scepticism as regards history. And his scepticism is focused especially on the question of causality. Is it not an absurd fiction, Ulrich states, to think of history as a billiard ball that follows its predestined, linear course? As if we only had to know all the initial conditions well enough in order to be able to calculate the whole process and its results; or, given the final results, to figure out all the factors and circumstances they were caused by? I am going to quote just one of these passages or digressions:

> The course of history was therefore not that of a billiard ball which, once it is hit, takes a definite line—but resembles the movement of clouds, or the path of a man sauntering through the streets, turned aside by a shadow here, a crowd there, an unusual architectural outcrop, until at last he arrives at a place he never knew or meant to go to. Inherent in the course of history is a certain going off course.[4]

A nice aphoristic observation indeed. But what is the reason for Ulrich's occupation with this sophisticated and misleading subject? First, his reflection is not as misleading as it seems to be: Ulrich's *bonmot* that history should be invented or simulated is exactly the credo of the Austrian "Parallelaktion" which fills the novel's first volume; and it also describes the relation Musil's novel establishes to its own "raw materials." On a second level, Ulrich's reflection is not misleading because it is misleading, namely misleading Ulrich; when he stops thinking about history at the end of the chapter, he realizes that he has lost his way, too. Thereby he confirms exactly what he has said about the similarity of progression and digression, or, of making history up as he goes along, as *he* is going off course.

Finally we should recognize that Ulrich's reflection and even the metaphors he uses do not pertain exclusively to this fictional character, they are part of the author's thinking, and for Musil the problem of causality is not an academic one. As we saw, this question only arose in the postwar situation, so that the whole passage can be read as an anachronistic insert from after the war. There are two metaphors Ulrich suggests for replacing the mechanical pattern of the billiard-ball: the way of history is like the way of a flaneur walking through the streets—which happened to be Ulrich himself; or, and this is a strange comparison, like the movement of the clouds. Does the movement of the clouds have anything in common with the course of history? Let us suppose that weather-forecasting probably was not as reliable in the twenties as it is today; so what makes meteorological phenomena comparable to the contingency of historical events is that they are almost unpredictable. To respect contingency means to admit that history is not predictable, that it cannot be processed by sheer deduction. A beginning can thus give us initial conditions, but it cannot determine what follows, although everything that actually follows is determined. A beginning therefore could be described as a starting point, "from which, remarkably enough, nothing develops" ("woraus bemerkenswerter Weise nichts hervorgeht").[5] So, why not start this beginning with the unpredictable *per se*, the movement of the clouds? "A barometric low hung over the Atlantic. It moved eastward toward a high-pressure area over Russia without as yet showing any inclination to bypass this high in a northerly direction.[6]

It took a long time to arrive here at the very beginning, to reach the novel's famous first words and the initial conditions they provide. Is there really nothing that develops from this beginning? Nothing but more than 2,000 pages. But is there anything that supplies the answer to our question about the possible ending?

As every "tick" is followed by its "tock," Frank Kermode's book on narrative endings was echoed by Edward Said's study on beginnings. Said points out that one of literature's primordial merits is its capacity of deliberate beginnings, of constructing beginnings. We do not have to speculate about origins anymore, Said writes; there is no origin, but there are lots of beginnings and a variety of ways to begin. On the one hand, there are the solemn ones, beginnings which do not just fall in medias res but try to emphasize in advance the kernel of the whole story; those beginnings pretend to be not only beginnings but principles, so that what follows can be deduced from this logical basis. For example: "It is a truth universally acknowledged, that a single man in possession of a good fortune must be in want of a wife" (Jane Austen's *Pride and Prejudice*). As that novel is about prejudice, it performs prejudice, in spite of its ironic mode: a beginning that claims to predestine all the following action.

The other way to begin emerges when irony and the self-consciousness of the narrator not only accompany the run of narrative but disturb and almost destroy the plot that is being told. The paradigm for this category is *Tristram Shandy*. A beginning that is postponed "with a kind of encyclopedic, meaningful playfulness which ... delays one sort of action for the sake of undertaking another."[7] But even in cases like that, Said declares, "the beginning is always a first step from which ... *something follows*."[8] Unfortunately, *The Man without Qualities* is not discussed in Said's study, so that it is up to us now to give evidence to that judgment.

Musil's first chapter seems to be located right in the middle between the solemn beginnings and ironic playfulness; in fact, it is a battlefield occupied by both of them. While nearly the whole first paragraph neglects and frustrates our conventions of beginnings with astronomical and meteorological details, its last phrase is willing to reconcile us to tradition: "It was a fine day in August 1913." ("Es war ein schöner Augusttag des Jahres 1913.")[9] It is only from both aspects together that we receive some indirect information about the novel's subsequent course and its ending. The first chapter mainly designates what M. Bakhtin called a chronotopos, it indicates that the following action starts in Vienna, capital of Austria-Hungary, in August 1913. Reading this in 1930 or later, it was almost impossible not to be reminded of what happened one year later. Now the crucial point in Musil's beginning is that he manages to say two things that are absolutely contradictory at the same time. He says: Look at our pretty town dozing in its peaceful summertime, there is no reason at all to be suspicious or scared. Not even the clouds are showing any inclination to move eastward toward that Russian high-pressure area, so to speak. But only a few moments later an accident happens that disturbs this sunny opening. Just as the accident that ends this beginning results from an unpredictable urban traffic system, the end of the novel would have been marked by the collective accident of war.

We know that the final point of the story would have been reached exactly when Ulrich's sabbatical year was reaching its end. In his very last years of writing, Musil tried to postpone, I guess almost unconsciously, this troublesome ending by repeatedly rewriting chapters that took place in previous parts of the story; that is, to extend both his hero's "leave of absence from his life" ("Urlaub von seinem Leben")[10] and Musil's own symbiosis with the world he had created. When Lyotard started to propagate the end of the master narratives, *The Man without Qualities* was one of his chief witnesses. But Musil's main problem was not the ending of narrative but rather the narrative of an ending. Referring to Kermode's book once more, it reminds us that to narrate "the end" was a central theological problem. As the last things were supposed to be transcendental, how could they be inserted into such inferior matters like narrative? What takes place in modernity, then, is a secularization of this everlasting apocalyptic imminence. Kermode says literature converts imminence into immanence, into small endings, so to speak. It seems to me that we can find something quite similar in Musil's novel: Although he was obviously hindered from reaching the final point, the showdown in August 1914, the plot offers small endings, like the first chapter's accident, like the telegram informing Ulrich about his father's death, or, at the end of the last volume published in Musil's lifetime, a series of four chapters entitled: "A great event is in the making" ("Ein großes Ereignis ist im Entstehen").[11] That was the point when the "Parallelaktion" tried to put a deliberate ending to its own history, in vain, as we know, because they were confounding endings with results.

In a diary note from September 1939 in Geneva, Musil recognized: "In my career as a writer, I never succeeded in going beyond beginnings" ("Ich habe nie etwas über die Anfänge hinausgeführt.")[12] When World War II started, not a single soul would care about those remote times that preceded the first one. Musil still did, for his own biography and his way of writing were too deeply and too persistently challenged by the experience of war. What was all the traditional lore of how to tell stories good for, when it was confronted with a new, technological warfare that did not operate in terms of individual fighting but of statistical destruction? The imminence of death did not appear as a personal fate anymore, but as a question of simple calculations.

Do you remember that conversation in the first chapter immediately after the accident, when individual suffering is countered by anonymous statistics? "People dispersed almost as if justified in feeling that they had just witnessed something entirely lawful and orderly. 'According to American statistics,' the gentleman said, 'one hundred ninety thousand people are killed there every year by cars and four hundred fifty thousand are injured.'"[13] Not even American statistics can be as enormous as Musil's imagination was. Lots of critics have not been able to find any convincing explanation for these totally mistaken and exaggerated numbers. I have to admit, I did not even try to find some American statistics which could reach an amount like that. But I received some statistics from Manfried Rauchensteiner, the director of the Museum of Military History in Vienna. In the first year of war, the Austro-Hungarian troops had had very high losses: exactly 490,000 wounded and 190,000 killed, counting from a beautiful day in August 1914—a crucial point that does not appear at the ending of Musil's novel, but that lies buried under its beginning.

Nothing but beginnings? Musil's narrative achieves what Austria failed to do: preparing for an end that is still hard to tell.

NOTES

1. Frank Kermode, *The Sense of an Ending: Studies in the Theory of Fiction* (New York, 1967), 44.

2. *Die Reichshaupt und Residenzstadt Wien: recte Robert Musil, Der Mann ohne Eigenschaften*, Adolf Frisé, ed. (Reinbek: Rowohlt, 1978), 9; *The Man without Qualities*. Translated by Sophie Wilkins and Burton Pike (New York: Alfred Knopf, 1995), 3.

3. Musil, *The Man without Qualities*, 388; "Seinesgleichen geschieht oder warum erfindet man nicht Geschichte?": *Der Mann ohne Eigenschaften*, 357.

4. Musil, *The Man without Qualities*, 392. "Der Weg der Geschichte ist also nicht der eines Billiardballs, der, einmal abgestoßen, eine   bestimmte Bahn durchläuft, sondern er ähnelt dem Weg der Wolken, ähnelt dem Weg eines durch die Gassen Streichenden, der hier von einem Schatten, dort von einer Menschengruppe oder einer seltsamen Verschneidung von Häuserfronten abgelenkt wird und schließlich an eine Stelle gerät, die er weder gekannt hat, noch erreichen wollte. Es liegt im Verlauf der Weltgeschichte ein gewisses Sich-Verlaufen." *Der Mann ohne Eigenschaften*, 361.

5. Musil, *The Man without Qualities*, 3; *Der Mann ohne Eigenschaften*, 9.

6. Musil, *The Man without Qualities*, 3. "Über dem Atlantik befand sich ein barometrisches Minimum; es wanderte ostwärts, einem über Rußland lagernden Maximum zu, und verriet noch nicht die Neigung, diesem nördlich auszuweichen." *Der Mann ohne Eigenschaften*, 9.

7. Edward W. Said, *Beginnings. Intention and Method* (New York: Columbia University Press), 44.

8. Ibid., xvi.

9. Musil, *The Man without Qualities*, 3; *Der Mann ohne Eigenschaften*, 9.

10. Musil, *The Man without Qualities*, 44; *Der Mann ohne Eigenschaften*, 17.

11. Musil, *The Man without Qualities*, 1078; *Der Mann ohne Eigenschaften*, 994.

12. Musil, *Tagebücher*, Adolf Frisé, ed. (Reinbek: Rowohlt, 1983), volume I, 943.

13. Musil, *The Man without Qualities*, 5. "Man ging fast mit dem berechtigten Eindruck davon, daß sich ein gesetzliches und ordnungsgemäßes Ereignis vollzogen habe. 'Nach den amerikanischen Statistiken,' so bemerkte der Herr, 'werden dort jährlich durch Autos 190.000 Personen getötet und 450.000 verletzt.'" *Der Mann ohne Eigenschaften*, 11.

MICHAEL ANDRÉ BERNSTEIN

Robert Musil:
Precision and Soul

W hen Robert Musil died in exile in Geneva on April 15, 1942, he was virtually a forgotten figure, his reputation fading even among his fellow refugees from Nazism, and his masterpiece, *The Man without Qualities* (*Der Mann ohne Eigenschaften*),[1] on which he had labored for over twenty-five years, nowhere near completion. Only eight people attended his cremation, and except for a few scattered and laconic notices, the literary world ignored the event completely.

This lack of attention was not simply a natural consequence of the war's all-consuming hold on the imagination, in comparison with which the fate of one individual author could scarcely be expected to arouse much interest. Fifteen months earlier, for instance, James Joyce's death in Zurich was marked by an outpouring of articles in mass-circulation newspapers as well as in literary journals. Moreover, even after the defeat of the Third Reich had restored a German-speaking readership to other émigre authors like Thomas Mann and Bertolt Brecht, Musil remained largely unread and unpublished. Many of his most important texts were published only posthumously, and the first postwar edition of *The Man without Qualities* did not appear until 1952. It took another decade and a half before his works began to be widely translated and anything resembling a consensus about his importance as one of the preeminent European writers of the century emerged.

Today, though, there is little doubt that Musil belongs in the great

From *Five Portraits: Modernity and the Imagination in Twentieth-Century German Writing.* © 2000 by Northwestern University Press.

constellation of novelists like Joyce, Proust, and Kafka, writers who both redefined the formal possibilities of their medium and, in the process, reshaped the ways we use storytelling to make sense of our experience. *The Man without Qualities* is now regularly ransacked for its striking epigraphs and historical aperçus, and it is routinely invoked as one of the especially revelatory documents that nourish our ongoing fascination with the final days of the Austro-Hungarian Empire. But we are still only beginning to comprehend the scrupulous lucidity with which Musil transformed the well-made European novel into an open-ended thought experiment, a "testing ground" for problems whose pertinence is no less powerful today than when he was writing. The reaction of even a generally sympathetic critic like J. P. Stern is typical of the deep-seated ambivalence that Musil's formal, as well as thematic, originality continues to arouse: To the question whether what he has written is a great novel there is, I think, only one answer: it is great, but it is not a novel."[2] Clearly, then, if the recognition of Musil's mastery has taken so long to secure, this is not due merely to resistance against the intrinsic difficulty of his work. Instead, the whole nature of his achievement, the ways in which his work is both difficult and rewarding, constitutes so singular a case that even a thorough grounding—and delight—in the complexities of the other great modernist authors does little to prepare one for an encounter with a body of writing like his.

It is his unprecedented combination of eroticism and rationality, mysticism and scientific rigor that distinguishes Musil from even the most brilliant of his contemporaries. Like many thinkers in the first third of the twentieth century, Musil was tormented by the sense that modern consciousness was becoming increasingly splintered and fragmentary, lacking the kind of central, synthesizing principles that could command the simultaneous allegiance of mind and heart. In the lapidary formulation of one of his *Diary* entries, "The facts of contemporary life have outgrown the concepts of the old."[3] But in an epoch when thinking itself was becoming ferociously politicized and ideological, Musil had only contempt for the catastrophic simplifications of totalitarian movements, whether they came from the left or the right wing. Nor did a purely aesthetic solution hold any appeal for him; he never aimed just to create another significant work of art, but rather to use all the resources of both his scientific training and his literary imagination to find a way out of the sterile oppositions of his era. Musil kept looking for a way to make sense of himself and the world that would not be compartmentalized into discrete domains. The new ethical, moral, and sexual dispensation he sought would have to reflect the scientific, practical world modern men and women inhabit, but also be able to overcome its isolating and dehumanizing effects.

The decisive initial difference between Musil and most of the other modernist literary masters is the fact that he came to literature from science and demanded from his own fiction the intellectual rigor and precision that he had learned in the laboratory. He was a true polymath, as expert in theoretical physics, experimental psychology, and mechanical engineering as in strictly literary or philosophical questions. The prewar Austrian intelligentsia placed a much higher value on a rigorous scientific education than did their counterparts in England, France, or the United States. One need think only of Ludwig Wittgenstein, who was initially trained in mechanical engineering and first came to England in 1908 to study aeronautics at Manchester before finally turning to philosophy relatively late in his education. Like Wittgenstein, but far more understanding of the vicissitudes of sexual desire, Musil sought throughout his whole life to combine a commitment to the most stringent principles of mathematical logic with a mystical yearning for a new, less alienated way of living. Musil despised the widespread habit of substituting a grandiloquently soulful rhetoric for the kind of disciplined intellectual labor that understanding oneself and the world requires. "Anyone who is incapable of solving an integral equation, anyone who is unable to perform a laboratory experiment, should today be forbidden to discuss all spiritual matters" is a characteristically pugnacious formulation in Musil's play *The Enthusiasts* (*Die Schwärmer*).[4] And in his principal work, *The Man without Qualities*, the conventional insistence that true inwardness is incompatible with logical rigor is one of the reasons that Ulrich, the book's eponymous hero, was first attracted to the hard sciences: "one thing ... could safely be said about Ulrich: he loved mathematics because of the kind of people who could not endure it."[5] So when Diotima, the novel's society hostess, discovers to her delight that she has a profoundly yearning soul, the narrator mordantly comments on such self-serving pretensions to spiritual inwardness: "What is a soul? It is easy to define negatively: It is simply that which sneaks off at the mention of algebraic series."[6]

Musil's early preparation for his quest to unite mathematics and mysticism was as idiosyncratic as the project itself. He was born in Klagenfurt, Carinthia, in 1880, the son of a gifted, hardworking, and emotionally distant civil engineer with a distinguished career in academic and administrative appointments, and a mother whose temperament was flamboyantly sexual and self-dramatizing. In 1882, when Musil's mother openly took a lover, Heinrich Reiter, her husband seems to have accepted the situation without a struggle, and in 1890 Reiter accompanied the Musil family as their regular "house guest" to Brünn (Brno), where Alfred Musil moved to become professor of mechanical engineering. This permanent and oddly domestic ménage à trois lasted without any serious disruptions until Hermine Musil's death in 1924. Although an outstanding student, Robert suffered from severe attacks of nerves throughout his childhood, and biographers have speculated, often based only on the ambiguous evidence of his fiction, about the links between his recurrent emotional crises and his family's eccentric sexual configuration. What is indisputable, though, and perhaps even stranger, is how Musil was haunted by the image of his "lost" sister, Elsa, who died at less than eleven months old, four years before his own birth. The motif of a vanished and then rediscovered sister, a twin with whom all intimacy is possible but at the risk of transgressing into the illicit and demonic, became central to *The Man without Qualities*. The most moving relationship in the novel, indeed the only one whose potential the book takes seriously, is the sexually charged affinity between Ulrich and his sister, Agathe, siblings "who are doppelgängers, who have two souls, but are one."[7] Their mutual attachment is characterized by Agathe herself, with only the faintest trace of the normal Musilian irony, as "no longer a love story; it is the very last love story there can be."[8]

Like many boys of his social class, Musil was sent to boarding schools as an adolescent. For three years he attended the famous cadet institution in Mährisch-Weißkirchen, and although he was only somewhat happier there than Rilke had been a few years earlier, Musil was able to draw on his experiences at the school for his first significant writing. *Young Törless*, Musil's first novel, was published to considerable critical acclaim in 1906 and contains a bitter account of the boarding school's atmosphere of claustrophobia, snobbism, homosexual brutality, and intellectual nullity. He abandoned his plans for a military career in 1898, after just one year in Vienna at the Military Academy of Technology, and returned to Brünn to take up civil engineering. Once back in Brünn, though, he also began to attend lectures on literature and philosophy, and he became more systematic about noting down his personal impressions and projects in a series of diaries that he continued to keep for the rest of his life. In 1902 he obtained an assistantship at Germany's most advanced laboratory for mechanical engineering, the Technical Institute in Stuttgart, but a year later, he was already bored with his research and moved to Berlin to begin doctoral studies in philosophy (particularly logic) and experimental psychology. Musil continued to read widely in literature, while simultaneously applying his engineering skills to patent a new design for a color wheel used in experimental psychology tests. In Berlin, Musil studied with Carl Stumpf (to whom Edmund Husserl later dedicated his *Logical Investigations*), and in 1908 he received his doctorate in philosophy, physics, and mathematics for a thesis on Ernst Mach, the Austrian physicist and philosopher for whom the Mach number, representing the ratio of the speed of an object to the speed of sound in the atmosphere, was named.

But to the disgruntlement of his family, which was still supporting him financially, Musil rejected the academic post that he was offered in Graz in order to devote himself entirely to writing. In 1911, he married Martha Marcovaldi, née Heimann (1874–1949), a Jewish-born Berliner who had been married twice before and was seven years his elder. Martha had been trained as a visual artist, and her studies had included classes at a school founded by Lovis Corinth. She became the one indispensable partner on whom Musil would rely, both for his writing and his emotional well-being. Although Agathe in *The Man without Qualities* differs in many ways from Martha Musil, it is fascinating to see how often Musil referred to his wife as his "married sister." The short stories he was writing during these years, "The Perfecting of a Love" and "The Temptation of Quiet Veronica," seem almost collaborative works, so clearly can one sense the perspective and voice of Martha in the texture of both narratives. Indeed, Musil, along with Joyce, is one of the few important modern novelists to have made eroticism in marriage a central part of his reflective preoccupations. Despite Musil's initial literary success, however, his refusal of an academic career left the couple in precarious circumstances throughout his life, and neither his regular work as a reviewer, an editor, and a cultural critic for leading journals in Berlin and Vienna, nor his brief stints at the Library of the Technical University in Vienna (1911–14) and at the Press Office of the Austrian Foreign Ministry (1919–20), assured him any financial stability. Musil served with distinction throughout the First World War in some of the harshest conditions the Imperial Army faced, but when he returned to civilian life, his long-term prospects were even less secure than they had been in 1914. In *The Man without Qualities*, Ulrich has sufficient means to take off a year from his work as a mathematician in order to live free of external constraints, and there is no doubt that his fictional hero's economic independence represents the wish fulfillment of Musil's own unrealized longings.

Musil continued to publish essays in both Germany and Austria on an enormous range of topics, including politics, art, cinema, metaphysics, and the nature of essayistic thinking. The best of these—they are available in English as *Precision and Soul*—contain some of the century's most searching discussions of the breakdown of the European intellectual and imaginative order. Sentences like "We do not have too much intellect and too little soul, but too little intellect in matters of the soul" (from "Helpless Europe")[9] and "If I want to have a worldview, then I must view the world" (from "The German as Symptom")[10] are gradually becoming as much a part of the German aphoristic tradition as the most memorable of Nietzsche's and

Schopenhauer's epigrams. But even the relative success of his two plays, *The Enthusiasts*, published in 1921, and the still-untranslated *Vincent and the Mistress of Important Men* (*Vinzenz und die Freundin bedeutender Männer*), which appeared in 1923, did little to improve his financial position. The need for a steady income became all the more pressing as Musil began to devote himself with ever increasing determination to his great novel. Musil's diary entries show that elements of *The Man without Qualities* began to crystallize in his mind well before the outbreak of World War I. By 1919 he had already blocked out many of the book's fundamental themes and specific situations, and by 1924 he was working on it full time.

Beginning in 1925, Musil was receiving regular, if modest, advances for the novel (still tentatively called "The Twin Sister") from his publisher, Ernst Rowohlt, and in 1926 Musil gave the first extensive interview in a literary journal about his forthcoming book. In October 1930, at the urging of the increasingly impatient Rowohlt, Musil published the first volume of *The Man without Qualities*, 1,075 pages containing all of parts 1 and 2 ("A Sort of Introduction" and "Pseudoreality Prevails"). In 1933, again yielding to pressure from Rowohlt, Musil reluctantly published a second volume of 608 pages, comprising a portion of part 3 ("Into the Millennium" ["The Criminals"]). Musil strongly resented having to publish his work piecemeal. He was afraid that once a significant portion was in print, he would be locked into formulations and character descriptions that did not fully satisfy him, without having the chance to revise these parts in the light of subsequent realizations. Since he regarded his novel as a kind of experiment in progress, he was as reluctant to publish his "results" prematurely as he would have been to circulate an early draft of a paper in mathematics or logic.

At almost the same time as the second volume appeared, Robert and Martha left Berlin for Vienna, appalled by Hitler's accession to power. After the Nazi annexation of Austria in 1938, the Musils again fled, this time to Switzerland, where they lived on increasingly depleted resources until the writers death in 1942. A third volume of *The Man without Qualities* had been prepared by Musil for publication in 1938, in an effort to keep alive some public interest in his work. The book contained twenty chapters intended as a continuation of part 3, not as its conclusion, but Musil withdrew them when they were already set in galleys. No further parts of *The Man without Qualities* appeared during Musil's lifetime, but in 1943 Martha had the withdrawn chapters, along with a very small selection from his voluminous drafts and fragments, published at her own expense in Lausanne as volume 3. Since 1952, under the editorship of Adolf Frisé, who had become fascinated with Musil's novel in the 1930s and contacted Martha after the war to inquire about the state of the manuscripts, *The Man without Qualities* has appeared in increasingly expanded and revised editions, incorporating more of Musil's posthumous fragments and draft chapters (the *Nachlaß*). The latest of these editions was published in 1978 and serves as the basis of the 1995 English translation by Sophie Wilkins and Burton Pike, but almost everything about the *Nachlaß*, from the internal order of the chapters to their degree of relative completeness, remains conjectural, and every new edition has occasioned fierce and often highly technical controversies in which vital interpretative, as well as purely bibliographic, issues are at stake. Like the narrative of *The Man without Qualities*, the physical book itself, as a material product, turns out to have remained open-ended and subject to limitless revision.

More than most long and complex novels, *The Man without Qualities* resists being summarized. Far from coming together to form a coherent plot, the book's diverse incidents become increasingly more disparate and fragmented as the novel unfolds. Indeed, the inability of separate stories, motifs, and perspectives to coalesce into a meaningful pattern is one of Musil's major themes. *The Man without Qualities* may be understood as a series of events in search of a plot, just as the Habsburg Empire itself is shown as a haphazard political amalgam engaged in a hopeless search for some unifying meaning or identity.

At the center of all these stories, and providing the novel's sustained focus and source of continuity, is Ulrich, the "man without qualities." An ex-soldier, an experimental scientist, a brilliant mathematician, and a casual womanizer, Ulrich decides, at the age of thirty-two, to take a yearlong "vacation from life" so as to discover in himself the intellectual rigor, spiritual intensity, and emotional depth that, he has grown to feel, must underlie any meaningful action. He has many talents, but he has no qualities, in the sense that his acute self-awareness detaches him from his own attributes and gives them, in his eyes, a kind of impersonal and even transitory nature. If the other characters in the book have a stable identity and the conviction that whatever belief system bolsters their position in the world must be universally beneficent, Ulrich deliberately resists the reassurance of such stability; he does not want to assume a possessive stance toward the qualities he has, nor use them to take a proprietary attitude toward the world. Everyone in the novel is certain both how to think and what truly merits being thought about except Ulrich, who is certain about neither.

The Man without Qualities opens in August 1913, less than a year before the assassination of Franz Ferdinand, the presumptive heir to the Habsburg throne, triggered the outbreak of the First World War. The specific historical situation is central to the novel's unfolding, since Ulrich is prodded by his anxious father, a judge with aristocratic connections, and by his beautiful, ambitious cousin, Ermelinde Tuzzi (nicknamed "Diotima"),[11] to assume the position of secretary for a grandiose but incoherent plan—the Parallel Campaign (*Parallelaktion*)—to celebrate the seventieth anniversary of Emperor Franz Joseph's coronation, which is due to fall on December 2, 1918. Conceived as a patriotic response to the already formulated German idea of honoring their monarch, Wilhelm II, on July 15, 1918, with a national festival celebrating his thirty years on the throne, the Austrian scheme is pathetically, even risibly, futile, since Franz Joseph was to die in 1916, and in 1918 both the Austrian and the German empires would collapse and be replaced by republics. The only "parallel action" that will actually take place is the almost simultaneous downfall of both dynasties.

In the first two parts of the novel, Ulrich is drawn into the frantic but essentially vacuous activities set into motion by the Parallel Campaign. Diotima's salon becomes the campaign's unofficial headquarters, and since almost every section of Austrian society wants to influence the direction of the planned jubilee, Musil is able to paint a rich portrait of the epoch's leading character types and their ideas. At Diotima's receptions, Ulrich encounters everyone from members of the imperial government and army General Staff to career diplomats, bourgeois plutocrats, and arriviste poets, and in these chapters Musil comes close to creating a kind of updated, Balzacian human comedy of the Habsburg Empire in its final months. In a separate development, Ulrich also begins to follow the trial of an obsessed sex murderer named "Moosbrugger," who exerts a hold on the Viennese imagination of the day somewhat as Charles Manson did on the American imagination not long ago. Moosbrugger becomes the locus where all the competing discourses of the day pitch their claims for interpretive authority (religious, medical, juridical, philosophical, mystical, etc.), and we hear how each of these discourses fails to incorporate or to convincingly contest the perspective of its rivals. And just as the Parallel Campaign provided Musil with a central focus for the political and economic machinations of Austria's ruling classes, so the Moosbrugger trial turns the novel in a different direction, toward the themes of madness and messianic delusions as these haunt both Ulrich himself and a circle of his private acquaintances, from his frustrated childhood friends Walter and Clarisse to the young right-wing Germanic nationalist Hans Sepp. These minor characters are often deeply compelling in their own right, especially Moosbrugger and Clarisse, whose craziness is disturbingly close to Ulrich's own glimpses of a "second consciousness." Ulrich's thinking strives to break down the binary oppositions that structure the way people make sense out of the world; he is no longer able to believe in the solidity of such antithetical pairings as science versus soul, male versus female, freedom versus necessity, or reason versus imagination. The problem is, though, that a number of other figures in the book not only want to but actually have succeeded in their efforts to break down those oppositions—only these characters are mostly pathological and dangerous. Tracing the separate stories of these characters simultaneously enriches the breadth of the novel's social canvas and, more important, brings into focus the riskiness of Ulrich's decision not to settle for a partial solution to his search for a meaningful new "science of feeling."

But his father's death and his own increasing indifference to the world of power and high politics distance Ulrich more and more from the campaign. In the third, unfinished section of the work ("Into the Millennium"), he gives up his position as the campaign's secretary, temporarily abandons his concern with Moosbrugger, and withdraws almost completely from society in order to pursue his quest for a way to heal the rupture between scientific precision and mystical intensity. His sister, Agathe, whom he rediscovers during the settling of their father's estate, decides to divorce her husband and set up house with Ulrich, and together the two siblings dedicate themselves to learning how "to hold fast to their intimations ... [of a] second reality ... a day-bright mysticism ... [that] mustn't ever be more than an hour old!"[12] The mysticism that Ulrich and Agathe seek is not "a secret through which we enter another world, but only ... the secret of living in this world differently." Musil never finished his description of Ulrich and Agathe's joint search, but the notes he left behind suggest that this quest, too, ultimately would have failed. In its isolation from the rest of humankind, even as sublime a passion as Ulrich's and Agathe's ends up exhausting itself on the unstable borderline between the ecstatic and the solipsistic.

"Unfortunately, nothing is so hard to achieve as a literary representation of a man thinking."[13] This rueful admission by Musil's narrator crystallizes both the main difficulty as well as the originality of *The Man without Qualities*. To an extent unprecedented in Western literature, large stretches of the book contain neither a forward-moving action nor inward character development. In their place, we are often given extended sections of pure intellectual-moral speculation, reflections that exist less to illuminate the private passions of a character than to follow the inner logic of a concept with its own independent claims on our attention. This is a kind of novelistic "essayism," a term that exactly translates Musil's loan-word *Essayismus*.

Consider, as a particularly appropriate example of one of the novel's "essays," these passages from a lengthy meditation on the nature of *Essayismus* itself:

[E]verything he encounters behaves as though it were final and complete. [Yet] he suspects that the given order of things is not as solid as it pretends to be: no thing, no self, no form, no principle, is safe, everything is undergoing an invisible but ceaseless transformation, the unsettled holds more of the future than the settled, and the present is nothing but a hypothesis that has not yet been surmounted ... later ... this became an idea no longer connected with the vague word "hypothesis" but with the concept he oddly termed ... "essay." It was more or less in the way an essay, in the sequence of its paragraphs, explores a thing from many sides without wholly encompassing it—for a thing wholly encompassed suddenly loses its scope and melts down to a concept ... such an expression is always risky, not yet justified by the prevailing set of affairs, a combination of exact and inexact, of precision and passion.... Philosophers are despots who have no armies to command, so they subject the world to their tyranny by locking it up in a system of thought. But ... there was something in Ulrich's nature that ... resisted all logical systematizing ... it was also connected with his chosen term, "essayism" ... The accepted translation of "essay" as "attempt" contains only vaguely the essential allusion to the literary model, for an essay is not a provisional or incidental expression of a conviction capable of being elevated to a truth ... or of being exposed as an error ... An essay is rather the unique and unalterable form assumed by a man's inner life in a decisive thought ... There have been more than a few such essayists, masters of the inner hovering life [and] ... their domain lies between religion and knowledge, between example and doctrine, between *amor intellectualis* and poetry.... A man who wants the truth becomes a scholar; a man who wants to give free play to his subjectivity may become a writer, but what should a man do who wants something in between?[14]

Essayism is so crucial to Musil because it allows him to express the fullest possible range of human consciousness while avoiding the sterility of premature closure. Since the novel shows us a society caught in a helpless pendulum between sclerosis (Leinsdorf) and cataclysm (Moosbrugger), there is a compelling need for some new, more flexible principle of order. Musil's essayism is no longer a question of genre, it is a way of thinking about and experiencing the world as an unfixable, variegated, and constantly self-transforming phenomenon. Ulrich himself could just as easily be called "the Essayistic Man," and Musil makes clear that the concepts of "essayism" and being "without qualities" are simply twin ways of accounting for the same cast of mind. Even Ulrich's project of taking a year's absence from normal existence in order to explore new ideas and ways of living is itself already a kind of essay. Ulrich's gift as a "master of the hovering life" is to be able to listen to diverse and formally irreconcilable systems of thought without either prejudging them or forcing them into a premature synthesis, and his sharpest irony is reserved for those who insist that only their own explanatory terms are really "true" and "complete." It is only for the insane that everything falls into place, like Moosbrugger, whom Ulrich views as "a rampant metaphor of order."[15] For the truly mad, the whole universe is just a manifestation of their demand for an absolute order based on the impoverished categories of their own egos. Thus, during Moosbrugger's time in jail, Musil gives us a terrifying glimpse of a too-ordered consciousness at its most pathological:

> If Moosbrugger had had a big sword, he'd have drawn it and chopped the head off his chair. He would have chopped the head off the table and the window, the slop bucket, the door. Then he would have set his own head on everything because in this cell there was only one head, his own, and that was as it should be. He could imagine his head sitting on top of things ... The table was Moosbrugger. The chair was Moosbrugger. The barred window and bolted door were himself.[16]

The chapter from which this quote is taken, called "Moosbrugger Dances," is an uncanny glimpse of the implicit danger in a state of mind that many of the century's most powerful writers had depicted as entirely beneficent. Moosbrugger's delirium is close to a sinister parody of Rilkean inwardness; when the table, chair, window, and door become Moosbrugger, the language has some of the same rhythms and intensities as the epiphanies of "real seeing" in Rilke's *Notebooks of Malte Laurids Brigge*. In his prison cell, Moosbrugger achieves something eerily like the Angel's perspective in the *Duino Elegies* for which Rilke himself spent decades longing. It was crucial for Musil to show the pathological extension of such visionary moments as well as their extraordinary attraction. For a poet like Yeats, the question "How can we tell the dancer from the dance?"[17] is always purely celebratory: the merging of one's inner world with the externally given environment and the perfect interplay of body and spirit are exemplary of a transcendent realization achieved only in rare moments of utter focus like in a dancer's performance or a mystic's trance. In many ways, Musil shared Yeats's and Rilke's conviction that breaking down the difference between self and world is an essential step in attaining the kind of unitary wisdom for which all three writers were seeking. But he is aware, in a way neither Rilke nor Yeats was, that the collapse of boundaries is always also deeply perilous, and that the effects of trying to achieve such a collapse, both for individuals and for societies, have often been catastrophic. Moosbrugger is both inside and outside of normal distinctions. Musil finds a brilliantly unexpected image, one consonant with Moosbrugger's own physically vivid conceptual repertoire, to illustrate the strain required not to let one's consciousness expand until it merges violently with everything it encounters:

> It was just that the rubber bands were gone [for Moosbrugger].
> Behind every thing or creature, when it tries to get really close to
> another, is a rubber band, pulling. Otherwise, things might finally
> go right through one another. Every movement is reined in by a
> rubber band that won't let a person do quite what he wants. Now,
> suddenly, all those rubber bands were gone.[18]

It is the hard work of maintaining proportion and balance on which passages like this insist. For all his analysis of the limitations of prosaic reasonableness, Musil is the only one of the five figures treated in this book for whom it was not inherently beneath serious consideration. Indeed, at several points in the novel, Musil suggests that the long-standing Habsburg distaste for extreme measures and radical innovations, combined with its undeniable intellectual and political philistinism, probably contributed as much to the empire's longevity as did any of its more edifying characteristics. The breakdown of that mildly cynical Habsburg accommodationism and its replacement by shrilly competing absolutist ideologies were a far more serious harbinger of crisis than the supposed laxness and decadence with which critics habitually charge the last years of the empire. *The Man without Qualities* makes it clear that far from being too indolent and pleasure-seeking, almost everyone in Vienna is as obsessed with finding his or her own all-transforming new ways of living as are Ulrich, Moosbrugger, and Clarisse. No one, from wealthy industrialists to adulterous housewives, is without a solution to the problems of the age. Ulrich's own skeptical and bemused intelligence needs to be emphasized so strongly in the essayistic passages of parts 1 and 2 in order to balance the reader's awareness that his longing for a mystical "oneness with the world" in which "all affirmations express only a single surging experience"[19] shares an unwelcome family resemblance with Moosbrugger's ecstatic delirium and Clarisse's swirling fantasies.

The similarities between Ulrich and the other characters also ensures that the book is not simply condescending to everyone except its hero. At their best, the essayistic parts of the novel really are essays; that is, they have no absolute authority over any other sections of the book and do not add up to one single, overarching argument. Hence the element of irony in the essays, an irony that is aimed as much at Ulrich's cherished ideas as at the more obviously mockable opinions of the minor characters or of Austrian society in general. This is very different from the essays in novels like Tolstoy's *War and Peace* or Hermann Broch's *The Sleep-Walkers*, which are largely without irony about the novel's serious themes and which, consequently, read more like treatises than true essays. Tolstoy's and Broch's essays are unmistakable vehicles for ideas that advance the argument of the book as a whole—so much so that they risk making the rest of the narrative seem more like an illustration or instantiation of the judgments reached in the "essays" rather than an independent carrier and revealer of meaning. In one of the late entries in his *Diaries*, Musil tried to define his distinctive kind of irony: "Irony has to contain an element of suffering in it. (Otherwise it is the attitude of a know-it-all.) Enmity and sympathy."[20] In *The Man without Qualities*, even the deranged characters are rarely seen without that crucial "element of suffering." But clarity is ultimately even more important than sympathy, and Musil shows us that figures like Moosbrugger and Clarisse, who mistake their moments of phantasmagoric inward illumination for universal truth, can only react with murderous rage or total dissociation whenever their beliefs are thwarted. On the other hand, our long familiarity with Ulrich's essayism, with its insistence on the provisional character of any realization, helps us trust his experiences of transcendent wholeness in part 3, while still, like the narrator himself, keeping a certain critical distance from the full sweep of Ulrich's and Agathe's "second reality." Because Ulrich's scientific and mathematical skepticism coexists with equally powerful yearnings for a condition in which feeling and knowledge would act in concert, neither perspective can ever be sacrificed. Ulrich is no more willing to abandon the rational, analytic categories of pure thought than he can find satisfaction solely within their terms.

Ulrich's essayism may incline toward the merging of exterior and interior perceptions, but it cannot inhabit them exclusively. Unlike Moosbrugger's or Clarisse's delusions, which are always in part compensatory for their thwarted desires and which are regularly redirected by random physical sensations and external stimuli, it is often impossible to specify what prompts a particular chain of thinking in Ulrich. Indeed, it is the absence of any readily categorizable motivation for their speculations that distinguishes Ulrich and Agathe from the other figures in the book, whose delight in large, philosophical-sounding pronouncements is wickedly satirized by having the self-serving and self-referential function of their ideas laid bare. The Habsburg aristocrat, Count Leinsdorf, for example, is a marvel of quiet complacency, memorably described as being unable to recognize anything in what he reads, "other than agreement with or mistaken divergence from his own principles."[21] Musil's most vividly realized secondary characters, like the great industrialist and occasional writer of philosophical-cultural tracts Paul Arnheim (modeled after the German tycoon and Weimar foreign minister Walter Rathenau [1867–1922]), all *use* ideas to validate their particular class or professional interests, while society figures like Diotima try on important cultural issues like pieces of prized jewelry designed to confer distinction on whoever wears them. For men with virtually unlimited qualities like Arnheim, the dilemmas that torment Ulrich are only transient, topical disturbances, and Arnheim's self-satisfaction is grounded in the conviction that he already embodies the very synthesis for which Ulrich is futilely searching. When Arnheim loftily declares that what the modern world requires is to unite "capital and culture" (*Besitz und Bildung*), he does so with the comforting knowledge that he possesses both in abundance: "Arnheim's books also had the same kind of self-assurance: the world was in order as soon as Arnheim had given it his consideration."[22]

Each of the secondary characters has fashioned a prison for himself or herself through a false and partial or, more accurately, false *because* partial, worldview. Fundamentally there is something similar between letting one's madness (Moosbrugger and Clarisse) or one's ideology (Leinsdorf and Arnheim) think for one. Moosbrugger, Clarisse, Arnheim, and even the emperor, Franz Joseph himself, want, in their different ways, to be all inclusive—all of them, not just Moosbrugger, are actually "rampant principles of order." Whereas men like Leinsdorf and Arnheim familiarize everything in their world by viewing it as an extension of themselves, Ulrich programmatically defamiliarizes whatever he encounters. While they bring everything back to the expected, to the already known and available formulations, Ulrich tears everything out of its customary frame of reference and makes it part of a deliberately inconclusive new essay. To contest the certainties of the other characters, Ulrich relies on four closely related techniques of resistance. First, he extends what he is given in an unexpected direction. Second, he considers it from a completely different system of thought (e.g., if it is a cultural idea, he will give it a scientific or economic explanation, if it is an economic one, he will analyze it from the perspective of moral theory), thereby creating a cross-analysis of discursive fields in which commonplace assumptions are destabilized as well as defamiliarized. Third, he assigns an inverse moral and psychological value to current ideas in order to test the consequences if what is assumed to be positive is provisionally regarded as negative and vice versa. Fourth, he makes people confront their own stake in whatever system of explanation they cling to, thereby bringing to light its inherently ideological and self-interested function. One odd result of such corrosive scrutiny is that as soon as one of the other characters voices an idea whose attraction we have heard Ulrich himself proclaim, he is immediately driven to challenge it. To Ulrich, these ideas have value only as single elements of an undiscovered new compound, when he suspects that they are being held up as the total solution, they temporarily lose all their appeal.

But the refusal to exploit ideas ideologically, to inflate the limited and fixed perspectives of a class or character into a totalizing explanatory system, greatly raises both the stakes and the potential self-contradiction in the book's quest for *das rechte Leben*, the right life and the right way to live that life. The plot of *The Man without Qualities* is not so much philosophically driven as it is propelled by the search for a philosophy sufficient to motivate a meaningful story. At its core, the novel is continuously about judgment—it is actually about nothing but judgment, about how and what to judge—and yet it ruthlessly and continuously undermines all existing criteria of judgment. How, then, can we judge at all, when what we are looking for are precisely criteria of judgment? The novel keeps reflecting on its own possibility of existing, but since that question is also the point of origin of the whole narrative, there is a sense in which the story not only can't end but cannot even properly begin. When Ulrich says that "we really shouldn't demand action from one another; we should create the conditions that make action possible,"[23] he is not merely speaking of his own quest, but also of Musil's dilemma as a novelist. Several times in the novel, in such passages as "he had always ended up feeling trapped in endless preparations that would never come to fruition,"[24] Ulrich's destiny, Musil's personal anxieties, and the fate of *The Man without Qualities* itself are clearly linked. Musil increasingly came to feel that it was an impossible task simultaneously to depict actions while exploring the preconditions that would make those actions truly meaningful. The very concept of *das rechte Leben* implies a hierarchic stability that is counter to the infinite openness and provisional nature of essayism, of remaining "without qualities." If the partiality of Arnheim's and Leinsdorf's ideas is what makes them vulnerable to Musil's irony, why is Ulrich's dedication to finding *das rechte Leben* any less subject to a critique of its absolutist claims? One of the central problems of Ulrich's quest, and thus of the novel as a whole, is that at its deepest level it wants mutually exclusive things, and in that sense Ulrich's project is dangerously similar to the hopelessness of the *Parallelaktion*. Paradoxically, though, what rescues the novel from the dangers of its own totalizing ambition is its very "failure" to reach any conclusion. The essayism that fractures its surface and disrupts any movement toward closure is also what gives *The Man without Qualities* its permanent freshness and sense of intellectual and imaginative daring. The book's density of historical description and social observation are important not merely for the inherent novelistic pleasure they provide, but as the indispensable counterpart to what would otherwise risk becoming a kind of free-floating spiritual autobiography. Ulrich continues to remain socially a man without qualities, not merely a solitary consciousness, both because the world he inhabits is realized with such vivid specificity and because that world keeps generating so many fascinating and preposterous, but historically plausible, characters to set beside him. The book's attention is significantly wider than Ulrich's—hence the discrepancies between the narrators voice and Ulrich's—and it is able to include a critique of its hero's project as part of its own larger story. The essayistic temperament can never permanently privilege any single perspective, not even one "without qualities," and while the novel as a whole takes Ulrich's longing for *das rechte Leben* almost as seriously as he himself does, in the end, that search remains only the most important of the multiple, mutually antagonistic quests whose unfolding constitutes the book's real story.

*   *   *

Musil saw his Vienna as both uniquely itself and as "nothing but a particularly clear-cut case of the modern world."[25] But readers of *The Man without Qualities* know from the outset that the particular world the novel describes has very little time left before perishing in the conflagration of World War I. Yet Musil does not use the reader's knowledge of the empire's imminent dissolution as the basis for representing the actions and hopes of the characters in the book as absurd, nor is his ironic perspective on contemporary political events based on their eventual outcome.[26] The Parallel Campaign, for example, is not ludicrous *because* the emperor it planned to honor would be dead and his dynasty overthrown before the celebration's announced date. On the contrary, in its intellectual incoherence and ideological blindness, the campaign was already thoroughly ludicrous from the moment of its conception. In the salons and ministries of Vienna in the years before the war, the chance of a general European conflict is kept constantly in mind, but it is presented as only one of a wide range of possibilities, and avoiding such an outcome is, in fact, the chief purpose of many of the characters in Musil's book. Most of what takes place politically is a result of the law of unintended consequences, and nothing better illustrates this than the fact that the nebulous Parallel Campaign, originally conceived as an anti-Prussian maneuver, will soon give way to the all-too-real parallel action of the Austrian and German armies marching as allies to their joint destruction. *The Man without Qualities* is full of intimations of the coming war, but it is just as resonant with suggestions that such a cataclysm can be prevented. The important point is that Musil skillfully allows the whole range of ideas and hopes held by his characters *in 1913* to be heard clearly on their own terms. He regularly satirizes all of his characters' positions, but only when their blindness and self-deception are already fully demonstrable in the context of their own day, not when they fail to foresee the future accurately.

The Man without Qualities shows us that there is no inevitable trajectory to events: the Parallel Campaign stumbles toward the war quite against the intentions of most of its members. There is no overarching, secret authority or force planning everything and moving history along a predetermined path. Competing centers of power (foreign affairs [Tuzzi], the army [Stumm von Bordwehr], and international finance [Arnheim]) have separate and often competing agendas. They form temporary and rapidly changing alliances, often with groups whose purpose and raison d'être are actually antithetical to their own. At a certain point, it sometimes happens that the particular "local" alliances that have coalesced for that moment alone find themselves bound together for good into a single long-term aim by the pressures of a larger event that none of them had expected, like the outbreak of a continent-engulfing war. But it is important to recall that the alliances' individual members did not seek the war as their principal objective, nor did they envisage any permanent link to one another. For example, Austria's foreign service and army tried repeatedly to forge alliances that would prevent the Habsburg Empire from becoming Prussia's junior partner. Yet that is precisely what it did become, against all the aspirations of its most skilled leaders. In the course of the novel, we see how the fumblings of the Parallel Campaign helped cement a German–Austrian alliance, which was the one goal undesired by anyone involved in its initial conception.

Musil's novelistic solution to the epistemological problems raised by the narration of historical events whose outcome is already known is exemplary in its fairness. Since it is impossible for the reader to suspend a knowledge of the book's historical aftermath, the narrator deliberately plays on that knowledge, not to exploit it for the emotional intensities it might add to the story, but rather to undermine any sense of historical inevitability. The dense network of contradictory voices and ideas represented in the book makes the reader's faith in a superior, because subsequent, vantage point impossible. There are so many plausible scenarios for the future sketched out in *The Man without Qualities,* so many different hopes and expectations expressed by characters in a position to make astute forecasts, that the novel swarms with projections of mutually exclusive prospects. Inevitably, though, because we know which of these projected futures came to pass, we are tempted to pay special attention whenever any character seems to articulate as the likeliest possibility what actually happened in 1914. Musil is especially inventive at finding effective ways to subvert this impulse, to make clear, that is, the absurdity of judging his book's characters by the accuracy of their historical prognoses. For example, perhaps the most benevolently accommodating character in the entire novel is Ulrich's friend General Stumm von Bordwehr, who is sent by the General Staff to represent the army at Diotima's salon. Instead of the conventional postwar literary representation of senior officers as callous monsters, completely without any regard for human life, Musil goes out of his way to show Stumm as both kindhearted and utterly unbelligerent, all the while knowing that the novel's readers can never entirely forget that it is precisely men like Stumm who will shortly be leading the Imperial Army into mass slaughter. Musil then complicates this already subtle play between the novel's and the reader's different temporal horizons by having the usually ridiculous Diotima be more prescient than Ulrich when it comes to foreseeing the likelihood of a general war. It is Diotima who is right about what Stumm will end up doing. She says of him, "he makes me think of death," and when Ulrich lightheartedly replies, "an uncommonly life-loving figure of Death," Diotima's insistence that Stumm fills her "with an indescribable, incomprehensible, dreamlike fear" is decidedly more prophetic.[27] If either Ulrich or the narrator were to predict the coming war, their foreshadowing would risk endowing that outcome with the aura of historical inevitability. But since it is the usually self-deluded Diotima who guesses correctly, the war becomes just one of the possibilities in the air at the time. Musil repeatedly makes fun of the urge to endow a specific moment with greater portentousness strictly because of what actually ensued: "Time was making a fresh start then (it does so all the time).... there was great excitement everywhere around the turn of 1913–1914. But two years or five years earlier there had also been much excitement."[28]

The war is never seen as "inevitable" by Musil, for the very good reason that nothing in history can be so considered. The war is indisputably a pivotal turning point in world history, but its historical magnitude gives it no retrospective authority over the events narrated in *The Man without Qualities*. History is not destiny. The most satiric parts of Musil's novel describe a world in stasis or in a self-perpetuating muddle, rather than on the verge of disintegration. The Habsburg Empire that we actually are shown could just as easily have lasted for many years more, just as, for example, the Ottoman Empire survived for more than a century after observers were certain of its imminent dissolution. The disintegration certainly happened, but occurrence, as *The Man without Qualities* regularly instructs us, does not imply necessity.

Yet just as Ulrich is deeply frustrated by the gulf separating modern man's expert knowledge in the professional and scientific areas of life from the uncritical assumptions with which he interprets the world in his private psychological and moral life, so the novel as a whole seeks to undo the narrative conventions by which the reader imposes a linear, scripted pattern on the motility of historical events and individual psyches. Musil's irony works so effectively because he expects readers to approach a novel set on the eve of the Great War as though it would manifest all the familiar devices of deterministic inevitability. Thus we, too, are already "set up" by our own expectations to undergo the shock of realizing that everyone, not just the book's characters, indulges in no-longer-credible patterns of thinking. What is satirized in Musil's descriptions is not the psychological makeup of the characters, but their habits of thought, and since those same habits still largely govern how we make sense of our world, we are denied the position of superiority usually occupied by readers of satires. Musil's typically ironic/serious way of insisting on the speciousness of fixed interpretive categories is to deny the attribute of inevitability even to divine creation: "God Himself probably preferred to speak of His world in the subjunctive of possibility ... for God creates the world and thinks while He is at it that it could just as well be done differently."[29] And this aphorism exactly parallels the dilemma at the heart of the new kind of novel Musil was striving to create.

Musil undertook the perhaps irreconcilable duties of creating a fully plausible, densely realized world while still indicating that "it could just as well be done differently." And so, irrespective of some posthumous drafts in which Musil briefly tries out having Ulrich go into combat, it is unlikely that the war could have been inserted successfully into the novel. Only by setting his narrative before the outbreak of hostilities can Musil guarantee that neither his characters nor his narrator speaks with predictive historical certainty. Since Musil is so concerned to show that many things can be imagined as likely to happen, and that history is not driven by any rational principle or internal logic that would let the future be accurately predicted, he is also particularly careful not to allow the war to undermine the novel's fidelity to a sense of multifarious possibilities (*Möglichkeitssinn*). To include the war directly would risk giving it the privilege of being not just an *event* in the narrative, but rather its *meaning*, and this, precisely, is what Musil regarded as unacceptable. But simply at the level of composing a coherent work of art, Musil's refusal to use the war as an externally validated closure to his book left him with an impossible struggle to create a structure that would provide a narratable resolution to his theoretical and ethical requirements. That he failed to do so is clear not only from the incompleteness of the novel at the time of his death, but also from the nature of the last sections he actually published and the enormous mass of drafts and fragments he left behind. A variety of reasons—including depression over the lack of an audience, an intermittent but long-standing "writer's block," intellectual exhaustion, and the financial uncertainties of an exile's life—have all been advanced to explain Musil's inability to complete his book. But once Musil rejected ending the novel with the melodramatic thunderclap of the outbreak of war (say, for example, with the reading of a telegram announcing Franz Ferdinand's assassination at what would then obviously become the last meeting of the Parallel Campaign), the novel had to remain unfinished for strictly internal reasons.

The Man without Qualities is a work that, for all its biting irony, struggles to achieve not a distance from the world, but an adequacy to the world's inherent complexity. The problem, in its simplest terms, is that the exclusion of the war turns the various contradictory futures projected by the book's different characters into permanently available possibilities. That, in turn, makes the novel itself permanently unresolvable into an outcome of any kind, since the choice of an ending counter to the real, historical one would have the intolerable effect of relegating the entirety of The Man without Qualities to the realm of the fantastical. Musil was trapped between closure and counterhistory: closure would mean ending the story with the war, counterhistory would mean allowing the empire to continue indefinitely, and neither solution was acceptable. In The Enthusiasts, one of the characters cries out, "But then life always makes you choose between two possibilities, and you always feel: One is missing! Always one—the uninvented third possibility."[30] But Musil, to his dismay, found that his novel, too, was making him choose between two equally inadequate possibilities. Inventing a third one was the hopeless goal that he had set himself in order to end the novel on his own terms, and he preferred leaving everything in fragments rather than imposing an artificial solution in which he could not believe. The tension between closure and counterhistory is actually symmetrical with that of wanting both the stability of das rechte Leben and the permanent fluidity of essayism. It is equally impossible to narrate the war or to trace the lineaments of a utopian way of life entirely "in the subjunctive case." Moreover, a resolution in the text that remained entirely private but had no correspondence in or influence upon the public world would have been unsatisfactory and, by Musil's standards, unprincipled. That is no doubt why he deliberately rejected what would have been the readily narratable, but purely aesthetic solution of having Ulrich decide to write about his failed attempt to find *das rechte Leben* in a book that we retroactively understand is the very novel we have just finished reading. Such a sub-Proustian strategy had no appeal for Musil, in part because he was unconvinced about the redemptive power of art and in part because doing so would risk collapsing the indispensable difference between Ulrich and the narrator. But precisely the same reasons make even the illuminations of what Ulrich and Agathe call their "holy conversations" on the nature of love impossible to use as a conclusion. Tempted though he clearly was to abandon the novel's public and historical issues for the inwardness of Ulrich's and Agathe's union, Musil ultimately decided, on what I think were primarily ethical grounds, to make clear that even these two marvelously prepared lovers ultimately fail to sustain the "incomparable birth of the spirit out of darkness."[31] If too much were claimed for it, Agathe's and Ulrich's love would end up providing an emotional-erotic "answer" to his quest in precisely the same way that a successful "slogan" would solve the Parallel Campaign's search for a unifying national theme, and hence it would be just as vulnerable to essayistic mockery.

And yet, because they are not made to serve as the climactic revelations on which the novel ends, the posthumous fragments about Ulrich's and Agathe's relationship are able to contain some of the book's most moving passages. The satiric tone of the earlier portions drops away. Musil's spiritual yearning begins to penetrate Ulrich's and Agathe's discussions, and so does his extensive reading in the Church Fathers and Christian mystics. Finally their "understanding gives way to irrepressible astonishment."[32] Their love story encompasses intellect, sexual passion, transcendence, and rootedness in the world in a way that, with the sole exception of Rilke's late poetry, is unique in postmedieval literature. Many of their dialogues are set in the garden of the house they now share, and in Ulrich's astonishment at his unexpected happiness, Musil undoubtedly intended us to hear an echo of the Song of Solomon's wonderful phrase, "A garden inclosed is my sister, my spouse" (Song of Sol. 4:12, King James Bible). The intense inwardness of some of Ulrich's and Agathe's meditations come close to finding a prose equivalent for the interpenetration between subject and object, self and world, that the *Duino Elegies* celebrate. Sometimes, in reading these chapters, it is as if we are encountering a consciousness simultaneously imbued with the ecstatic longing of a great mystic and the fastidious rationality of a master logician:

> Not only do external relationships melt away and re-form in the
> whispering enclosures of light and shadow, but the inner

relationships, too, move closer together in a new way ... And it is not the mouth that pours out its adoration but the body, which, from head to foot, is stretched taut in exaltation above the darkness of the earth and beneath the light of the heavens, oscillating between two stars. And the whispering with one's companion is full of a quite unknown sensuality, which is not the sensuality of an individual human being but of all that is earthly, of all that penetrates perception and sensation, the suddenly revealed tenderness of the world that incessantly touches all our senses and is touched by them.[33]

For the first time in the book, there are extended dialogues in which it is not always Ulrich's voice that is endowed with expository authority. Agathe often helps Ulrich understand his own experiences by giving him a series of images that come closer to what he is feeling and thinking than any of his own attempts at a more comprehensive formulation:

I suggest you try looking at a mirror in the night: it's dark, it's black, you see almost nothing at all; and yet this nothing is something quite distinctly different from the nothing of the rest of the darkness. You sense the glass, the doubling of depth, some kind of remnant of the ability to shimmer—and yet you perceive nothing at all![34]

How do you bring closure to what is, by definition, provisional? At their best, these fragmentary chapters are working toward a new mode of writing that might be called ecstatic essayism, so deliberately do they take up and rework in a heightened key some of the fundamental motifs of earlier sections. The startling shifts in Musil's tone, from analytic to imagistic, and from aloofly ironical to soaringly impassioned, come very close to fashioning a convincing linguistic correlative for the union of lucidity and self-transcendence that Ulrich and Agathe set out to find. But Musil's language also shows the gradual winding down of that transcendence, its erosion by the forces of exhaustion and enervation. A private revelation, even one as intense and as seemingly earned as Ulrich's and Agathe's, is shown to be as vulnerable to the laws of entropy as the society the lovers had sought to leave behind. Nowhere is Musil's integrity more visible than in his refusal to make these two figures, in whom he himself had clearly invested so many of his own hopes as well as the whole destiny of his novel, emerge as convincing alternatives to the quotidian, historical reality of the other characters. Musil's novel lets us glimpse the flicker of a possible, redemptive integrity, but at the end, it returns us to the moment before the catastrophe with which the whole book began. In a way, nothing has happened in the course of this immense, incomplete, and uncompletable novel. But like Agathe's mirror, we are profoundly different for having looked at that nothing with receptive eyes. In its deliberate failure to cohere into a definable plot, *The Man without Qualities* explicitly reveals itself, in a way few novels of comparable ambition do, to be written not only *about* history, but from *within* it as well.

Earlier, I quoted Musil's injunction to himself never to permit his sense of irony to serve as merely the facile demonstration of an isolate superiority. Musilian irony must always "contain an element of suffering in it,"[35] precisely because irony and suffering are the direct emotional and stylistic correlates of Musil's demand for precision and soul. The whole of *The Man without Qualities* shows how simultaneously potent and fragile that amalgam can be. Musil placed extraordinary, indeed impossible, demands on himself as a writer and thinker, but he understood better than almost anyone else how much still remained to be done before we can achieve a way to talk about what matters most to us without relying on outworn premises and discredited conventions. For Musil, everything, including the shape and rhythm of our own sentences, should have the freshness of a new discovery. His definition of good writing in the *Diaries* has a generosity of responsiveness to the specific moment that is almost profligate in its refusal to keep anything back: "Something is well-written if, after some time, it strikes one as alien—one would be incapable of writing it that way a second time. Such an idea (expression) did not come from the fund that is available for daily expenditure."[36] To read Musil is to encounter both the risks and the sheer excitement of that kind of writing.

NOTES

1. Robert Musil, *Der Mann ohne Eigenschaften. Roman*, 2 vols., ed. Adolf Frisé (Reinbek: Rowohlt, 1978); *The Man without Qualities*, 2 vols., trans. Sophie Wilkins and Burton Pike (New York: Alfred A. Knopf, 1995). All subsequent references are to these editions and will be acknowledged with the German volume and page number first (as *MoE*), followed by the English volume and page number (as *MwQ*).

2. Stern, *Dear Purchase*, p. 182.

3. Musil, *Tagebücher*, vol. 1, p. 667; *Diaries: 1899–1942*, p. 328.

4. Musil, "Die Schwärmer," in *Prosa und Stücke*, p. 392; *The Enthusiasts*, p. 88.

5. Musil, *MoE*, vol. 1, p. 40; *MwQ*, vol. 1, p. 37.

6. Musil, *MoE*, vol. 1, p. 103; *MwQ*, vol. 1, p. 106.

7. Musil, *MoE*, vol. 1, p. 905; *MwQ*, vol. 2, p. 982. Musil here wittily inverts one of the most famous tag lines in German literature: Faust's outcry that "two souls, alas! are living in my breast / Each one longs to be severed from the other" (*Faust*, part 1, lines 1112–13).

8. Musil, *MoE*, vol. 2, p. 1094; *MwQ*, vol. 2, p. 1190.

9. Musil, "Das hilflose Europa," in *Prosa und Stücke*, p. 1092; "Helpless Europe," in *Precision and Soul*, p. 131.

10. Musil, "Der deutsche Mensch als Symptom,"; in *Prosa und Stücke*, p. 1359; "The German as Symptom," in *Precision and Soul*, p. 155.

11. The function of the various nicknames applied to the characters, especially to the women in the book (Diotima, Bonadea, etc.) deserves fuller consideration than it has so far received in the critical literature.

12. Musil, *MoE*, vol. 2, pp. 1130, 1084, 1089; vol. 1, p. 755; *MwQ*, vol. 2, pp. 1229, 1179, 1184, 820.

13. Musil, *MoE*, vol. 1, p. 111; *MwQ*, vol. 1, p. 115.

14. Musil, *MoE*, vol. 1, pp. 247–57; *MwQ*, vol. 1, pp. 267–77.

15. Musil, *MoE*, vol. 1, p. 653; *MwQ*, vol. 1, p. 712.

16. Musil, *MoE*, vol. 1, p. 394; *MwQ*, vol. 1, p. 427.

17. W. B. Yeats, "Among School Children," in *The Collected Poems of W.B. Yeats* (New York: Macmillan, 1956), p. 214.

18. Musil, *MoE*, vol. 1, p. 394; *MwQ*, vol. 1, p. 427.

19. Musil, *MoE*, vol. 2, p. 1084; *MwQ*, vol. 2, p. 1179.

20. Musil, *Tagebücher*, vol. 1, p. 973; *Diaries: 1899–1942*, p. 485.

21. Musil, *MoE*, vol. 1, p. 89; *MwQ*, vol. 1, p. 90.

22. Musil, *MoE*, vol. 1, p. 178; *MwQ*, vol. 1, p. 190.

23. Musil, *MoE*, vol. 1, p. 741; *MwQ*, vol. 2, p. 805.

24. Musil, *MoE*, vol. 1, p. 593; *MwQ*, vol. 1, p. 647.

25. Musil, *Tagebücher*, vol. 1, p. 354; *Diaries: 1899–1942*, p. 209.

26. I have analyzed this aspect of the novel at length in *Foregone Conclusions: Against Apocalyptic History* (Berkeley: University of California Press, 1994).

27. Musil, *MoE*, vol. 1, p. 466; *MwQ*, vol. l, p. 507.

28. Musil, *MoE*, vol. 1, pp. 20, 359; *MwQ*, vol. 1, pp. 15, 390.

29. Musil, *MoE*, vol. 1, p. 19; *MwQ*, vol. 1, p. 14.

30. Musil, *Prosa und Stücke*, p. 311; *The Enthusiasts*, p. 16.

31. Musil, *MoE*, vol. 2, p. 1084; *MwQ*, vol. 2, p. 1179.

32. Musil, *MoE*, vol. 2, p. 1090; *MwQ*, vol. 2, p. 1186.

33. Musil, *MoE*, vol. 2, p. 1084; *MwQ*, vol. 2, p. 1179.

34. Musil, *MoE*, vol. 2, p. 1089–90; *MwQ*, vol. 2, p. 1185.

35. Musil, *Tagebücher*, vol. 1, p. 973; *Diaries: 1899–1942*, p. 485.

36. Musil, *Tagebücher*, vol. 1, p. 722; *Diaries: 1899–1942*, p. 378.

STEFAN JONSSON

A Story with Many Ends:
Narratological Observations

M usil's hero enacts an existential attitude and an ethical program. In the previous chapter I analyzed Ulrich in this role. I treated him as a human-like figure and explained how he responds to the rationalized lift world of urban modernity. But Ulrich is also a lens, a perspective, and a point of view. He is not only part of the subject matter but also the cognitive and narrative instrument through which the reader accesses the world of the story. That Ulrich is such a dodging figure is because he occupies a dual position, both the human-like character and the frame within which the other characters are portrayed.

The Musilian subject must consequently be interpreted on several levels. In order to find out what the novel says, we must learn how it works. In this chapter I will examine how the narrative form generates a temporal and spatial experience, from which we may deduce a certain structure of subjectivity. In brief, I want to analyze the subject as an effect of narrative production. My focus will be on the first nineteen chapters of the novel, which constitute the section called "A Sort of Introduction," because it is here that Musil's narrator establishes the laws of time and space that govern the novelistic representation as a whole.

From *Subject Without Nation: Robert Musil and the History of Modern Identity*. © by 2000 Duke University Press.

Expressive Realism and Beyond

Every reader senses that *The Man without Qualities* does not conform to the mimetic representations that can be found in, for instance, nineteenth-century realist novels. Also, it deviates from Musil's early prose, the novel *Die Verwirrungen des Zöglings Törless* (1906; *The Confusions of Young Törless*) and the two novellas *Die Vollendung der Liebe* (*The Completion of Love*) and *Die Versuchung der sullen Veronika* (*The Temptation of Quiet Veronika*) that he published in 1911 under the title *Vereinigungen* (*Unions*), in which a mimetic rendering of the external world is punctuated by astounding sections of psychological narration. Nothing in *The Man without Qualities* can be trusted as true or real. The novel speaks in several voices, each contesting the others. The text operates with satire, irony, and self-irony. Undermining every reliable arrangement of events, it shakes the foundations of reality. Indeed, there is no privileged viewpoint from which to discern the causes of the subtle displacements that gradually transform the political and social sphere of Vienna, a sphere populated by people living among illusions and motivated by illusions, who move forward with the same slow sureness as Hermann Broch's sleepwalkers, until they stumble on the threshold of war.

A passage at the beginning of the novel describes this state of affairs: "Time was on the move.... But nobody knew where time was headed. And it was not always clear what was up or down, what was going forward or backward" (*MWQ* 7 / *MoE* 13). This passage is meant to capture a specific zeitgeist. It is a preliminary diagnosis of that "mysterious malady of the times," evoked a few chapters later, which lies at the core of the complications rendered by the plot. Yet, the passage also draws attention to a formal feature of the representation: this is a narrative that relativizes categories like *up* and *down*, *forward* and *backward*, *truth* and *falsity*, *good* and *bad*. The meaning of these categories comes to depend on what perspective the reader assumes.

True, the narrative structure of every novel integrates a multiplicity of perspectives, often linked to different characters, who serve as mouthpieces of different worldviews. Although these perspectives may be contradictory, they are in general balanced by the narrative structure as such, for they are all organized by a central voice and vision. In Catherine Belsey's words, there is a "hierarchy of discourses." The privileged discourse is normally that of the narrator, who has the power to arrange and evaluate the other discourses incorporated into the novel, typically by presenting them as thoughts or statements coming from the characters.[1] This structure, moreover, is modeled on a certain conception of reality and human character to which both the narrator and the reader must adhere if the mimetic illusion is to hold. As long as the narrator does not violate his poetic license, making sure he does not transgress the limits of an established conception of reality, his status as the omniscient, implicit author manipulating his fictitious figures is concealed behind the mimetic illusion itself, which now assumes a lifelike quality, and its characters start to address the reader as human beings of flesh and blood.[2]

The narrative form resulting from this ordering of various discourses and characters may be called "classical realism." According to Philippe Hamon, the realist text is characterized by a double tendency, driving the text in two directions at once.[3] First, the novel charts a social world with its specific topography, habits, conflicts, and symbolic systems. This is the horizontal tendency of the text, through which it establishes an inventory of a particular social sector. This tendency is strongly felt in *The Man without Qualities*, which presents a broad panorama of Viennese life and thought.[4] But a novel cannot just keep adding material, characters, and events, or else it would become a formless encyclopedia. This is why there must also be a vertical tendency at work, one that organizes and interprets the surface of society, stabilizing its various manifestations by leading them back to a deeper law or structure. In order to realize this tendency, the narrative usually turns an object or a character into a representative of the social body as a whole. In this way, the object and character in the realist novel fulfill two functions. On the one hand, they are knots in a web of numberless other elements that make up the extensive totality of the world. On the other hand, they are signs indicating those deeper social structures, historical processes, or psychological laws that constitute the meaning of the represented totality.

The successful coordination of the two tendencies results, in Hamon's view, in a realist narrative. In such a narrative, each object and character is independent and self-sufficient, and at the same time an expression of a hidden totality, a symptom of a concealed infrastructure that gives meaning and stability to the ephemeral present moment of the story. Hamon's definition of realism confirms what I said about the bildungsroman in the first chapter. The bildungsroman demonstrates a convergence between the horizontal axis—the detailed account of the complicated and multifarious social world through which the characters move—and the vertical axis— which ascribes a historical and symbolic meaning, a specific "typicality," to certain characters and events. The realist novel turns the two axes into mirrors of one another. Joining forces, they construct a mimetic illusion that is as convincing as reality itself, and which, moreover, shows that this reality is meaningful.

What happens if the formal innovations of *The Man without Qualities* are analyzed against the background of this model of realist expressivity? As we shall see, the novel does not coordinate the horizontal and the vertical tendencies. On the contrary, it brings them into contradiction. The process by which the realist novel turns the individual and the social into expressions of one other is inverted in *The Man without Qualities*; indeed, subject and society negate each other.

THE IMPOSSIBLE ART OF REPORTING THE WEATHER

Musil's novel establishes a perplexing ambiguity already from the beginning. Although the first chapter has the title "From which, remarkably enough, nothing develops," it makes at least two things clear. First, it introduces us, in some awkward way, to the setting: Vienna, 1913. Second, and more important, it institutes a discrepancy between an authoritative representation purporting to convey objective knowledge and a narrative mode accounting for the perspective of the particular individual.[5] In the opening paragraph, there is first an extensive account of the meteorological situation over Europe: "A barometric low hung over the Atlantic. It moved eastward toward a high-pressure area over Russia without as yet showing any inclination to bypass this high in a northerly direction." Saturated by a terminology intelligible only to the specialist, this description expands over almost half a page. Suddenly, it is translated into ordinary language: "It was a fine day in August 1913" (*MWQ* 3 / *MoE* 9). The first register is scientific and seemingly objective; the other anthropocentric and invested with human emotion and intentionality, as indicated by the adjective "fine" (*schön*).

When the narrator juxtaposes the individual's ordinary experience of the weather with an enumeration of the countless climatological factors that make this experience possible, the result is, of course, a demonstration of the insufficient precision of the former. This feature is then amplified in the following chapter. A fairly precise description of the architectural style of Ulrich's palace is juxtaposed with the individual reaction to the same building ("Ah!"), thus highlighting the sheer banality of a subjective experience that cannot communicate the richness of reality.

As the first chapter unfolds, these two discursive registers generate two narrative modes running side by side. One is fixed to an impersonal perspective, scanning reality from above. The other accommodates the perspective of the individual character. The textual fabric constituted by these two narrative modes may easily be untied. By erasing the sentences generated by the opposite mode, we may transcribe chapter 1 in two versions. The first would look like this:

A barometric low hung over the Atlantic. It moved eastward toward a high-pressure area over Russia without as yet showing any inclination to bypass this high in a northerly direction.... Automobiles shot out of deep, narrow streets into the shallows of bright squares.... Hundreds of noises wove themselves into a wiry texture of sound.... Like all big cities it was made up of irregularity, change, forward spurts, failures to keep step, collisions of objects and interests, punctuated by unfathomable silences; made up of pathways and untrodden ways, of one great rhythmic beat as well as the chronic discord and mutual displacement of all its contending rhythms.... Something had spun around, falling sideways, and come to a skidding halt—a heavy truck, as it turned out, which had braked so sharply that it was now stranded with one wheel on the curb.... Now the siren of an approaching ambulance could be heard.... The victim was lifted onto a stretcher and both together were then slid into the ambulance.... People dispersed, almost with the justified impression that they had just witnessed something entirely lawful and orderly. (*MWQ* 3ff.* / *MoE* 9ff.)

If this is the view of an eye observing things from a great distance, a more pedestrian experience of the same reality generates a different story:

It was a fine day in August 1913 ... in the Imperial and Royal City of Vienna.... The two people who were walking up one of its wide, bustling avenues ... belonged to a privileged social class, which could be seen on their distinguished bearing, style of dress, and way of conversing with each other.... Their names might have been Ermelinda Tuzzi and Arnheim.... The pair now came to a sudden stop when they saw a rapidly gathering crowd in front of them.... The lady and her companion had also come close enough to see something of the victim over the heads and bowed backs...... "According to American statistics," the gentleman said, "one hundred ninety thousand people are killed every year by cars and four hundred fifty thousand are injured." "Do you think he's dead?" his companion asked, having still the unjustified feeling that she had experienced something unusual. (*MWQ* 3ff.* / *MoE* 9ff.)

The impersonal tone of the first version makes it sound like a news report communicating facts. The second conforms to the codes of the narrative discourse of the classical novel. The narrator could of course have constructed a narrative in which the two registers were inseparable, letting the whole give meaning to the part, and using the description of the part to enhance the understanding of the whole. But in *The Man without Qualities* there is no such gradual rapprochement. The novel evinces the fractures between the two narrative modes. Passing from the panoramic survey of the city to the perspective of an individual within that city, the narrator makes a point of indicating all other similar and equally possible passages between general and particular. Thus we are told that it is a beautiful day in August 1913. Juxtaposed with the meteorological account, however, this piece of information also transmits the opposite message: it could have been any year. We are told that the city in question is Vienna. But the narrator states that the city's name is unimportant, for it could have been any city. And as soon as the pedestrians seem to have been identified ("Let us assume," the narrator suggests, "that they are called Arnheim and Ermelinda Tuzzi"), this identification is ruled out as an impossibility—"because in August Frau Tuzzi was still in Bad Aussee with her husband and Dr. Arnheim was still in Constantinople" (*MWQ* 4 / *MoE* 10). Therefore, the narrator continues, we are "left to wonder who they were." But of course, the names of these persons are enigmatic only insofar as they could be anybody. The point is that their names do not matter. They are ants in an anthill. What counts in this case study of street life is not any particular identity or personality but the description of a position that could belong to any person with any identity. The particular—be it a place, an individual, or an object—becomes an accidental instance of a general totality which is independent of its parts. Consequently, a narrative representation focalized through these parts conveys no knowledge about the whole which nonetheless determines them.

If this applies to the individual, the place, and the object, it also applies to the status of the event within the depicted social world. Just as the specific identities of the pedestrians add nothing to the whole, the accident they witness does not have any significance in itself. It is merely an example of normal life in the era of crowds and traffic—"something entirely lawful and orderly." Reducing the injured man to a statistical fact, the gentleman witnessing the accident is the mouthpiece of the objective and authoritative voice organizing most of the chapter. However, the lady accompanying him makes a contrary assessment of the same event, "having still the unjustified feeling that she had experienced something unusual." The narrator now steps in to evaluate these opposing ways of judging the event. To see it from the standpoint of the general, as "entirely lawful and orderly," is said to be justified (*berechtigt*). The feeling of having witnessed something unique, a feeling attributed to the woman, is, on the other hand, an "unjustified feeling." Comparing the experiential "feeling" (*Gefühl*) with the impersonal "impression" (*Eindruck*) of the same event, the narrative suggests that an adequate account of it rules out individual experience, which is rendered as a bizarre deviation or a too personal view.

Yet, in order to invalidate individual experience by proving its insignificance within a broader view of society, this experience must all the same be evoked as a narrative event in its own right. Thus, through the perspective of the woman, individual experience is at least momentarily affirmed. The tension inherent in the dual narrative mode organizing the text is thereby preserved. The two representations of that beautiful day in August 1913 remain disjunctive. Scientific objectivity and subjective experience are displayed as two incommensurable approaches to the world.

The conflict between *objective knowledge* and *experiential knowing* is a key theme in Musil's work. According to Musil, the natural sciences were ahead of other realms of thought, which did not operate with the same precision. However, Musil did not see the difference between the two as a distinction between rationality and irrationality. Rather, the difference was constituted by the fact that objective science, linking fact to fact and argument to argument, circumvents the self and excludes subjective factors. Objectivity is therefore necessarily abstract, Musil states in his essay "Helpless Europe" (1922). It sacrifices the inner aspects of objects: "*We exclude our ego, our self, from our thoughts and actions.* Therein lies, of course, the essence of our objectivity; it connects things one with the other, and even where it sets us in relation to them, or, as in psychology, takes us as its very object, it does so in a way that excludes the personality" (*PS* 131 / *GW* 2:1092).

The epistemological conflict in the first two chapters is thus not merely a collision between belief and knowledge, or delusion and reality. It is a confrontation between subjectivity and objectivity, as Musil defines it in the passage above. In the novel, the function of each of these epistemologies is to bring the opposing one into crisis by contradicting it. In his discussion of so-called *narrative moods*, Gérard Genette has indicated how conflicts of values and knowledge are articulated in literary texts. Just as verbs have grammatical moods, Genette argues, so is each narrative governed by a certain *mood*, which determines the "point of view from which the life or the action is looked at."[6] In contradistinction to the more general *mode*, a narrative mood thus designates a specific narratological device, which always entails a *perspective*. The tension we have observed in Musil's novel can hence be described as a result of a narrative that shifts between two narrative moods, each corresponding to a particular perspective on the world, one invested with feeling and interest, the other without such qualities.

Crucially, this entails another opposition, also at play in Musil's text. For the same abstraction that is carried out with respect to the perceiving subject can also be executed with regard to the object perceived. An object or an event can be seen either as a unique phenomenon characterized by its own irreducible essence, or as a relationally determined effect of the whole. On this level, the conflict between objective knowledge and experiential knowing becomes a conflict between perceiving an event or a person as a structurally determined fact or as an expression of essence.

In a narrative text, moreover, the issue of perceiving is of course transformed into a question of representing, or narrating. In fact, the first paragraphs of the novel constitute a subtle attempt to write a narrative of facticity, a story purged of experiential aspects. This narrative mood is juxtaposed with a subjective and perceptual mood according to which the world is vibrating with human intentions. The two narrative moods can be characterized by literally distinguishing the two perspectives involved. The first is a story told from the point of view of a cloud. The second is a story told from the point of view of a person experiencing the weather. The first evokes the countless circumstances contributing to a particular meteorological situation and suggests that the addition of new factors would have created a different situation, thus conveying an idea of other possible situations, which could just as well have been realized. The second tells how the subject responds to a situation that he or she must accept as a necessary reality.

Already in the first chapter, then, the narrative's horizontal tendency, enumerating the factors that affect a particular situation, is brought into conflict with its vertical tendency, accounting for the meaning of this situation. We no longer have two perspectives complementing each other and expressing a totality that encompasses both of them; we have two perspectives that are mutually exclusive.

ON THE DIFFERENCE BETWEEN AN ACCIDENT AND AN INCIDENT

The first two chapters of *The Man without Qualities* suggest the presence of a solar eye looking down on the world. Having observed the meteorological situation over Europe, the narrator's perspective narrows. It settles over Vienna, fixes a particular street, and follows two persons walking toward the crowd gathered around the man who has been hit by a lorry. In chapter 2, the narrative trajectory moves further along the same street until it finally stops in front of "a sort of little château with short wings, a hunting lodge or rococo love nest of times past" (*MWQ* 6 / *MoE* 12). Scanning the exterior of this building, the ocular imagery of the narrative directs the reader toward a certain window of the house. Standing in the window, and now introduced for the first time, is the man without qualities.

It would seem as if the divine machinery, having launched the narrative and targeted the window, is dismantled as soon as the man in the window, Ulrich, appears and begins to act on his own. Strangely, however, Ulrich continues the same visual operation, as though the narrator had only cut to a new camera angle in his protocinematographic spectacle.[7] Like the solar eye observing Europe from above, Ulrich scientifically examines the vehicles and pedestrians in the street below, reflecting on the "antlike" character of the crowd. What catches his attention is the enormous amount of energy expended on trivial acts such as crossing the street or rushing to catch the trolley. Ulrich's interest is arrested not by any individual phenomenon but by the process as a whole. He perceives the world as a scientist collecting data. Imagining himself as part of the machinery, he then makes a discouraging summation: "'No matter what you do,' the man without qualities thought with a shrug, 'within this mare's nest of forces at work, it doesn't make the slightest difference!'" (*MWQ* 7 / *MoE* 13). Here, too, as in chapter 1, individual agency is negligible when seen from the perspective of the observer who reduces individuality and particularity to statistical facts.

Yet, this conclusion, too, is challenged as the narrative switches to another mood or perspective. A few pages later it so happens that Ulrich is victimized by the same street life he previously surveyed with the cool gaze of the scientist. One night on his way home, he is knocked unconscious and robbed by three hooligans. This assault, which leaves Ulrich injured on the sidewalk, echoes the accident in chapter 1. The assault brings out the contradictory nature of Ulrich's attitude. In his role as a detached observer in chapter 2, he formulated a maxim: "No matter what you do, it doesn't make the slightest difference." Still, as soon as he walks out into the street, he must violate his own maxim, thus reasserting the importance of agency and individual experience. His actions are no longer indifferent. He must react on the actions of others, and he must, indeed, react in the "right" way, or else he may not get home without being robbed of his wallet. There are no intermediary stages between these attitudes in Musil's novel. In fact, the narrator emphasizes the discontinuity between them and implies that this generates two different stories. In chapter 1, a serious accident is reduced to a mere incident. In chapter 7, an incident—Ulrich's fight with the hooligans—is presented as a matter of life and death.

Meanwhile, we notice that the tension is transposed from form to content as the narrative moves from chapter 1 to the episodes involving Ulrich in chapters 2 and 7. In the first chapter, the tension occurs at the level of cognition and narrative modality. The event is represented as both negligible and exceptional, depending on whether the narrator uses the detached account of the scientist or the omniscient vision of the narrator of the classical novel. In chapters 2 and 7 the same tension reappears as Ulrich's ambivalent attitude toward his involvement in social affairs, or even as a choice between two ethical programs: stoic resignation or committed vocation. Thus what previously presented itself as two cognitive, perceptual, and narrative moods is now recorded as two ethical or even ontological moods, that is, as a conflict between two ways of *acting* and *being*. Crucially, Ulrich cannot be situated on either side of this tension. He embodies the struggle, is the container of opposing attitudes toward the world.

The presence of two conflicting narrative moods is hence linked to the presence of two conflicting ethical standards. On the one hand, the subject can be seen as the origin and source of meaning, knowledge, action, and history. In this view, social formations are constituted by free subjects expressing themselves and associating with others, gradually realizing an essence inherent in their human nature. On the other hand, the subject can be seen as a product of already existing social and cultural formations, as bound by tradition, habits and history. In this view, the subject becomes a replicable unit. My analysis in the previous chapter showed that Ulrich was left in suspension between these two notions of subjectivity. The expressivist notion that regards the subject as the inner source of meaning was just as unacceptable as the functionalist notion that defines it as a product of external pressures.

THE NARRATION OF EVENTS

Some chapters later, Ulrich visits his old friends Walter and Clarisse, who are now introduced to the reader. Ulrich and Clarisse go for a stroll in the garden. They have barely begun talking when the scene suddenly is interrupted by a long retrospective section providing information about Walter's life. Serving as a summary of the past, this analepsis covers some three pages. It ends as abruptly as it started, and the reader awakens anew to the present moment of the story, realizing that the conversation between Ulrich and Clarisse still goes on; the narrator's swift move to another temporal level was just an interruption. In this way, a scene with a duration of no more than a few minutes envelops a narrative sequence representing many years.

As the chapter ends, the conversation seems concluded. In the following chapter, the narrator abandons Ulrich and Clarisse as well as the mimetic mode of representation, reflecting instead on the "cultural revolution" at the turn of the century. Then comes a chapter containing a similar reflection, now presented from Ulrich's point of view. The conversation between Ulrich and Clarisse seems firmly anchored in the story's past. But in the next chapter the reader is oddly enough transported back to the same evening. Again, we must conclude that everything told since we last saw Ulrich and Clarisse was an intermission in the story. Two chapters have passed, decades have elapsed, the cultural situation has been thoroughly analyzed, yet Ulrich and Clarisse still remain, exchanging thoughts, in the same corner of the garden. The present moment expands to enclose decades of action. To be sure, this is a general strategy of modernist narrative, masterly developed by Proust and Woolf, and perhaps most congenially expressed in Joyce's *Ulysses*, where twenty-four hours equal eternity.

Had the narrator adhered to the codes of the classical novel, he would perhaps have used the mimetic scene depicting Ulrich and Clarisse's dialogue as a narrative device to communicate the information that is now conveyed by his own voice. In Musil's novel, however, scenes of mimetic representations are rare. They mostly function as narrative relays leading from one discursive and diegetic section to another. But they also constitute brief periods of rest as they bring the narrative back to the story's present: they provide temporal and spatial coordinates that build the narrative's syntagmatic axis. Thus they help the reader retain the impression of a narrative progression and regain his or her orientation in the fictional universe.

The mimetic representation of dialogue is only one of a number of comparable narrative devices developed in the realist novel that *The Man without Qualities* reappropriates for new purposes. The nineteen chapters in the introductory part rely on the entire tool kit of the old storyteller. Ancient and approved narrative conventions—codes designed to begin a story, to present a character, a scene, a setting, or an event—are picked up and rehearsed, only to be dropped, much in the same way as happens in chapter 14, where that otherwise privileged form of novelistic narration, the dialogue, in this case of Ulrich and Clarisse, is abandoned as soon as it is put to use.

We have already seen how a standard opening clause—"It was a fine day in August 1913"—is held up to ridicule when confronted with the narrator's amassing of meteorological data. The same fate befalls conventional phrases of similar kinds, presented only to be undermined: "The man without qualities whose story is being told here" (*MWQ* 13 / *MoE* 18); "When he set about putting his house in order, as the Bible has it" (*MWQ* 14 / *MoE* 19); "At the age when one still attaches great importance to everything connected with tailors and barbers" (*MWQ* 26 / *MoE* 31); "It turned out that Bonadea, too, yearned for great ideas" (*MWQ* 38 / *MoE* 41); "The Moosbrugger case was currently much in the news" (*MWQ* 67 / *MoE*

67); "So the time passed" (*MWQ* 77 / *MoE* 77). The satirical effects of Musil's narrative are to a large extent produced by the witty insertion of older narrative idioms; the obsoleteness of which is revealed when confronted with the realities of modern life.[8] *The Man without Qualities* exhausts battalions of received ideas and literary paradigms that once gave meaning to human existence. Its use of conventional narrative codes to wrap a content or an argument for which these conventions are insufficient creates comic effects that produce a state of indeterminacy, in which various discursive registers collide and are undone.

The point is that the narrator can neither make do with these codes, nor do without them. They are inadequate for representing modern experience, and yet indispensable because they are the only ones at hand. One crucial aspect of their indispensability has already been mentioned. These codes constitute the text as a recognizable aesthetic artifact, continually checking and confirming the contract between reader and narrator. But they also establish a certain measure of internal coherence, without which the text would become a mosaic of fragments.

There are, to be sure, strong tendencies of fragmentation in *The Man without Qualities*. In the first part of the novel there is no unfolding through time and no plot, but a constellation of narrative segments—biographical material, psychological analyses, political overviews, historical expositions, scenes from bourgeois life, a report of a criminal case, and a letter to Ulrich from his father—which all contribute their shares to the story. These pieces do not form an integrated whole. Yet together they construct something like a hero, a subject. It would be wrong to call this construction a montage, however. In modernist textual montages, plot disappears or goes underground. What is left on the manifest level is the other material of the narrative—segments of dialogue, disconnected pieces of traditional narrative paradigms, mimetic scenes where characters act and speak, ideas picked from the storehouses of cultural history—which the reader must recombine in conformity with a subtext that he or she must invent.[9]

In *The Man without Qualities*, traditional plot is also disrupted. But this does not produce a plotless representation. The fragmented character of Musil's novel derives not from the fact that the story is hidden underground but from the fact that the story is continuously interrupted. Ernest Hemingway once said that his stories only showed the tip of an iceberg, nine-tenths of the action being situated under the surface. In Musil's novel, these nine-tenths erupt to the surface. What in the realist novel used to be a finite sequence of long mimetic scenes is in Musil transformed into a series of disconnected frames through which the narrator breaks in as he wishes, in order to supply an ongoing interpretation of characters, scenes, and events.

It is not without reason that most critics have observed how *The Man without Qualities* sways uneasily between a comedy of manners and a philosophical treatise, while the author himself admitted that he was not interested in specific facts and events. "What interests me is the culturally typical!" (*GW* 2:939). The narrated moments that construct the story are thus reduced to a subordinate role. They seem to emerge from a discursive magma consisting of an infinite narratorial commentary that constructs its own temporality and assumes any perspective.

This is how the repeated interruption of the conversation between Ulrich and Clarisse finally should be understood. Their conversation constitutes a segment of an unfolding story. But this story is just a grid, the squares of which are filled in by the narrator's commentary. In most novels, mimetic scenes constitute the greater part of the text. Individual and society are stitched together by a story that represents their continual interaction. In Musil, the real action takes place when interaction is postponed, during the intermissions, when the narrator is left to himself.

As we saw in the previous chapter, social reality in Musil's novel equals the dull and repetitive realm of das Seinesgleichen. The point of the narrator's constant interruptions of the story is precisely to defamiliarize this realm. The representation of society, which was the main object of the realist novel, hence becomes Musil's pretext for entering an underlying space of possibilities that are suppressed by das Seinesgleichen. It is in order to articulate these possibilities that the Musilian narrator exposes the vacuity of the narrative frames that make the story of the realist novel cohere.[10] This is the reason for his continuous negation and ironic subversion of cultural codes, discourses, ideas, and habits. This cultural debris must be cleared away, for it hides more than it reveals.

THE NARRATION OF TIME

The reader of *The Man without Qualities* may get the impression that the story, just like any other novel, unfolds through time. First, the hero, Ulrich, is introduced. Second, the hero is characterized: he is a man without qualities who has already begun several careers without liking any of them and who has now chosen to take a year's leave from life in order to reach a decision about his future. Third, the hero is sent out on a mission: he receives a letter from his father urging him to make appointments with influential persons. On closer consideration, the reader realizes that temporal coordinates dissolve.

In the order of events there is, apart from the supposed ending of the story, August 1914, only one fixed point of reference, August 1913. This date is mentioned on the first page. Chapter 3 states that Ulrich, has recently returned to Vienna and relates how he furnishes his new home. The novel states that he had rented his château, as he "some time ago" (*vor einiger Zeit*) had returned from abroad (*MWQ* 8* / *MoE* 13). One might thus divide the events of Ulrich's life as happening either before or after this return to Vienna. Given that August 1913 is the present moment of the story, Ulrich's return can then be located earlier in 1913. This is a plausible interpretation of "some time ago."

In chapter 13, the narrative again apparently refers to this event in Ulrich's life, revealing his resolution "to take a year's leave of absence from his life" (*MWQ* 44 / *MoE* 47). This decision is made "in another city and street from where he was now, but only a few weeks ago" (*aber erst vor wenigen Wochen*) (*MWQ* 43 / *MoE* 46). Obviously, then, this resolution is made a few weeks before the present of the story time, August 1913, and also before Ulrich moves to his château. However, the narrator has already informed the reader that Ulrich moved to his château "some time ago," and according to a common phenomenological presumption—that the measurement of a period of time becomes less precise the longer that period is—"some time ago" designates a longer period of time than "only a few weeks ago." In order to make sense of Ulrich's past, we must, however, assume the opposite, that "only a few weeks" is more time than "some time" (*einiger Zeit*). Otherwise, Ulrich's decision to return to Vienna would, paradoxically, take place after he had already carried out that decision.

Of course, we can assume that "only a few weeks" signifies more time than "some time." But such a claim is neither reasonable nor practical. Given other instances where the chronology is notoriously vague, it seems plausible to regard this ambiguity as a deliberately fabricated temporal enigma serving to destabilize Ulrich's personality. This impression is magnified by all the chapters where the historical "now"—August 1913—and the temporality of the story are simply abandoned, chapter 4 being the first case in point. There are places in Musil's narrative—Genette would call them instances of *achronic* time—where linear chronology is simply irrelevant. Political and biographic histories implode into one great atemporal event.

With regard to tense and duration, the nineteen chapters in the first section can be divided into three categories: (1) summaries of past events, that is, events taking place before August 1913; (2) mimetic or diegetic representations of events taking place in the present of the story time, that is, in or after August 1913; and (3) "achronic" discourses without any specific temporal relation to the story.

The chapters containing summaries of the past together form a story in which Ulrich emerges as the hero. There is a brief biography of Ulrich's father, fragments of Ulrich's past, particularly of his consecutive careers as officer, engineer, and mathematician. Finally there are the reminiscences of his friendship with Walter at the turn of the century. These pieces of information may readily be organized into one extended, chronologically unfolding narrative following Ulrich from cradle to the age of thirty-two. This is precisely how the life of Ulrich's father is narrated in chapter 3, as an evolutionary history of a person advancing toward maturity and social eminence, as though life were a fulfillment of fate. The difference between this and the representation of Ulrich's life is conspicuous, and this is of course the point. Compare the ease with which the father adjusted to society with the smoothly flowing biographical narrative of chapter 3. Ulrich's father could well be a hero of a bildungsroman or a classical realist novel. By contrast, the labyrinthine character of Ulrich's life, advancing by way of sidetracks and detours, corresponds to the constantly interrupted narrative through which his past is related. As we have seen, the narrative provides different versions of his past, and the order in which this past is narrated is different from the order in which it was lived. Above all, there are no connections demonstrating how one stage in life led to the next, which makes it appear as if the link were gratuitous, decided by chance rather than will, and certainly not by any intrinsic essence expressing itself as personal destiny. Pierre Zima observes that the consecutive accounts of Ulrich's "three attempts to become a great man" should be read as three beginnings, or three variations on the same theme: "that of the bourgeois career."[11] Yet the final product of the story is three equally possible variations of the bourgeois subject—the once unitary individual divided in three. Incidentally, this conforms to the self-understanding of the hero himself. Looking back at his past, "thinking over his time up to that point today, Ulrich might shake his head in wonder, as if someone were to tell him about his previous incarnations" (*MWQ* 35 / *MoE* 38).

This absence of connections and temporal indications also characterizes the chapters dealing with the present of the story time, the second category above. The setting of the first two chapters is the August day in 1913. Then follows a series of chapters describing Ulrich's mistresses, Leona and Bonadea. Finally, chapters 14 through 17 relate Ulrich's visit to Walter and Clarisse, which I have already discussed. Each of these sequences has its own internal chronology, but there is no chronology that establishes the order among them. Does Ulrich's visit to his friends occur before or after that beautiful day in August? Does this take place before or after meeting Bonadea? It is impossible to know. The narrative discourse neglects, even distorts, the temporality of the narrated story. As a result, the narrative logic yields a temporality of its own, independent of historical causality.

This temporal discrepancy is visible not only in the arrangement of the chapters, however. It is even more striking at the microlevel of the text, where the reader finds numerous temporal data but never the overall temporal structure that would allow for a reconstruction of the "real" order of events. Consider the following sentences. "Two weeks later Bonadea had been his mistress for fourteen days" (*MWQ* 26 / *MoE* 30). "The next morning Ulrich got out of bed on his left foot and fished halfheartedly for his slipper with his right" (*MWQ* 43 / *MoE* 46). "Since his return, Ulrich has already been a few times to see his friends Walter and Clarisse, for these two had not left town, although it was summer, and he had not seen them for a number of years" (*MWQ* 45 / *MoE* 47). Such phrases abound in most novels. In order to make sense, however, they must be related to a general chronological table. This table is conspicuously absent from Musil's novel, which makes such seemingly precise chronological data enigmatic, if not absurd. Typically, the reader turns back a few pages, searching in vain for the piece of missing chronological information, only to conclude that Musil's narrator refuses to establish a consistent temporal order.[12]

Events assumed to happen in temporal sequences are thus reshaped by a strong tendency to expand the present to the point where it swallows the past, transforming the latter into raw material for retrospections and interpretations through which the present, in turn, is abolished as a discrete and chronologically identifiable moment. Thereby, the order of das Seinesgleichen is again dissolved, and another level of experience is gradually uncovered. What is left after this derealization is a narrative that does not correspond to familiar models of reality: an event in the near past is located in two different temporal dimensions; a biography is cut in pieces, and the pieces are presented as if they belonged to different protagonists; the present of the story has no progression, constituting instead an achronic space where decades elapse in the course of a conversation. Turning now to the novel's representation of character, I will discuss that particular human subject who may experience time in this peculiar way.

THE NARRATION OF CHARACTER

Let us return to Ulrich and Clarisse and their conversation in the garden on the outskirts of Vienna. Beginning as a dialogue, the scene is interrupted by the narrator, who makes a lengthy digression, only to return suddenly to the same scene, finding Ulrich and Clarisse where he left them some pages earlier. Their dialogue continues, or so it would seem. Yet no words are pronounced. What appears to be said is merely thought, and what is thought, moreover, has the same transparency and intelligibility as anything spoken.

But then again, Ulrich and Clarisse are silent, just observing each other while smoking:

> "How much does Ulrich know about this?" Clarisse wondered on her hummock. "Anyway, what could he possibly know about such struggles?" She remembered how Walter's face fell apart with pain, almost to extinction, when the agonies of music and lust beset him and her resistance left him no way out; no, she decided, Ulrich knew nothing of this monstrous love-game on the Himalayas of love, contempt, fear, and the obligations of the heights. She had no great opinion of mathematics and had never considered Ulrich to be as talented as Walter. He was clever, he was logical, he knew a lot; but was that any better than barbarism? She had to admit that his tennis used to be incomparably better than Walter's, and she could remember sometimes watching his ruthless drives with a passionate feeling of he'll get what he wants, such as she had never felt about Walter's painting, music, or ideas. And she thought: "What if he knows all about us and just isn't saying anything?" Only a moment ago he had, after all, distinctly alluded to her heroism. The silence between them had now become strangely exciting.
>
> But Ulrich was thinking: "How nice Clarisse was ten years ago—half a child, blazing with faith in the future of the three of us." She had been actually unpleasant to him only once, when she and Walter had just got married and she had displayed that unattractive selfishness-for-two that so often makes young women who are ambitiously in love with their husbands so insufferable to other men. "That's got a lot better since," he thought. (*MWQ* 51f.* / *MoE* 53f.)

From which perspective is this language produced? Obviously, the sentences in quotation marks are thoughts registered by a narrator with complete access to both minds. In addition, there are pieces of what Dorrit Cohn has termed narrated monologue: "He knew a lot; but was that any better than barbarism?" But such instances are difficult to distinguish from passages where the narrator's reflections intervene, examples of what Cohn would call psychonarration.[13] Most likely, it is the narrator who supplies the information about how Clarisse felt when watching Ulrich defeating Walter on the tennis court. This would be the only explanation of the sudden insertion of a different mood, "she could remember" (*sie konnte sich erinnern*), signaling that Clarisse does not actually recall this as she sits there smoking a cigarette, but that the episode still is a good way of capturing her relationship to these men, whence the narrator can take the liberty of inserting it. But who is responsible for the peculiar analogy comparing the love play of Walter and Clarisse to the peaks of Himalaya? Is it really Clarisse who likens it thus? Is it the narrator's interpretation of her feelings? And who feels that the silence between them is "strangely exciting"? Clarisse? The narrator? Ulrich? Indeed, it is impossible to tell, for the narrative moves imperceptibly between these three points of focalization. We are dealing with yet another textual space marked by indeterminacy.

Confronted with cases like this, narratological typologies of character depiction and point of view run up against their limits, revealed as the abstractions they always were. If only negatively, however, in revealing their own insufficiency, such categories remain useful. Without them, it would be impossible to register the deviations in the Musilian narrative. Discussing the novella *Die Vollendung der Liebe* (1911; "The Completion of Love"), Cohn points out that Musil's ways of rendering thoughts and feelings make the narrating consciousness fuse with the mind of the heroine. The line separating them is blurred.[14] We can never tell with certainty whether an association originates in the mind of the narrator or in that of the protagonist. Musil's friend Franz Blei was so bewildered by the floating perspective in the novella that he asked the author who the narrator really was. A very interesting question, Musil replied. "The point de vue is not in the author and not in the constituted person, there is in fact no point de vue at all, the stories have no central point of perspective" (*T* 2:943).[15]

Taken as a whole, the first nineteen chapters of *The Man without Qualities* are marked by the same confounding feature. After chapter 14, from which I have just quoted, there follows a chapter in which the narrative appears to be unfocalized. The narrator steps back to depict the cultural atmosphere at the turn of the century, the formative years of Walter and Ulrich. As this chapter ends and a new one begins, a barely perceivable shift in perspective turns the depiction upside down. This is the transition between the chapters:

> Something went through the thicket of beliefs in those clays like a single wind bending many trees—a spirit of heresy and reform, the blessed sense of an arising and going forth, a mini-renaissance and -reformation, such as only the best of times experience; whoever entered the world then felt, at the first corner, the breath of this spirit on his cheek.
>
> *A Mysterious Malady of the Times*

> So they had actually been two young men, not so long ago—
> Ulrich thought when he was alone again—who, oddly enough,
> not only had the most profound insights before anyone else did,
> but even had them simultaneously. (*MWQ* 54 / *MoE* 56)

The text explains the intellectual intimacy between two young men captured by the zeitgeist. The most interesting element in the passage is, however, the first, inexplicable word in the new chapter: "So" (*also*). This chapter is entirely focalized through Ulrich; what is said is attributed only to him, including the word "so." But this word refers back to the end of the previous chapter, which, however, is entirely rendered by the narrator. This is to say that a character here steps in to bring out the conclusion of the narrator's account. An odd inversion of romantic irony: it is no longer the narrator informing the reader about things unknown to figures in the story; it is a figure in the story entering the scene behind the back of the narrator to rectify his information, which implies that Ulrich somehow must have been listening to what the narrator stated in chapter 15. Or perhaps chapter 15 never was anything but the narrated monologue of Ulrich himself, but in that case the narrator forgot to indicate that this was so, thus making us mistake a diegesis rendered through Ulrich's perspective for the unfocalized discourse of the narrator. The point is, again, that we cannot tell. The narrative attributes the same discourse to two sources at once, much as it earlier situated one discrete event at two separate moments in time.

An even more peculiar instance of this follows shortly afterward. Ulrich, pondering his past, argues with himself. But what perspective governs this passage?

> It seemed to Ulrich that with the beginning of his adult life a
> general lull had set in, a gradual running down, in spite of
> occasional eddies of energy that came and went, to an ever more
> listless, erratic rhythm. It was very hard to say what this change
> consisted of. Were there suddenly fewer great men? Far from it!
> ... Had life in general reached a standstill? No, it had become
> more powerful! Were there more paralyzing contradictions than
> before? There could hardly be more! Had the past not known any
> absurdities? Heaps! *Just between ourselves*: people threw their
> support to the weak and ignored the strong. (*MWQ* 55 / *MoE* 57;
> my emphasis).

The reversal revealing that the narrator's commentary could have been part of Ulrich's reflection is now reversed in turn, this time disclosing that

Ulrich's monologue may be ascribed to the narrator. What else is the import of the conspicuous apostrophe "Just between ourselves" (*Unter uns gesagt*)? To whom is it addressed? By whom is it enunciated? Is it Ulrich addressing himself, thus splitting himself in two? Is it Ulrich calling on an imaginary listener, perhaps the reader, thus usurping the role of the narrator? Is it Ulrich addressing the narrator, or the narrator addressing Ulrich? Or perhaps it is the narrator who, disguised as Ulrich, addresses the reader from Ulrich's position, only forgetting to unmask himself before speaking?

In his discussion of Proust's *A la recherche du temps perdu*, Genette concludes that the novel works in three modes of focalization at once, "passing at will from the consciousness of his hero to that of his narrator, and inhabiting by turns that of his most diverse characters."[16] This is something quite different from the simple omniscience of the narrator of the classical novel, Genette continues, although he does not develop the distinction. Also, since this focalization transgresses a "law of the mind," being inside and outside consciousness at the same time, it defies realistic illusionism. Genette's description is valid also for Musil's narrative, but only in part. It is true that Musil's narrator moves into and out of the minds of the characters, situating them in a wider, intersubjective narrative space. But while the Proustian narrator unifies this space, creating an experiential totality, the discourses and idioms that invade Musil's novel cannot be integrated into any totality, since they offer contradictory representations of time, space, and subjectivity. The narrator keeps adding these perspectives, but they fail to add up to a unity, as they do when Marcel stumbles on the pavement, recaptures the past, and starts to record it in narrative form.

Genette calls Proust's modernistic mood of narration "polymodality" of focalization.[17] This is also a valid designation of the narrative strategy in *The Man without Qualities*, provided the qualification that the various modes never merge but are merely superimposed or juxtaposed. They do not supplement or replenish one another, nor are they unified in a more comprehensive order of consciousness. They just expose the limits of one another. As regards the question of how to represent human experience, then, Musil's narrator demonstrates that each system of inscription, perspective, and order is partial and arbitrary.

Musil's novel reverses the process by which the realist novel integrates individual and society into a meaningful totality. In Hamon's view of the realist text, as well as in Lukács's and Moretti's respective accounts of the bildungsroman, the social events on the narrative surface are given meaning by the life story of the individual, while the individual is socialized through his exposure to these events. In *The Man without Qualities*, there is no reciprocity between society and subject. The truth of Musil's characters is not disclosed by representing them in situations of social interaction. They are not sufficiently autonomous to express themselves as free agents. Each encounter with the social world empties them, so as to show that outside the social systems and discourses that each character articulates, he or she is unintelligible. As J. P. Stern points out, "the very indeterminacy of the hero's personality makes it difficult to say where that personality ends and the social ambience begins." A planned indeterminacy, Stern adds, is the author's first intention.[18]

So even if Musil's protagonist has no trouble making his way through the social world, in a deeper sense he has no place there. As a social being Ulrich is portrayed as exchangeable and one-dimensional, consisting only of the discourses that he articulates. Prefiguring the post-structuralist idea that the subject is an effect of discourse, Musil played with the idea of putting together a human being entirely from citations.[19] The only way to represent such a character truthfully is to peel away layer after layer of the social material of which he is made. Hence these extended pauses where the narrator interrupts mimetically represented scenes and derealizes the situation. Hence the irony that undercuts every assertion. Hence the satirical destruction of the illusions of "the realist novel. The narrator appears to unlock a passage to unexplored territories of human reality. The urge to represent these landscapes engenders the achronic time, the polymodal focalization, and the floating psychonarration, which are characteristic of the Musilian narrative.

In his essay on the position of the narrator in the modernistic novel, Adorno approaches this narrative process in more general terms: "The world is imperceptibly drawn into this interior space—the technique has been given the name 'interior monologue'—and anything that takes place in the external world is presented ... as a piece of the interior world, a moment in the stream of consciousness, protected against refutation by the objective order of time and space."[20] The real is reconstructed inside a psychic universe. The result is what Adorno calls an "Innenraum," an interior space, which forces external reality to disappear beyond the narrative horizon and sets itself in its place as a new, internal reality. Yet Adorno's remark neglects one crucial feature. Musil's narrative shows that the psychic space described by Adorno cannot be ascribed to any particular psyche. Strictly speaking, this psychic space cannot be an "Innenraum," for such a notion presupposes a subject with a defined interiority. In the case of Musil, authentic subjectivity has neither interiority nor exteriority; it floats unanchored between the social roles and discursive matrices that it must use to articulate its being, but without ever finding any single role or idiom that can capture its desire for meaning and identity.

My discussion in chapter 2 of the subject's relationship to social and urban space is thus supported by this investigation of the narrative form: the

Musilian subject must be conceptualized not as intrinsic substance nor as a socially imputed function; but rather as a barely tangible Zwischenraum that cannot be reduced to or explained by either of these.

I will conclude this analysis of Musil's narrative discourse with a brief discussion of chapter 18, in which Moosbrugger is introduced to the reader. Apparently, this episode relates how Ulrich runs into Moosbrugger in the street. This encounter then turns out to be a fake, another instance of the narrator's mocking treatment of narrative codes:

> When Ulrich first laid eyes on that face with its signs of being a child of God above handcuffs, he quickly turned around, slipped a few cigarettes to the sentry at the nearby court building, and asked him about the convoy that had apparently just left the gates; he was told ... Well, anyway, this is how something of the sort must have happened in earlier times, since it is often reported this way, and Ulrich almost believed it himself; but the contemporary truth was that he had merely read all about it in the newspaper. It was to be a long time before he met Moosbrugger in person, and before that happened he caught sight of him only once during the trial. The probability of experiencing something unusual through the newspapers is much greater than that of experiencing it in person; in other words, the more important things take place today in the abstract, and the more trivial ones in real life.
>
> What Ulrich learned of Moosbrugger's story in this fashion was more or less the following.... (*MWQ* 68f. / *MoE* 69)

The narrator here limits Ulrich's field of knowledge and experience. The experience offered him is abstract; it is what he happens to read in the newspaper.[21] His personal investment in reality is thereby ruled out. The narrator then promises to deliver this kind of abstract experience ("[it] was more or less the following"). What follows, however, is not a compilation of news reports, not even a montage of clippings of the kind that other modernists of the period experimented with, notably Döblin in *Berlin Alexanderplatz* and John Dos Passos in his *U.S.A.* trilogy. What follows in Musil, on the contrary, is in fact a passage that is focalized through Moosbrugger himself. If this is what Ulrich experienced through the news, it must be remarkable news, for it amounts to an account of what it is like to be Moosbrugger, having his memories, feeling his feelings, perceiving with his senses, executing his actions, even killing his victim:

Then he felt something hard, in her pocket or his. He tugged it out. He couldn't say whether it was a scissors or a knife; he stabbed her with it. He had claimed it was only a pair of scissors, but it was his own knife. She fell with her head inside the booth. He dragged her partway outside, onto the soft ground, and kept on stabbing her until he had completely separated her from himself. Then he stood there beside her for maybe another quarter of an hour, looking down at her, while the night grew calmer again and wonderfully smooth. (*MWQ* 74 / *MoE* 74)

This is surely not what Ulrich experienced by reading the newspaper but a narrative of Moosbrugger's murder focalized through the murderer himself. Yet, the narrator explicitly states that this is what Ulrich "experienced" in the newspaper. What we see in this chapter on Moosbrugger, then, is a mode of narration that would seem to affirm the gap between experience and journalism. But as soon as this difference is established, the narrator offers an account that cancels it.

Looking at the chapter as a whole, we see how its perspective shifts among the narrator, Ulrich, Moosbrugger, and the judges. The impact of this polymodal focalization is amplified by a constantly changing distance and a voice sometimes sympathetic, sometimes sharply ironic—all of which contribute to the coming into being of an ambiguous space, at once social and psychic, in which several discourses collide and in which the representation of reality must be patched together from contradictory perspectives. As Anne Longuet Marx has argued, this is a primary trait of Musil's narrative. It does not follow an itinerary, much less an intrigue; it is regulated by a disposition, or a mood, which sutures discursive registers that are absolutely heterogenous.[22] In this way, the narrative process dissolves every authoritative account of reality, contrasting it with a set of alternative but conflicting perspectives. Meanwhile, the character is emptied of its traditional contents, liberated from any firm identity, and instead affirmed as an agency suspended in a state of mobility and possibility.

THE NARRATIVE PROCESS OF *THE MAN WITHOUT QUALITIES*

The Man without Qualities is narrated by a disembodied and placeless voice whose irony cuts in all directions. I have argued that the narration refuses to give any authoritative account of events, objects, and characters. An event signifies different things, depending on the perspective from which it is seen. The meaning of an object varies with the discourse used to describe it. A character can obey contradictory principles, depending on the situation, and

he or she is also equipped with alternative pasts. Furthermore, nothing in
this novel acts or functions on its own accord but only in relation to the
systems in which it is inserted. No epistemological paradigm is privileged.
No particular narrative mood governs unchallenged over the representation.
The laws of causality are suspended. The temporal structure is blurred. The
absence of a superordinate narrative and temporal order creates the
impression that everything happens more or less simultaneously: the
narrative creates an achronic space. The absence of a central perspective and
a predominating epistemology allows several perspectives and symbolic
systems to coexist: the narrative generates a heterologic and polycentric
space. Importantly, Musil's novel evokes this achronicity, heterology, and
polycentricity in and by the *movement* of narration.

The narrator's swift changes of perspective, his instantaneous passage
from one focus to another, serve to demonstrate that the choice of a
particular focus, character, event, object, narrative code, or discursive
register is arbitrary. The result is a textual practice demonstrating the seams
and joints in the narrative surface, thus indicating that the frame within
which a certain representation is fabricated is but one among an infinite
number of other no less interesting frames. This creates what Genette would
call "an iterative narrative" (*un récit itératif*): various possible narrative
beginnings and developments are tested but they cannot be arranged along a
unitary narrative line.[23] Stated in more technical terms, the syntagmatic axis,
on which the narrative events are ordered in succession so as to drive the
story forward, is eclipsed by the paradigmatic axis of combination.[24]
Themes, scenes, and events no longer succeed one another in time but are
evoked as various, sometimes contradictory possibilities of the same
paradigm, and as a set of possible but mutually exclusive continuations of the
story. Along each narrative thread actually chosen in the weaving of the story,
the narrator thus pulls a bundle of others, the vibrations of which create
strange resonances. It is not surprising that Jean-François Lyotard, in his
book on the postmodern condition, enlists *The Man without Qualities* to
support his account of "the decomposition of the great narratives."[25]

This narrative modality is central to Musil's conception of subjectivity,
which can partly be seen as an effect of the narrative logic that I have
examined here. The narrative structure of Musil's novel and the structure of
subjectivity presented in the novel refuse the firm frames of existing reality.
And they do so in order to preserve the possibility of different realities.[26]

My account of how Musil's narrative generates a polyvalent
Zwischenraum thus merges with the conclusion reached in the previous
chapter. As we saw there, the novel responds to social reification by
postulating the possibility of another mode of experience, the other

condition, which transcends the conflict between intellect and feeling, rationality and nonrationality. In the most beautiful passages of the novel, this mode of being is made concrete as an ethical and existential posture in which Ulrich momentarily recaptures a sense of meaning and presence, the barriers separating his self and the world suddenly falling away.

It should be added that Musil also linked the other condition to the possibility of reorganizing human life as a whole. Consequently, this condition suggested a path to social improvement. Art had an important pedagogic function in this project, for it provided the medium through which the articulations of the other condition could be explored. In his essays, especially "The German as Symptom" (1923), Musil attempted to substantiate this idea, tying the ethical and aesthetic qualities of the other condition to related ideas in human history, drawing on research in experimental psychology as well as the tradition of mysticism: "We have a great many accounts of this other condition. What seems to be common to all of them is that the border between self and nonself is less sharp than usual, and that there is a certain inversion of relationships.... Whereas ordinarily the self masters the world, in the other condition the world flows into the self, or mingles with it or bears it, and the like" (*PS* 186 / *GW* 2:1393).

This is an articulation, within the existential and ethical register, of Musil's imaginary solution of the historical dilemma of modernity. It is described as a state of being characterized by a transgression and reversal of boundaries. The same dilemma, then, is inscribed in the form of the Musilian narrative. The transgression of temporal order and the ironic subversion of discursive matrices contribute to the generation of a space of indeterminacy and potentiality that dissolves the mimetic representation of a lifelike character moving through a solid external reality.

The ethics of the other condition and the functioning of the Musilian narrative can thus be seen as two articulations of the same mood. If Musil's narrative mood were projected onto the level of the narrative content and turned into an existential strategy, the result would be similar to what Musil describes as the other condition. Correspondingly, if the other condition could be converted into a narrative attitude, the result would be the kind of representation of time, space, and character that we find in Musil's novel: an achronic, polycentric, and heterologic Zwischenraum, in which subjectivity, no longer determined by social identities, floats in an experiential flux.

Interestingly, the same modality of a subject without identity emerges in even purer form in Hermann Broch's last novel, *The Death of Virgil* (1945). A boundless subject governs two of the main sections in this lyric novel. This subject is comparable only to the writing process itself, in the ways in which it rejuvenates itself with each additional letter and steps outside itself with each new phrase. Like Musil's subject in the other condition, Broch's subject floats "beyond the expressible as well as the inexpressible"; it penetrates the world and is simultaneously penetrated by it; it is a "no thing," a mere borderline of energy, which nonetheless fills up the empty consciousness and floods the universe.[27] As we shall see, the similarities between Broch's and Musil's renderings of this *ecstatic* mode of subjectivity indicate their common origin in Austria's postimperial culture.

Still, the difference between the narratological and the existential-philosophical articulations of this mood cannot be erased. On the one hand, there is the representation of Ulrich—or in Broch's case the dying Virgil—who ascend to this state of mind in transient epiphanies, or in the moment of death. Musil's Ulrich also turns it into the basis of an existential program that is necessitated by modern society and yet cannot be realized in this society; this gesture of aesthetic refusal is typical of modernist literature, as we saw in the first chapter. On the other hand, there is the narratological Zwischenraum that emerges through a continuous narrative production and an irony that derealizes language and identities.

On the level of content, then, the other condition is an ideological closure. On the level of form, by contrast, the narrative mood articulating the other condition can never constitute any closure, for it is the very generating force of the narrative—a process, not a fixed existential structure. It is important to distinguish these two levels of the problem. If we narrowly focus the content, we arrive at an ideological solution from which we may learn no more, and no less, than from any treatise on mysticism. If we compare this to what goes on on the level of narrative production, we see that the closure is constantly unmade, that the narrator must resist the solutions which he cannot but keep fabricating and project onto the world. Ulrich, as a character, is precisely a projection of that kind. As such, he is marked by the restrictions of his era and his society.

The Musilian narrative elaborates preestablished models of character representations in a number of conspicuous ways, in order to arrive at an atemporal and polymodal representation of human subjectivity. Yet the tension between this representation and the expressivist and realist convention that it negates remains in place. In order to make Ulrich play his role as a literary character, Musil was dependent on the categories and models that conditioned a novelistic representation of subjectivity at his historical moment. Hence, his novel cannot avoid articulating the expressivist paradigm of subjectivity, which, in Musil's time, determined the range of possible answers to the questions of identity and human nature. The point, however, is that Musil was unsatisfied with all available answers to this question, and he therefore tried to imagine new ones. In doing this, he used

Ulrich as the vehicle for his new answers, thus projecting the hero beyond the narrative, psychological, and philosophical categories that in his period circumscribed the notion of the human.

Ernst Fischer once stated that Musil wrote "in the twilight of an era suspended between dying and becoming."[28] Indeed, seen from the point of view of the expressivist paradigm, the novel depicts what Broch summed up as "the almost mystical disintegration of a culture."[29] Ulrich consequently exemplifies the disappearance of established codes of "normal" behavior. Seen from the perspective of as yet unrealized possibilities, on the other hand, the novel inaugurates a time to come. Ulrich then becomes an example of a human subject fit to meet the demands of a truly modernized world. The latter aspect alone accounts for Musil's unique aesthetic and philosophical innovations. An interpretation that applies this perspective therefore affords a richer and more complex view of the novel. Burton Pike has suggested, rightly, that while "Thomas Mann stands at the end of an old tradition, there is reason to believe that Musil stands at the beginning of a new one."[30]

NOTES

1. Catherine Belsey, *Critical Practice* (London: Routledge, 1980), 70.

2. Ibid.

3. Philippe Hamon, "Un Discours contraint," in *Littérature et realité*, by Roland Barthes et al. (Paris: Seuil, 1982), 159f.

4. This panorama has been mapped by several Musil scholars, for example, Cornelia Blasberg, *Krise und Utopie der Intellektuellen: Kulturkritische Aspekte irr Robert Musils Roman "Der Mann ohne Eigenschaften"* (Stuttgart: Hans-Dieter Heinz, 1984); Alexander Honold, *Die Stadt und der Krieg: Raum- und Zeitkonstruktion in Robert Musils Roman "Der Mann ohne Eigenschaften"* (Munich: Wilhelm Fink, 1995), 281ff.; Götz Müller, *Ideologiekritik und Metasprache in Robert Musils Roman "Der Mann ohne Eigenschaften"* (Munich: Wilhelm Fink, 1972); and Karl Corino, *Robert Musil: Leben und Werk in Bildern und Texten* (Reinbek bei Hamburg: Rowohlt, 1988).

5. There are numerous interpretations of chapter 1 of *The Man without Qualities*. Bernd-Rüdiger Hüppauf focuses on the contrast between the narrative's employment of two incommensurate registers of language and knowledge. In his view, there is a hierarchy of discourses in which the concrete account focalized through the individual is linked to "empirical reality," which is then subordinated to the abstract register, which is said to be metaphorical and conceptual. Hüppauf thus makes an ontological distinction between two realms of the real. By contrast, I want to argue that Musil's differentiation is less concerned with separate domains of reality than with a separation of two epistemological approaches to the same reality. Hence, the novel preserves the tension between these approaches, avoiding positing one of them as more "truthful" than the other (*Von sozialer Utopie zur Mystik: Zu Robert Musils "Der Mann ohne Eigenschaften"* [Munich: Wilhelm Fink, 1971], 90–98). Other useful interpretations are offered by Hartmut Böhme, "Eine Zeit ohne Eigenschaften: Robert Musil und die Posthistoire," *Natur und Subjekt* (Frankfurt am Main: Suhrkamp, 1988), 308–333; Ulf Schramm, *Fiktion und Reflexion: Überlegungen zu Musil und Beckett* (Frankfurt am Main: Suhrkamp, 1967), 13–19; Honold, *Die Stadt und der Krieg*,

25–94. Ulrich Karthaus, *Der andere Zustand: Zeitstrukturen im Werke Robert Musils* (Berlin: E. Schmidt, 1965); Helga Honold, "Die Funktion des Paradoxen bei Robert Musil" (Ph.D. diss., Tübingen, 1963); and Wolfdietrich Rasch, *Über Robert Musils Roman "Der Mann ohne Eigenschaften"* (Göttingen: Vandenhoeck und Ruprecht, 1967). See also Jochen Schmidt, *Ohne Eigenschaften: Eine Erläuterung zu Musils Grundbegriff* (Tübingen: Max Niemeyer, 1975), 70–78; and Beda Alleman, *"Musil": Ironie und Dichtung* (Pfullingen: Neske, 1956), 177–220. A more questionable interpretation is Günter Graf, *Studien zur Funktion des Ersten Kapitels von Robert Musils Roman "Der Mann ohne Eigenschaften": Ein Beitrag zur Unwahrhaftigkeits-Typik der Gestalten* (Göppingen: Göppingen Arbeiten zur Germanistik, 1969), 14–23, 239–241.

6. Gérard Genette, *Narrative Discourse: An Essay in Method*, trans. Jane E. Lewin (Ithaca: Cornell University Press, 1980), 161; "Discours du récit," in *Figures III* (Paris: Senil, 1972), 183.

7. For a discussion of the relation between Musil's narrative and early cinematography, see Christian Rogowski, "Ein andres Verhalten zur Welt: Robert Musil und der Film," *Sprachkunst: Beiträge zur Literaturwissenschaft* 23 (1992): 105–118.

8. For an analysis of Musil's satire, see Helmut Arntzen, *Satirischer Stil: Zur Satire Robert Musils im "Mann ohne Eigenschaften,"* 3d ed. (Bonn: Bouvier, 1983).

9. Fredric Jameson's analysis of Alain Robbe-Grillet deals with this tension between surface and subtext in high modernist narratives. See "Modernism and Its Repressed; or, Robbe-Grillet as Anti-Colonialist," *The Ideologies of Theory: Essays 1971–1986* (Minneapolis: University of Minnesota Press, 1988), 1:167–180.

10. Similarly, Schelling, Kühn, and Schramm have demonstrated that the style and organization of Musil's novel continually "derealize" social reality. According to Schelling and Kühn, the narrative works by way of "analogy," inserting unexpected and alogical contrasts and connections through which the "pseudo-real" order of things ("das Seinesgleichen") is undone, so as to disclose a more basic level of reality. Since these critics associate this level with a "true" representation of reality, they ascribe to Musil an expressivist notion of the subject, because they define the subjectivity that Musil, allegedly, is searching for as an expression of this authentic realm of reality. See Ulrich Schelling, "Das analogische Denken bei Robert Musil," in *Robert Musil Studien zu seinem Werk*, ed. Karl Dinklage (Reinbek bei Hamburg: Rowohlt, 1970), 170–199; Dieter Kühn, *Analogie und Variation: Zur Analyse von Robert Musils Roman "Der Mann ohne Eigenschaften"* (Bonn: Bouvier, 1965); and Schramm, *Fiktion und Reflexion*.

11. Pierre V. Zima, *L'ambivalence romanesque: Proust, Kafka, Musil*, rev. ed. (Frankfurt am Main: Peter Lang, 1988), 291.

12. Cf. Ulrich Schelling: "Musil treats the external course of events which runs through time and space, with its fixed locations, topographical order, and chronological relations, its motivations and causal links, just as carelessly as any narrator of romanticism" ("Das analogische Denken bei Robert Musil," 170). See also Massimo Cacciari: "Time explodes into a myriad of moments that accompany, upon complete disenchantment with any eschatological perspective, maximum attention to the *fact*, the event, the moment" (*Posthumous People: Vienna at the Turning Point*, trans. Rodger Friedman [Stanford: Stanford University Press, 19961, 200f.). And Hüppauf, *Von sozialer Utopie zur Mystik*, 25ff.

13. Dorrit Cohn, *Transparent Minds: Narrative Modes for Presenting Consciousness in Fiction* (Princeton: Princeton University Press, 1978), 14. The categories are defined in this way: (1) psychonarration: the narrator's discourse about a character's consciousness; (2) quoted monologue: a character's mental discourse; (3) narrated monologue: a character's

mental discourse in the guise of the narrator's discourse. Quoted monologue would here correspond to Joyce's stream-of-consciousness or "monologue interieur."

14. Ibid., 43.

15. I am here benefitting from Walter Moser's discussion of Musil's correspondence ("R. Musil et la mort de 'l'homme liberal,'" in *Robert Musil*, ed. Jean-Pierre Cometti [Paris: Editions Royaumont, 1986], 195).

16. Genette, *Narrative Discourse*, 210; "Discours du récit," 223.

17. Ibid.

18. J. P. Stern, "'Reality' in *Der Mann ohne Eigenschaften*," in *Musil in Focus: Papers from a Centenary Symposium*, ed. L. Huber and J. J. White (London: Institute of Germanic Studies; University of London, 1982), 77.

19. Musil notes this same idea twice in his journals: "Einen Menschen ganz aus Zitaten zusammensetzen!" (*T* 1:356, 443)

20. Theodor W. Adorno, "The Position of the Narrator in the Contemporary Novel," in *Notes to Literature*, ed. Rolf Tiedemann, trans. Shierry Weber Nicholsen (New York: Columbia University Press, 1992), 1:33; "Standort des Erzählers im zeitgenössischen Roman," in *Noten zur Literatur*, in *Gesammelte Schriften* (Frankfurt am Main: Suhrkamp, 1970–1978), II:67.

21. The irony is, of course, that Musil constructed Moosbrugger from newspaper reports. Moosbrugger borrows his traits from the murderers and mental patients Christian Voigt, Fritz Haarmann, and Florian Grossrubatscher, who stirred the imagination of the Viennese public. See Karl Corino's articles "Ein Mörder macht Literaturgeschichte: Florian Grossrubatscher, ein Modell für Musils Moosbrugger," in *Robert Musil und die kulturellen Tendenzen seiner Zeit*, ed. Josef Strutz (Munich: Wilhelm Fink, 1983), 130–147; and "Zerstückt und durchdunkelt: Der Sexualmörder Moosbrugger im 'Mann ohne Eigenschaften' und sein Modell," *Musil-Forum* (Saarbrücken) 10 (1984): 105–119; as well as Corino's remarks in *Robert Musil: Leben und Werk*, 358.

22. Anne Longuet Marx, "La Rhapsodie Musilienne," *Europe* 69, nos. 741–742 (January–February 1991): 16.

23. Genette, *Narrative Discourse*, 113–127; "Discours du récit," 145–156.

24. Zima uses this terminology in *L'Ambivalence romanesque*, 219–308.

25. Jean-François Lyotard, *The Postmodern Condition: A Report on Knowledge*, trans. Geoff Bennington and Brian Massumi (Minneapolis: University of Minnesota Press, 1984), 15; *La Condition postmoderne: Rapport sur le savoir* (Paris: Minuit, 1979), 30f.

26. Cf. Stern, "'Reality' in *Der Mann ohne Eigenschaften*," 79.

27. Hermann Broch, *The Death of Virgil*, trans. Jean Starr Untermeyer (New York: Pantheon, 1945), 481; *Der Tod des Vergil*, in *Kommentierte Werkausgabe* (Frankfurt am Main: Suhrkamp, 1976), 4:454

28. Ernst Fischer, *Von Grillparzer zu Kafka: Sechs Essays* (Vienna: Globus, 1962), 277.

29. Hermann Broch, "Nachruf auf Robert Musil," in *Kommentierte Werkausgabe* (Frankfurt am Main: Suhrkamp, 1975), 9, bk. 1:98f.

30. Burton Pike, *Robert Musil: An Introduction to His Work* (Ithaca: Cornell University Press, 1961), 199.

AUSTIN HARRINGTON

Undivided, Not-United: Robert Musil's Community

I would like to propose a reading of Robert Musil's *The Man without Qualities* that views Musil as ironising our received image of modernity's evils of alienation, anonymity and occupational specialisation by exposing the extent to which this image betrays traces of naivety and complacency inherent in Enlightenment humanist discourses of Bildung and the "authentic self." Through the voice of Ulrich, Musil asks us to consider whether the ideal of "authenticity" (*Eigentlichkeit*), of the "many-sided-personality" possessing "qualities" (*Eigenschaften*), able to live at one with the world by "appropriating" the products of his or her actions in the world in an organic "totality" of personal attributes and achievements, might not be an all-too-comforting illusion, impossible to realise in an age of irreducible complexity and indeterminacy, and whether the "authentic" response to modern social conditions, if there is one, might not instead lie in affirming constitutive ambivalence, difference and multiplicity, and not limiting the possibilities of cultural and ethical conduct to any single governing project or moral law. Musil here by no means bids farewell to Enlightenment ideals of personal well-being through rational social transformation, but he subjects these ideals to a kind of reflexive questioning that helps us to become clearer about what the central aspirations and problems of modernity fundamentally are—and he does so by means of a peculiarly literary mode of

From *Angelaki* 8, no. 1 (April 2003). © 2003 by Taylor & Francis Ltd. and the editors of *Angelaki*.

communication that exploits devices of irony, ambivalence and aesthetic distance in order to communicate, thoughts about the social conditions, movements and contradictory identities of modernity that could not otherwise be expressed in the abstract discursive language of social science.[1]

In the present context, I want to look at some of the limits of Ulrich's irony. I want to look at the point where, through Ulrich, irony turns back on itself and acknowledges the risks and responsibilities of its own logic. This concerns Ulrich's much-discussed relationship to his sister Agathe in the last part of the published text and the long unfinished chapters of the *Nachlass*. I examine here (i) the logic of this irony, (ii) its bearing on Ulrich's and Agathe's "utopia," and its implications for Musil's views about (iii) ethics, (iv) love and community, and (v) self-identity in the modern world.

I. IRONY: ON CONJUGATING "P" WITH "NOT-P"

In *The Man without Qualities*, Musil is at once novelist and essayist, poet and theorist. His subject is the subject of modernity: "the man without qualities." This is Ulrich; but it is, also, woman: Agathe, Clarisse, Diotima; and it is equally the elite and the reactionary (Leinsdorf, Stumm, Tuzzi); the bogus and the complacent (Arnheim, Hagauer); the insane (Moosbrugger) and the fanatic (Meingast, Hans Sepp); and it is the Jew (Fischel), the servant girl (Rachel) and the slave boy (Soliman); and not least, it is the mass and the multitude of the city, nation and state. In all these guises, Musil examines the subject of modernity in its contradictory states of identity and difference.

Through his portraits of characters such as the bourgeois couple Walter and Clarisse, and the salon lady Diotima, and, perhaps above all, her lover Arnheim—universal charlatan of *Bildung und Besitz* (Culture and Capital), modelled on the Weimar industrialist Walter Rathenau—Musil shows us how there can be no simple restoration of meaning in the midst of rationalised disenchanted social order. Musil shows how there can be no simple recourse to religion to patch up the holes in a scientised lifeworld, or to universalising moral systems to resolve the complexities of ethical situations, or to the brute certainties of "lived experience," national belonging or time-honoured cultural heritage to provide a sense of direction in life. In a "royal and imperial" land of Kakania that relies on some notion of its own dignity as "kaiserlich and königlich" or "k. & k."—Musil's satire on the insignia of a rotting Austro-Hungarian empire—tradition is already ideology. As with "Ukania"—in Tom Nairn's canny linking of Kakania to another not-so-united caca-dom of king, country and populist politics known as the UK—tradition here is already squalid and shabby in its resort to mediated identities masquerading as "organic solidarity" (cf. Nairn 2000).

But more than this, Musil tells us that even once we have become good Kantians and completed our Copernican turn, come to terms with disenchantment and got beyond substantive religion, regressive nationalism and self-indulgent *Lebensphilosophie*, we may yet have more work to do. For if modernity has been said to be about that search for autonomy of the subject "without dependence on an other" of which Kant speaks in the essay on enlightenment, Musil here seems to be enjoining us to inject a dose of irony into our confidence about our powers of autonomy and self-determination after the "end" of tradition. For if modernity is not itself to become a new kind of traditionalism, ossifying back in its own automatic reflexivity, as Beck et al. (1994) warn in their treatise on "reflexive modernisation," we need, as subjects of modernity, to be continually attentive to our ontological conditionality and never to take our cherished moral and epistemological sovereignty for granted. We need to stand back from ourselves, in comic self-mockery, and consider that we may yet be "dependent on an other," yet determined by the heteronomous: by such things as drugs, neurones, water molecules, motor cars, quarks, computers, telephone cables, statistics and other imaginary magnitudes.

To say, however, that Musil "ironises" Enlightenment humanist discourses of autonomy and authenticity is not to say that he proclaims them null and void. In "ironising" depth, wholeness and sincerity over against illusion, surface and dispersion, Musil does not flatly cancel the former values. Since Kierkegaard and Friedrich Schlegel, philosophers have long stressed that to ironise is not to stop taking seriously the things we want to laugh about. To flirt with irony is easy; to live with it is difficult—and the difficulty arises from the problem that to ironise "p" is not simply to assert "not p." An ironised "p" is not the antithesis of "p"; and nor is it some happily Hegelian synthesis of "p" and "not p." Rather, it is some kind of paradoxical conjugation of "p" and "not p." Thus, rather than debunking Enlightenment discourses, Musil invites us to seek ways of critically rescuing them through a dialogue with their negation. Irony in this sense for Ulrich becomes a work of impossible thinking, a work of the self that challenges the self to find autonomy, authenticity and ethical togetherness with others by means of a critical journey into the reverse of these values, so as to dig out the dogmas subtending them whenever we assert them without circumspection.

I suggest this is at least part of the import of Ulrich's later transformation in Part III of the novel in the union with Agathe. For here Musil demonstrates Ulrich's partial rediscovery of authenticity in his relation to woman, in his ethical reflections on the limits of aesthetic withdrawal, and in his attempt to face the infinite burden of responsibility for reason and "precision in matters of the soul" (1953, II: 348f.). Here, Ulrich desperately wants to close his irony, desperately wants to stop playing Socrates. Ulrich recognises that he cannot continue playing for ever the scientist, the positivist and the sceptic, and that he needs to re-engage with the imperatives of life and curtail his probabilistic philosophies of indeterminism and the "abolition of reality" (1953, I: 11f.). Yet still he cannot find closure. Even as he experiences the infinite conversation with Agathe about God, love, ethics, goodness, community and "the other condition" there is no final resolution of aporia, no final overcoming of alienation in the union with his sister, which Musil describes as at once "undivided and not-united," *ungetrennt und nichtvereint* (1978, II: 1337). Certainly, Ulrich mellows and learns to find community of a sort with others; but there is no decisive return of Ulysses to Ithaca, no final reconciliation after some long *Wanderjahre* in an ideal "odyssey of mind." Ulrich's fate remains equivocal and undecidable—and this is his suffering. This is the pathos we must understand in Musil's unfinished novel that cannot commit itself to commitment or to uncommitment, to engagement or to detachment, to "p" or to "not-p."

Earlier in *The Man without Qualities*, Ulrich appears to be enjoying his experimental life as a *flâneur* in the salons of Viennese high society. But already he is conscious of himself as "a man whom something compelled to live against his own grain, although he seemed to let himself float along without any constraint":

> There was something attracting him to everything there was, and something stronger that would not let him get to it. Why did he live so vaguely and undecidedly? ... There was something in him that had never wanted to stay anywhere, but had groped its way along the walls of the world, thinking: "There are still millions of other walls." (Musil 1953, I: 176, 178)

After several years' silence, Ulrich meets with his sister in the house of their recently deceased father. They must organise the funeral, sell the house and thank for condolences. From this point on, Ulrich finds the beginnings of a trail toward self-understanding. Time passes as Agathe settles in with Ulrich, refusing the summons of her arid second husband, the professorial Hagauer. Ulrich and Agathe now begin to discover a possibility of living, dreaming and thinking that Musil famously calls *der andere Zustand* (the other condition). What species of utopia is this "other condition" and what might it tell us about our contemporary utopian thinking?

II. INNERWORLDLY AND OTHERWORLDLY UTOPIANISM

The sociologist Peter Berger (1970) interprets Musil's "other condition" through the lens of Alfred Schütz's phenomenological concept of "multiple realities." Berger reads Musil as inquiring into the ontology of everyday life, into the problem of how there can be an everyday reality when knowledge of this "everyday," this "paramount reality" in William James's pragmatist sense, is itself dependent on consciousness of myriad other registers of experience, such as the aesthetic, the religious, the mystical and the pathological. Knowing the everyday requires experiencing some rupturing of this phenomenological continuum. The other condition in this sense represents some passing state of sensory enlightenment, a momentary privilege of insight suspended in time and space between discrepant everyday worlds, like the surrealist collage or the religious experience of the borderline. This, according to Berger, makes Musil's novel neither a "historical report," nor the "description of a society" but an analysis "presented to us with the intention of bringing out certain key features of *any* society, ... of delineating the essential structure of everyday reality" (Berger 1970, 216). The everyday reality of our lifeworld is that which we can take for granted "until further notice": a reality of subjective chances and probabilities confirmed by routine, as Max Weber and Schutz tell us. But this reality is only an "*epoché* of the natural attitude" (Schutz 1962) based on a deliberate suspension of doubt: it is a very dull and repetitious *theatrum mundi*, which collapses as soon as we are accosted in the street or knocked over by a tram. Very often we seek flight from this everyday reality, in mysticism, obscurantism and nationalism—Diotima's Platonism, Hans Sepp's fascism—or we defy it—Moosbrugger's criminal reality, Clarisse on the brink of madness. But equally often we seek refuge in it and acquiesce in it. Musil teaches us the necessity of this illusion of the everyday even as he lays bare its insufficiency. With Nietzsche, he explicates our reality as a reality of perspectives and appearances, of utopian no-places, that we somehow have to fit together into a meaningful cartography of experience.

Berger reminds us here that Ulrich's and Agathe's other condition is not explicitly recognisable as a political utopia. Part III of the novel, when Ulrich and Agathe enter "Into the Millennium," certainly marks a break with the earlier chapters, which seem to roll by like minor episodes in a soap-opera, in an eternally recurrent circulation of the same familiar characters conversing in enclosed domestic interiors. The earlier chapters at the same time gesture vaguely toward some higher standpoint of cosmic meaning, some much-sought-after but obscure understanding of historical totality beyond myth and ideology. Yet this expectation is continually deferred and only in part fulfilled. Certainly there is no clear sense of some social utopia free from violence. The novel does not appear to conclude with what Adorno calls, at the end of *Minima Moralia*, that "light of knowledge that is shed on the world from the standpoint of redemption." When Adorno (1974, 247) writes that "perspectives must be fashioned that displace and estrange the world, reveal it to be, with its rifts and crevices, as indigent and distorted as it will appear one day in the messianic light," Ulrich reaches a state of enlightenment that is perspectival in Adorno's sense but not one apparently founded in any material transformation of practices.

Nonetheless, I would like to argue that it would be wrong to follow Berger in interpreting Ulrich's condition solely in some perceptual-aesthetic sense, solely in terms of his winning of some privileged pair of phenomenological spectacles, without wider practico-normative significance. For Ulrich's ethic of seeing and sensing possibilities is still tied to a possibility and necessity of *doing*. For all his loathing of Arnheim's Goethean humbug of "the deed," *die Tat*, Ulrich practises a "utopia of the inductive attitude" (1953, I: 29f.) that wants keenly to find a way of tying vision and imagination to action through experience. Thus his fate ought not to be compared to the comically resigned one of Don Quixote, as Berger proposes.

One way of thinking this inter-meshing of action and perception in Musil's conception might be to consider some recent reflections on utopianism in art by the German aesthetician Martin Seel. Seel (2001) has proposed that we view utopias as "impossible possibilities that make possible possibilities visible"; Seel suggests that "utopias make distant possibilities foreseeable so that possibilities graspable in the here and now become visible" (2001, 747; my trans.). This implies that works of art are not to be viewed in the Adornian manner as hermetic *intimations* of utopia, as broken mimetic capsules of a possible totality. Rather, they should be understood as sensuous repositories of ways of revisiting our ordinary experience in the *hic et nunc* that transfigure our horizons of possibility, through our communicative engagements with them. Works of art thus impart utopia in the sense of releasing transformative possibilities of everyday praxis. Distinct from fantasy and wishful thinking, a work of art's aesthetic utopia allows us, and requires us, to mediate the possible with the impossible, in rigorous ways, in ways that must be (i) logically thinkable (not like squared circles), (ii) fulfillable (something we can really want to live with, for a long time), and (iii) achievable (something not absolutely beyond reach, but not reachable either by mere approximation or mere reform over time). One might suggest that this paradoxical mediating of the possible with the impossible is precisely Ulrich's worldview in respect of action, utopia and the question of "how to go on." It is his "precision in matters of the soul," his "daylight mysticism" (1978, II: 1089; my trans.), his "god-free" (1978, II: 1092; my trans.) but not god-less existence, his Weberian ethic of "intellectual integrity," which is "value-free" in its abstention from unconditional belief but "value-relevant" in its passionate commitment to meaningful conduct of life under the regimen of clarity and transparency (Weber 1949). With Agathe, Ulrich practises an aesthetic utopia that is neither nowhere wholly *outside* of the world—not some transcendent communistic beyond—nor nowhere wholly *within* the world—not some comfortable bourgeois bohemia.

III. ETHICAL EQUIVOCATION: DOING AND BEING GOOD

Spending their time in this equivocal position between innerworldly and otherworldly utopianism, Ulrich's and Agathe's conversations turn to questions of ethics. At the centre of the narrative in these passages stands Ulrich's and Agathe's implied crime of incest, which clearly rises in importance throughout the later chapters of Part III about "The Criminals." However, some while before their relationship becomes in any way erotic, another "crime" occurs, raising ethical questions of its own. This is Agathe's action of tampering with her father's will so that none of the inheritance falls to her—and therefore none to her husband Hagauer—but all of it to Ulrich.

A young widow after the death of her first husband (whom she loved), Agathe's second marriage is indifferent and perfunctory, "neither especially wonderful nor especially unpleasant" (1953, III: 73). She even feels a trifle sorry for hurting this morally impeccable schoolmaster. For she supposes that he is "after all, a decent sort of man, a good man" (1953, III: 74). But then she reflects:

> Or rather, he was more one of those people who always do good, without having any real goodness in them ... Apparently the goodness disappears out of people in the same measure in which it turns into goodwill or good actions. How had Ulrich put it? A stream that turns factory wheels loses its force. Yes, yes, he had said that too, but it was not what she was trying to remember. Now she had it! "It seems it's really only the people who don't do much good who manage to preserve their goodness intact."
> (Musil 1953, III: 74)

Agathe's action is wrong: she has not tampered with the will in order to possess anything herself but she has tampered with it in order to spite

Hagauer, or because she cannot bear the thought of his continuing ownership over her; and she does not intend to return to him. Ulrich attempts to dissuade her, but his words only seem to lend her courage in her deed. Like all nice and respectable *Bildungsbürger* (educated citizens), Hagauer is a *Tugut* (do-gooder). He means good and he does good. He is not even a hypocrite, and his actions are faultless. But somehow his goodness is bogus, and he is a repulsive character.

Hagauer's is a morality of rules, prescriptions and universals, not a morality of dispositions and singular situations. It is not a morality capable of imagining that "Every good action for the sake of a bad end actually adds to the world a portion of goodness; every bad action for the sake of a good end actually adds to the world a portion of badness." This is Hannah Arendt's (1968, 148) formulation of an ethical precept in the writing of Hermann Broch, and it expresses an outlook rather closer to our contemporary ethical sensibilities.

Hagauer's conduct of life grates against our late- or post-modern sense that goodness is *expressed* in action more than it is *produced* by action; that goodness accrues more to the way of proceeding, the manner and style of acting, than to the end or the intention. Hagauer, Arnheim and the judges presiding over Moosbrugger practise a rigidified, automatised vestige of Kantian transcendentalism. They have the starry heavens above them, the moral law within them; but no real goodness in them. They are Zygmunt Bauman's legislators—not interpreters—of morality (Bauman 1987, 1993, 1995). Ulrich and Agathe, in contrast, have moved beyond both Bauman's traditionalistic universe of moral anxiety relieved by authoritative institutions and personnel—the church and the priest—and Bauman's modernist universe of the moral code, the system of formal rules, rights and obligations. Agathe commits a wrong deed; but with Ulrich she has a consciousness of the burden of freedom and responsibility in ineluctably ambivalent ethical situations. After the encounter with Lindner, another priggish pedagogue, most proud of himself for averting Agathe's attention as she apparently contemplates suicide, she and Ulrich seek to regain a sense of the complexity of Kant's conflict between body and law and the real difficulty of autonomy in the "broken middle" between morality-as-freedom and morality-as-obligation (cf. Rose 1992). Above all, Ulrich and Agathe are impressive not because of what they do but because of their disposition, their *Gemut*—although their life together is by no means *gemütlich* ("comfy"), and Agathe, for all her inwardness, has no Pietistic "beautiful soul." In the thread of ideological history that runs between the story of the beautiful soul in Wilhelm Meister and its reception by nauseating nineteenth-century German *Bürgertum*, Musil's ironic *Bildungsroman* tells us something about the condition of ethics in late modernity. He tells us something rather like Bernard Williams's conclusion at the end of *Ethics and the Limits of Philosophy*:

> How truthfulness to an existing self or society is to be combined with reflection, self-understanding, and criticism is a question that philosophy, itself, cannot answer. It is the kind of question that has to be answered through reflective living. The answer has to be discovered, or established, as the result of a process, personal and social, which essentially cannot formulate the answer in advance, except in an unspecific way. (Williams 1985, 200)

IV. ULRICH AND AGATHE IN THE *COMMUNAUTÉ DÉSOEUVRÉE*

After the episode with the will, Ulrich and Agathe begin to think about love and community. Recalling Aristophanes' speech in *The Symposium* about an original "androgynon" divided into two by Zeus, each a "symbolon" of the other, Ulrich and Agathe are twins in love, "Siamese twins" (1953, III: 275) in search of their original union. However, they know that absolute communion is neither possible nor thinkable. Union for them is at most a *Gleichnis*, an allegory, a shadowy impression of some higher beatitude. Not-united, they undivide their dividing; but their undividing is not their uniting.

Abjuring public sociability, Ulrich and Agathe slowly retreat from the *Gesellschaft* (high society) of the members of the organising committee for an Austrian "Parallel Campaign" to outshine the encroaching cultural pretensions of the Prussians. (This is Musil's amusing story of an imperial propaganda campaign to celebrate the expected seventieth anniversary of the Emperor Franz Joseph's accession to the throne in 1918, eclipsing Prussia's expected thirtieth anniversary of the Emperor Wilhelm II in the same year— of course neither anniversary occurs after the outbreak of the Great War.) The members of the organising committee are the small coterie of ruling notables who meet around the salon lady Diotima, who lament the loss of *Gemeinschaft* (community) and desperately hanker after some last refuge of *Kultur* against the poisonous new religions of science, industry, commerce and the "ant-like" (1953, I: 40) mass society. Ulrich and Agathe reject this false discourse of community, this KaKa-discourse of contrived *agape*. They seek an alternative community, a utopian community that hopes to symbolise some higher condition of reconciliation, some perfect socius—while all the time knowing that reconciliation without parting and division is untruth. No carefree decedents in a felicitous space of intimacy, they know that their love is problematic because they know that it is borne of non-unity. Not the love-community of the early Hegel's *Fragment on Love*, their community is not a substance or an essence in and through which they make themselves what they are. It is not a community of their "own work," not their own *Eigentum* (property). It is, as Jean-Luc Nancy tells us about our contemporary social condition, a *communauté désoeuvrée* (inoperative community).

To declare that community can only ever exist in a sharing that is at once a parting (*partage*), as Nancy (1986) writes in his celebrated book, is not itself a new insight in social theory. Social thinkers since the canonical figures of Durkheim, Weber and Simmel have long understood that the Tönniesian thesis of lost *Gemeinschaft* misreads the conditions of solidarity in modern complex societies insofar as it ignores the sense in which division (of labour, occupation, role and identity) fertilises the soil of interaction and integration between individuals just as much as it sows possible seeds of anomie. Nonetheless, Nancy's diagnosis of the metaphysics of community in twentieth-century communist discourse can surely help us excavate something of Musil's meaning here. Drawing on Bataille's explications of death, finitude and sovereignty of the self, Nancy proposes that *désoeuvrement* (unworking) describes a constitutive alienation of human beings from any compensating social totality that attempts to cover over the facticity of death as the absolute horizon of our finitude and responsibility for others. Dispossessed from any unifying collective oeuvre, *désoeuvrement* is our attempt to forge a relationship to the other and to the self in the knowledge of the failure of all immanence of community to the course of history. One might suggest that it is precisely this constitutive disqualification, this constitutive expropriation, that Musil relates in his novel about the end of grand projects and grand narratives, in his literary meditation on being-without-qualities as a condition of being-with-others and being-by-oneself in late modernity. For Musil's man without qualities is indeed *l'homme désoeuvré*, the man without a work or a project, who shows us how being without-work might be the very condition of our even having work, "owning" our own qualities, "possessing" our own properties.

In Musil's *communauté désoeuvrée*, love is an experience of separating in coupling and of unmaking in making, in which, as Ulrich says, every imparting (*Mitteilung*) is an envy-less parting (*neidlose Teilung*) and every giving a receiving—and yet a giving that leaves the self always thrown back on itself, in the solitude of its own body (Musil 1978, II: 1084). An entry in the *Tagebücher* from 1937 tells us that Musil read Max Scheler's *The Nature of Sympathy* while working over the chapters for the "Conversations on Love" in Part III (Musil 1976, I: 918). In the text, Ulrich and Agathe consider Scheler's idea of *Mitgefühl*, the notion of a "fellow feeling" that so lets people participate in the experiences of others that they apparently "share in," and "know," the others' feelings: the fellow feeling that apparently founds Christian charity (Scheler 1979). But they are disaffected with this *Mitgefühl* because they discern that it presupposes Neo-Platonism's dream of collective soul—which, since Aquinas, we know cannot be true because soul without individuation is without relation to the world, and individuation can occur only through the body, in spatio-temporal location. Ulrich and Agathe thus realise that it is our finite sensuous embodiment that opens us to the other even as it alienates and divides us from the other, and further that it is this mundane embodiment that consequently ruins all possibility of transcendental subjectivity, and transcendental intersubjectivtiy, à la Husserl. Ulrich and Agathe soon doubt their sublunary ec-stasis as both now appear to the other like nebulous apparitions behind solid bars, at once petrified in corporeal form and entirely formless. Agathe reads from a passage in a book about the sea of divine love that drowns us and liquidates our self-knowledge—the author of the passage is Farid-ed-Din Attar, as Goltschnigg (1974, 80) has shown—exclaiming to Ulrich:

> Are you yourself or are you not? I know not, I have no inkling, nor any inkling of myself. I am in love but in whom I do not know; I am neither faithful nor unfaithful. What am I then? I have no inkling even of my love; I have a heart at once full of love and empty of love. (Musil 1978, II: 1091; my trans.)

Responding, Ulrich wonders how Christianity's "love thy neighbour as thyself" can be true when any such love would seem to imply non-knowledge of my self and therefore non-knowledge of the other, my neighbour:

> Usually all people love themselves more than anything else, and know themselves less than anything else! So then "love thy neighbour as thyself" means: Love others without knowing them, and under all circumstances. For otherwise, interestingly enough, if you'll permit me the joke, neighbourly love, like every other love, would have to contain original sin: the evil of eating from the tree of knowledge! (Musil 1978, II: 1213; my trans.)

Probing their relationship, Ulrich and Agathe conclude that undifferentiated fraternal love, no less than erotic love, is blind, empty and suffocating whenever it is not articulated by knowledge of the dividing and non-uniting that is inherent in all relating to others. To love and have compassion for the other, we must have some knowledge of the other, and such knowledge requires acceptance of the unreachability of the other, of the retreat of the other into separate spatio-temporal embodiment. To accept this recession, and not to seek consolation for it in any totalising myth, religion or metaphysics of brotherhood, is the meaning of *désoeuvrement* and the real challenge of community.

V. MODERNITY AND SELF-IDENTITY:
SELF-RELATING WITHOUT SELF-POSITING

In this non-union of Ulrich and Agathe, Musil raises a further question about relating and relations: that of how to know ourselves in relating to ourselves. Musil considers how, as Dieter Henrich (1982, 1987) puts it in his explication of the actuality of German idealist philosophy, I can relate to myself, when relating myself to myself, as object to subject and subject to object, will never take me to the ground of my being. How can I achieve self—consciousness when knowing myself as an object, possessing myself, will only propel me into infinite regress of "unprethinkable being"-*unvordenkliches Sein*, in Schelling's resonant phrase? Ulrich asks us something similar:

> Today, when you think yourself entirely in possession of your self, if you were to ask yourself for once who you actually are ... you'll always see yourself from outside, like an object. You'll notice that one thing makes you angry and another makes you sad, just as one time your coat is wet and another time it's too heavy. However carefully you observe, at the most you'll get to "what's behind you," but you'll never get inside yourself. You remain outside yourself, you stand beside yourself, whatever you try to do about it, and the only exceptions are precisely those rare moments when somebody else would say you were "beside yourself." (Musil 1953, III: 278)

In Henrich's terms, Ulrich's question is that of how to find a way of relating to ourselves without *positing* ourselves. Somehow we have to find an appropriate mode of "self-keeping," of *Selbsterhaltung*, without sliding into the trap, the murderous other-destroying trap, of "self-assertion" or *Selbstbehauptung*. *Selbsterhaltung* implies attending to our being by recognising our dependency on others and otherness, our conditionality— but not "self-preservation," in some nightmarish seventeenth-century Hobbesian sense. Yet, in a further sense, Ulrich's question is also an invitation to rethink the classical sociological thematic of the "relation of the individual and society" without invidious assumptions about what makes for an "open" as against a "closed" self in the social structures of modernity. For

Musil shows us here how the "relation of the individual and society" must be a little bit more difficult a story to tell about modernity than any simple narrative of the depredations of *homo clausus* wreaked upon *homines aperti*—in Norbert Elias' (1978) venerable account of civilisation's skidding off course into alienation and atomisation after Descartes, secularisation and the spirit of capitalism. Musil interrogates what Weber (1948, 310) called modernity's desiccation into "formless sand heaps of individuals," into disaggregation and "subjectivisation," but he also discloses a sense in which every closing of the self upon itself is at the same time a possible opening of the self, just as every relating of the self to itself is always a relating through others: every closing of individuals is at the same time the condition of their opening to one another, the imbricating of their inside with their outside. Thus it can be said that Musil enjoins us to distinguish between at least two different species of alienation in our philosophical discourses of modernity. Musil presents us the *contingent* alienation that need not be and ought not to be: alienation from our universally shared ends of freedom, justice and peace—by power and capital. And he also presents us the *constitutive* alienation that marks the very condition of our relationship to ourselves as others, as beings-without-qualities insofar as we "have" qualities to call "our own," a calling to accomplish, or a work to fulfil. One might submit that if there is any "unfinished project of modernity," it is learning how to make this distinction, and making it—in theory and in practice.

NOTES

I acknowledge the support of a fellowship from the Leverhulme Trust in preparing this article, 2001–02.

1. See also Harrington (2002). My approach here owes something to the work of Boehme (1974), Luft (1980), Jonsson (1998, 2001), Bouveresse (1993, 2001), Frisby (1981), Müller (1972), Brokoph-Mauch (1992) and Kochs (1996), but tries to propose something original in its styling of Musil as a species of social theorist.

BIBLIOGRAPHY

Adorno, T. *Minima Moralia*. Trans. E. Jephcott. London: Verso, 1974.

Arendt, H. *Men in Dark Times*. Trans. R. Winston. New York: Harcourt, 1968.

Bauman, Z. *Legislators and Interpreters*. Oxford: Blackwell, 1987.

Bauman, Z. *Postmodern Ethics*. Oxford: Blackwell, 1993.

Bauman, Z. *Life in Fragments*. Oxford: Blackwell, 1995.

Beck, U., A. Giddens and S. Lash. *Reflexive Modernisation*. Cambridge: Polity, 1994.

Berger, P "The Problem of Multiple Realities: Alfred Schutz and Robert Musil." *Phenomenology and Social Reality*. Ed. M. Natanson. The Hague: Nijhoff, 1970.

Boehme, H. *Anomie und Entfremdung: Literatursoziologische Untersuchungen zu den Essays Robert Musils und seinem Roman "Der Mann ohne Eigenschaften."* Kronberg: Scriptor, 1974.

Bouveresse, J. *L'Homme probable: Robert Musil, le hasard, la moyenne et l'escargot de l'histoire.* Paris: Éclat, 1993.

Bouveresse, J. *La voix de l'âme et les chemins de l'esprit dix etudes sur Robert Musil.* Paris: Seuil, 2001.

Brokoph-Mauch, G. *Robert Musil: Essayismus und Ironie.* Tübingen: Francke, 1992.

Elias, N. *The Civilising Process.* 2 vols. Trans. E. Jephcott. Oxford: Blackwell, 1978.

Frisby, D. *Sociological Impressionism: A Reassessment of Georg Simmel's Social Theory.* London: Heinemann, 1981.

Goltschnigg, D. *Mystische Tradition im Roman Robert Musils: Martin Bubers "Ekstatische Konfessionen" im "Mann ohne Eigenschaften."* Heidelberg: Lothar Stiehm, 1974.

Harrington, A. "Robert Musil and Classical Sociology." *Journal of Classical Sociology* 2.1 (2002): 59–76.

Henrich, D. *Selbstverhältnisse.* Stuttgart: Reclam, 1982.

Henrich, D. *Konzepte.* Frankfurt am Main: Suhrkamp, 1987.

Jonsson, S. "Neither Inside nor Outside: Subjectivity and the Spaces of Modernity in Robert Musil's 'The Man without Qualities.'" *New German Critique* 72 (1998): 31–60.

Jonsson, S. *Subject Without Nation: Robert Musil and the History of Modern Identity.* Durham, NC: Duke UP, 2001.

Kochs, A.M. *Chaos und Individuum: Robert Musils philosophischer Roman als Vision der Moderne.* Freiburg: Alber, 1996.

Luft, D. *Robert Musil and the Crisis of European Culture, 1880–1942.* Berkeley: U of California P, 1980.

Müller, G. *Ideologiekritik und Metasproche in Robert Musils Roman "Der Mann ohne Eigenschaften."* Munich: Fink, 1972.

Musil, R. *The Man without Qualities.* 3 vols. Trans. E. Wilkins and E. Kaiser. London: Secker, 1953.

Musil, R. *Tagebücher.* 2 vols. Hamburg: Rowohlt, 1976.

Musil, R. *Der Mann ohne Eigenschaften.* 2 vols. Hamburg: Rowohlt, 1978.

Nairn, T. "Ukania under Blair." *New Left Review* 1 (2000): 69–103.

Nancy, J.-L. *La Communauté désoeuvrée.* Paris: Christian Bourgeois, 1986.

Rose, G. *The Broken Middle: Out of Our Ancient Society.* Oxford: Blackwell, 1992.

Scheler, M. *The Nature of Sympathy.* Trans. F Heath. London: Routledge, 1979.

Schutz, A. "On Multiple Realities." *Alfred Schutz: Collected Papers*, vol. 1: *The Problem of Social Reality.* Ed. M. Natanson. The Hague: Nijhoff, 1962.

Seel, M. "Drei Regeln für Utopisten." *Merkur* 630 (2001): 747–55.

Weber, M. "The Protestant Sects and the Spirit of Capitalism." *From Max Weber.* Ed. and trans. H.H. Gerth and C. Wright Mills. London: Routledge, 1948.

Weber, M. "The Meaning of 'Ethical Neutrality' in Sociology and Economics." *Max Weber: The Methodology of the Social Sciences.* Ed. and trans. E. Shils and H. Finch. New York: Free, 1949.

Williams, B. *Ethics and the Limits of Philosophy.* Cambridge, MA: Harvard UP, 1985

Chronology

1880	Robert Musil is born on November 6 in Klagenfurt, Carinthia, Austria, to Alfred Musil and Hermine Bergauer Musil.
1892–97	Attends various military schools.
1898–01	Studies mechanical engineering at a technical university in Brünn, where his father is a professor.
1901–02	Serves mandatory year in the Austrian military.
1902–03	Works as a voluntary assistant at the Technological University, Stuttgart.
1903–08	Studies philosophy, mathematics, physics, and experimental psychology at the University of Berlin; befriends psychologists; develops literary contacts; begins to contribute essays to various journals.
1906	Publishes first novel, *Young Törless*; invents the chromatometer, for use in psychological experiments with color perception.
1908	Receives doctorate in philosophy; turns down offer of academic post at University of Graz.
1910–14	Works as an assistant and a librarian at the Technological University in Vienna; marries Martha Marcovaldi on April 15, 1911; publishes *Unions*.
1911–14	Visits Italy; contributes to leading periodicals, including *Die Neue Rundschau*, Berlin; in 1914, he gains editorial post on this publication.

1914–18	Serves as an officer of the Austrian army in World War I;
1916–17	Musil is editor of the army newspaper; he is awarded various military decorations; in 1917, his father is elevated to nobility and Musil receives a title that is hereditary.
1919–20	Works for the Austrian Foreign Ministry in Vienna.
1920–22	Becomes Educational Consultant at the Austrian War Ministry.
1921–31	Is a theater critic, essayist, and freelance writer, primarily in Vienna; works on *The Man without Qualities*; in 1921, his drama, *The Visionaries* is published.
1923–29	He becomes vice president of an association of German writers in Austria.
1923	He is awarded the Kleist Prize for *The Visionaries*; *Vincent and the Mistress of Important Men*, a farce, published and performed in Berlin.
1924	His parents die within months of each other; he is awarded literature prize of the city of Vienna; publishes *Three Women*.
1927	Gives what has become his famous memorial speech for Rainer Maria Rilke.
1929	Suffers a nervous breakdown; first performance of *The Visionaries* in Berlin is given in a shortened and unauthorized form.
1930	Publishes first volume of *The Man without Qualities*; despite its success, continues to suffer financially.
1931–33	Moves to Berlin; continues to work on novel; Kurt Glaser and others found a Musil Society, with the aim of supporting Musil while working on the novel.
1933	National Socialist Party takes over government of Germany; *The Man without Qualities, Book II*, is published; returns to Vienna.
1934–38	After dissolution of Musil Society in Berlin, his friends form a similar group in Vienna; it provides regular financial support.
1936	Publishes *Legacy in My Lifetime*; suffers a stroke.
1938	German National Socialists invade Austria and take control of the government; he emigrates with wife to Zurich, Switzerland by way of Italy; his books are banned in Austria and Germany.

1939–42   Moves to Geneva in 1939; he continues work on novel, despite deteriorating finances. Receives some help from various sources. Attempts to emigrate first to Great Britain and then to the United States, with support of Thomas Mann, Hermann Broch, and Albert Einstein, but is unsuccessful.

1942   Robert Musil Dies suddenly on April 15 in Geneva.

1943   Martha Musil publishes unfinished portion of *The Man without Qualities*.

Contributors

HAROLD BLOOM is Sterling Professor of the Humanities at Yale University. He is the author of over 20 books, including *Shelley's Mythmaking* (1959), *The Visionary Company* (1961), *Blake's Apocalypse* (1963), *Yeats* (1970), *A Map of Misreading* (1975), *Kabbalah and Criticism* (1975), *Agon: Toward a Theory of Revisionism* (1982), *The American Religion* (1992), *The Western Canon* (1994), and *Omens of Millennium: The Gnosis of Angels, Dreams, and Resurrection* (1996). *The Anxiety of Influence* (1973) sets forth Professor Bloom's provocative theory of the literary relationships between the great writers and their predecessors. His most recent books include *Shakespeare: The Invention of the Human* (1998), a 1998 National Book Award finalist, *How to Read and Why* (2000), and *Genius: A Mosaic of One Hundred Exemplary Creative Minds* (2002). In 1999, Professor Bloom received the prestigious American Academy of Arts and Letters Gold Medal for Criticism, and in 2002 he received the Catalonia International Prize.

LOWELL A. BANGERTER teaches in the department of modern and classical languages at the University of Wyoming. He is the author of a book on Robert Musil and of *German Writing Since 1945: A Critical Survey*. He also has translated numerous works.

THOMAS HARRISON is the author of *1910: The Emancipation of Dissonance* and the editor of *Nietzsche in Italy*. He has also translated books and been a co-author.

ERIC WHITE teaches English at the University of Colorado, Boulder. He is the author of several titles, including *Kaironomia: On the Will-to-Invent*.

BURTON PIKE has taught at the City University of New York. He has edited and translated a book of Robert Musil's and also has translated another of the author's titles.

ROBERT ZALLER is a Professor at Drexel University. He is the editor of *Centennial Essays for Robinson Jeffers* and the author, joint author, and/or translator of other titles.

ALEXANDER HONOLD teaches at Humboldt-Universität Berlin. He is the author of a book in German on *The Man without Qualities* and also the co-author of other titles in German.

MICHAEL ANDRÉ BERNSTEIN is Professor of English and Comparative Literature at the University of California, Berkeley. He is the author of *Bitter Carnival:* Ressentiment *and the Abject Hero* and other titles.

STEFAN JONSSON is an independent scholar. He is the author of numerous books and essays and is a contributing editor at *Dagens Nyheter*, a major newspaper in Sweden.

AUSTIN HARRINGTON teaches at the University of Leeds in the United Kingdom. He has been an author and joint editor, with one of his titles being *Hermeneutic Dialogue and Social Science*.

Bibliography

Appignanesi, Lisa. *Femininity and the Creative Imagination: A Study of Henry James, Robert Musil, and Marcel Proust.* New York: Barnes and Noble, 1973.

Baumann, Gerhart. *Robert Musil.* Bern and Munich: Francke, 1965.

———. "Robert Musil." *Handbook of Austrian Literature.* New York: Ungar, 1973.

Beard, Philip H. "The 'End' of *The Man without Qualities.*" *Musil-Forum* 8 (1982): pp. 30–45.

Berger, Peter. "Robert Musil and the Salvage of the Self." *Partisan Review* 51–52, 4–1 (1984-1985): pp 638–650.

Bryan, David Hennington. "Robert Musil: Politics, Poetic Language and the Authoritarian Style." *Dissertation Abstracts International*, Section A 62, no. 8 (February 2002) 2774.

Coble, Don Kelly. "Inscrutable Intelligibility: Intelligible Character and Deed in Kant, Schelling, Mach, and Musil." *Dissertation Abstracts International* 60, 8 (February 2000): 2958–59.

Constantine, Peter; Philip Payne; and Burton Pike. "Letters on *The Man without Qualities.*" *Fiction* 16, no. 1 (1999): pp. 87–100.

Dowden, Stephen D. *Sympathy for the Abyss: A Study in the Novel of German Modernism: Kafka, Broch, Musil, and Thomas Mann.* Studien zur Deutschen Literatur. Tübingen: Niemeyer, 1986.

Enright, D.J. "An Unfinished Journey." *Times Literary Supplement* (November 30, 1979): pp. 57–58.

Epstein, Joseph. "The Man Who Wrote Too Much." *Commentary* 100, no. 6 (December 1995): pp. 48–54.

Erickson, Susan. "Essay/Body/Fiction: The Repression of an Interpretive Context in an Essay of Robert Musil." *German Quarterly* 56, no. 4 (November 1983): pp. 580–593.

Finlay, Mirake. *The Potential of Modern Discourse: Musil, Pierce, and Perturbation*. Bloomington: Indiana University Press, 1990.

Genno, Charles N. "The Nexus between Mathematics and Reality and Phantasy in Musil's Works." *Neophilologus* 70, no. 2 (April 1986): pp. 270–278.

———. "Musil's Moral and Aesthetic Principles." *Orbis Litterarum* 38, no. 2 (1983): pp. 140–149.

———. "Observations on Love and Death in Musil." *Neophilologus* 67 (1983): pp. 118–125.

Grill, Genese Elinor. "Ecstatic Experience, Crime and Conversion in Robert Musil's *Der Mann ohne Eigneschaften*." *Dissertation Abstracts International* 62, no. 3 (September 2001) 1038.

Hickman, Hannah. *Robert Musil and the Culture of Vienna*. La Salle, IL: Open Court, 1984.

Hissom, James. "Musil's Masterpiece at Last, Too Late?" *Bulletin of the West Virginia Association of College English Teachers* 18 (Spring 1997): pp. 46–52.

Huber, Lothar, and John D. White, eds. *Musil in Focus*. London: Institute of Germanic Studies, 1982.

Jonsson, Stefan. "Neither Inside nor Outside: Subjectivity and the Spaces of Modernity in Robert Musil's *The Man without Qualities*." *New German Critique* 68 (Spring-Summer 1996): pp. 31–60.

Keller, James R. "Arnheim and His Discontents in Musil's *Mann ohne Eigenschaften*." In *Weimer Culture: Issues of Modernity and the Metropolis*, edited by Caitlin Gannon and Scott Melton, pp. 49–58. Tuscon, AZ: University of Arizona, 1994.

Kimball, Roger. "The Qualities of Robert Musil." *The New Criterion* 14, no. 6 (February 1996): pp. 10–20.

Kundera, Milan. "The Legacy of the Sleepwalkers." *Partisan Review* 51–52: 4-1 (1984–1985): pp. 724–728.

Large, Duncan. "Experimenting with Experience: Robert Musil, *De Mann ohne Eigenschaften*.'" In *The German Novel in the Twentieth Century: Beyond Realism*, edited by David Midgley, 110–127. Edinburgh: Edinburgh University Press, 1993.

Luft, David S. *Robert Musil and the Crisis of European Culture, 1880–1942*. Berkeley: University of California Press, 1980.

Moser, Walter, "The Factual in Fiction: The Case of Robert Musil." *Poetics Today* 5, no. 2 (1984): pp. 411–428.

Payne, Philip. *Robert Musil's* The Man without Qualities: *A Critical Study*. Cambridge: Cambridge University Press, 1988.

———. *Robert Musil's Works, 1906–1924: A Critical Introduction*. Frankfort am Main; NY: Peter Lang, 1987.

Peters, Frederick G. *Robert Musil, Master of the Hovering Life: A Study of the Major Fiction*. NY: Columbia University Press, 1978.

Pike, Burton. *Robert Musil*. Ithaca, NY: Cornell University Press, 1961.

Prawer, S. S. "Robert Musil and the 'Uncanny,'" *Oxford German Studies* 3 (1968): pp. 163–182.

Restivo, Giuseppina. "Melencolias and Scientific Ironies in *Endgame*: Beckett, Walther, Dürer, Musil." *Samuel Beckett Today/Aujourd'hui* 11 (2001): pp. 103–11.

Rogowski, Christian. *Distinguished Outsider: Robert Musil and His Critics*. Columbia, SC: Camden House, 1994.

Rußegger, Arno. "Mental Anticipation of Hypertext-Structures: Robert Musil's Posthumous Papers." In *The Poetics of Memory*, edited by Thomas Wägenbaur, 379–390. Tübingen, Germany: Stauffenburg, 1998.

Saemmer, Alexandra. "Marguerite Duras and Robert Musil: A Feminist View on Violence. Proceedings of the Conference at Passau University, March 15–17, 2001." In *The Aesthetics and Pragmatics of Violence*, edited by Michael Hensen and Annette Pankratz, 225–232. Passau, Germany: Stutz, 2001.

Strauss, Walter A. "In Search of Exactitude and Style: The Example of Proust and Musil." In *Narrative Ironies*, edited by Raymond A. Prier and Gerald Gillespie, 3–19. Amsterdam, Netherlands: Rodopi, 1997.

Ulfers, Friedrich. "Friedrich Nietzsche as Bridge from Nineteenth-Century Atomistic Science to Process Philosophy in Twentieth-Century Physics, Literature and Ethics." *West Virginia Philological Papers* 49 (2002–03): pp. 21–29.

Acknowledgments

"Experimental Utopias: *The Man without Qualities*" by Lowell A. Bangerter. From *Robert Musil*: pp. 111–130. © 1988 by Lowell A. Bangerter. Reprinted by permission.

"Robert Musil: The Suspension of the World" by Thomas Harrison. From *Essayism: Conrad, Musil, & Pirandello*: pp. 56–86. © 1992 by The Johns Hopkins University Press. Reprinted by permission.

"Chance and Narrative in Musil and Buñuel" by Eric White. From *Chance, Culture and the Literary Text*, edited by Thomas M. Kavanagh: pp. 173–200. © 1994 by Michigan Romance Studies. Reprinted by permission.

"Robert Musil: Literature as Experience" by Burton Pike. From *Studies in Twentieth-Century Literature* 18, no. 2 (Summer 1994): 221–238. © 1994 by *Studies in Twentieth-Century Literature*. Reprinted by permission.

"Robert Musil and the Novel of Metastasis" by Robert Zaller. From *Boulevard* 13, no. 3 (Spring 1998): pp. 96–118. © 1998 by Opojaz, Inc. Reprinted by permission.

"Endings and Beginnings: Musil's Invention of Austrian History" by Alexander Honold. From *Austria in Literature*, edited by Donald G. Daviau: pp. 75–85. © 2000 by Ariadne Press. Reprinted by permission.

"Robert Musil: Precision and Soul" by Michael André Bernstein. From *Five Portraits: Modernity and the Imagination in Twentieth-Century German Writing*: pp. 35–56. © 2000 by Northwestern University Press. Reprinted by permission.

"A Story with Many Ends: Narratological Observations" by Stefan Jonsson. From *Subject Without Nation: Robert Musil and the History of Modern Identity*: pp. 97–129. © 2000 Duke University Press. Reprinted by permission.

"Undivided, Not-United: Robert Musil's Community" by Austin Harrington. From *Agelaki* 8, no. 1 (April 2003): pp. 109–118. © 2003 by Taylor & Francis Ltd. and the editors of *Angelaki*. Reprinted by permission.

Index